Praise for Safe to Love Again

"A groundbreaking book that redefines what it means to be in a safe, secure, and lasting relationship. If you have ever lost hope for love, this is the book to read." — **John Gray,** bestselling author of *Men Are from Mars, Women Are from Venus*

"Dr. Gary Salyer has written a game-changing book that skillfully explains and illuminates the origins of the blocks to love so many suffer with. This magnificent work offers practical, healing solutions that will put you on the path to deep and lasting love." — **Arielle Ford**, bestselling author of *The Soulmate Secret*

"If you want to trade in that pillow for a loving, wonder-full partner, *Safe to Love Again*, will give you a new "GPS" for doing just that. This book reads like a brand new kind of heart-to-heart conversation about love." — **SARK**, co-author of *Succulent Wild Love*, PlanetSARK.com

"The poet, Ben Johnson, once described second relationships as, 'The triumph of hope over experience.' Gary Salyer teaches those of us who've been bruised how to find hope again." — **Terry Real**, bestselling author of *The New Rules of Marriage*

"When Dr. Gary Salyer writes, I read. And underline. And note-take. And laugh. And learn. And borrow. *Safe to Love Again* is one of the best books ever written on love!"— **Paul Carrick Brunson**, elite matchmaker, mentor and television host

"Dr. Gary Salyer is addressing the tough question . . . is love worth the hassle ? If you are looking for a way to create a relationship that's safe from your own issues as well as your partner's, this book will guide you." — **Lisa Garr,** host of *The Aware Show.*

"Finally, a book that unlocks the mysteries of the brain in love. The path forward into safe, lasting love is laid out for all to follow! This is a must read for anyone who ever wanted to fall in love and stay there." — **Dr. Scott Mills,** evolutionary business coach

"*Safe to Love Again* extends far beyond your finding and keeping that one special person in your life, as the book so beautifully empowers you to do. What Dr. Salyer reveals goes to the very heart of why we as individual and coupled souls were put here . . . to the meaning of life itself!"— **Dr. Michael R. Norwood,** bestselling author of *The 9 Insights of the Wealthy Soul* and *Speaking Your Truth*

"*Safe to Love Again* is a book for everyone who feels befuddled by love, who longs for love to be the safe harbor it was meant to be, and for all who may be anywhere along that spectrum of hope. I will highly recommend this to clients and friends alike." — **Alexandra Saperstein,** marriage and family therapist

"This book will revolutionize relationship counseling, and expand people's horizons when it comes to dating, mating, and relating. *Safe to Love Again* makes attachment theory practical to the reader. It needs to be a part of every therapist's toolkit." — **Edie Weinstein,** psychotherapist

"This book will help you gather the courage and strength to empower yourself to say "Yes!" to love and open yourself and your heart to the possibilities a healthy relationship can create."— **Dr. Rhoberta Shaler,** clinical psychologist, author of *Escaping the Hijackal Trap*

"Dr. Gary's unique and powerful approach is breathtaking and awe inspiring! This is a must read for those who are ready to feel safe enough to love and be loved deeply!" — **Dr. Mary Ozegovich,** marriage and family therapist, radio host

"As I read *Safe to Love Again,* I experienced a place of possibility I had not felt before. Dr. Salyer guides us on a journey of discovering how deep, fulfilling and safe real love can be. Read this wonderful book!" — **Julie Renee Doering,** brain rejuvenation expert

"I sat down to *read* Safe to Love Again. It wasn't a *read;* it was an *experience!* Dr. Salyer talked to my heart. I now know what it feels like to be in a secure love. I could not put down this book!" — **Rochelle,** nurse and health coach

"Dr. Salyer's book is a brilliant, deep dive into the inner workings of relationships. If you're interested in how to find love and be loved in the deepest possible way—this is a must read!" — **Patrick,** business coach

"*Safe to Love Again* forever changed the way I look at my relationships, myself, and my life. I can honestly say that I was one person when I started reading the book and another when I finished it." — **Andrea,** entrepreneur

"Dr. Salyer's book transformed my love life in a way I never imagined possible. I almost gave up on finding happiness in love until I decided to take a chance on his promise of becoming safe to love again. I freed myself from toxic relationship patterns and am now happily busy finding my soulmate." — **Michelle,** attorney

"I couldn't stop reading this book! This book blows other self-help books out of the water. It's amazing the clarity this book has given me and how it has pointed me in a totally different direction for finding love." — **Josh,** police officer

"Dr. Salyer has really created something quite revolutionary; an approach to understanding the search for love, based on the scientific research of Attachment Theory. He seems to have gotten to the heart of what makes us who we are, both as individuals and as couples."
— **Kenya,** engineer and corporate trainer

"If I had to go back in time and choose only one book to read my whole life, it would be *Safe to Love Again*. It eloquently expresses the full scope of what love really is in a way that shortcuts years of learning, and will immediately benefit me and my clients."
— **Brenda,** executive coach

"Long-term relationships aren't easy, and given all the variables that make them up, they aren't meant to be. Consequently, at different times we all struggle with them. Dr. Gary helps us navigate through the rough spots so we can all feel safe and secure in our love."
— **Mark,** trainee adult and CEO

"*Safe to Love Again* is a rigorous, decade-in-the-making sojourn to answer a basic question: "How can I feel safe to love and be loved?" He gives you the keys to understanding how to answer the question for yourself and find the secure love your heart desires."
— **Lysha,** organizational psychologist

"*Safe to Love Again* helps us move beyond our past hurts to reclaim what is our birthright—a deeply committed relationship that both feels good and lasts. However you feel about your current or past relationships, Dr. Salyer will show you how love is meant to feel."
— **Joan**, freelance editor

"Dr. Salyer's new book was the missing piece for me in my marriage. He illuminates so many facets of what makes not only a relationship work but also what creates an integrated *We*. This book is a relationship game changer!" — **Alexandra,** coach

"The work Gary talks about in *Safe to Love Again* changed my life. If you want to rewire your brain for secure love, this book will show you how." — **Elizabeth**, entrepreneur

"If you have ever felt unlucky in love and relationships, this book is worth the investment. Dr. Salyer brilliantly explains how luck has nothing to do with relationships. If you would like to take chance out of the equation, and take control to create your own experience in love, this book is for you." — **Michael**, attorney

"This book has been life changing. Using this skill set, I was able to create lasting positive changes for my children and myself. With heart-warming stories of clients who found their way back to safe, loving relationships, *Safe to Love Again* is an inspiring and practical guide to reclaiming the power of love for everyone." — **Joseph**, real estate developer

"Dr. Salyer brings together a synthesis of different fields of study at a time when both singles and couples are aligning their core being to have enlightened relationships in all areas of their life. Read this book and your world will shift to a place of rightness and deep love." — **Annie**, elementary teacher

"*Safe to Love Again* takes you on a journey of self-discovery that illuminates your love patterns. Dr. Salyer equips you with insightful tools to help you make the inner transformations that change the landscape of your life forever." — **Rihab**, physics professor

"This book showed me a road map to emotional freedom. I'm a self help book junky, but I have never come across the golden wisdom like in this book. I don't have to prove every day that I'm worthy to be here! I'm reclaiming my life one right at a time and no words can describe how freeing that is." — **Liliya**, nurse

"*Safe to Love Again* changed my life. I'm now in alignment with reality when it comes to love, romantic relationships and finding my soulmate. Wow! This is freedom." — **Stephanie**, artist

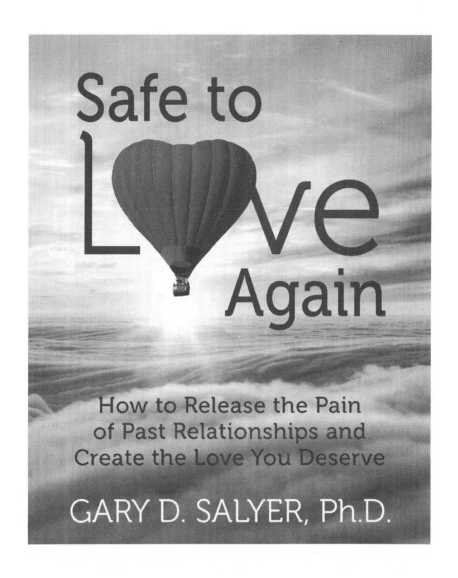

Safe to L♥ve Again

How to Release the Pain of Past Relationships and Create the Love You Deserve

GARY D. SALYER, Ph.D.

Belle Amoris Press

Belle Amoris Press, P.O. Box 30282, Walnut Creek, CA 94598
Published in the United States by Belle Amoris Press, Walnut Creek, California.

Safe to Love Again: How to Release the Pain of Past Relationships and Create the Love You Deserve/Gary Dean Salyer, Ph.D.

pages cm

Library of Congress Control Number: 2018966359

ISBN 978-1-7329778-0-8

ePub ISBN 978-1-7329778-1-5

Mobi ISBN 978-1-7329778-2-2

Printed in the United States of America

Cover Design by Michelle Radomski

First Paperback Edition

Author Website: www.garysalyer.com

DEDICATED TO

JAYNE AND KENNY

MAY YOU ALWAYS NURTURE YOUR DREAMS

SO YOUR SOULS CAN SHINE

"YOUR TASK IS NOT TO SEEK FOR LOVE,

BUT MERELY TO SEEK AND FIND

ALL THE BARRIERS WITHIN YOURSELF

THAT YOU HAVE BUILT AGAINST IT."

— Rumi

"WE ARE NOT HELD BACK BY THE LOVE

WE DIDN'T RECEIVE IN THE PAST,

BUT BY THE LOVE WE'RE NOT EXTENDING

IN THE PRESENT."

— Marianne Williamson

Table of Contents

Foreword

by Paul Carrick Brunson

My careers as an investment banker, matchmaker, and entrepreneur have taught me one thing for sure; communication is everything!

Seventeen years as a husband and eight as a father have proven it to me. And if my almost forty years on this earth as a son, friend, mentor, coach, and life-long learner have taught me anything, it's that good communication skills make all other skills secondary.

Communication is the skeleton key for the answers to life's questions. It affects all of our endeavors and relationships, no matter if we're at work or play, having a heart to heart with loved ones, or keynoting a crowd of a hundred thousand people.

How we communicate matters. In Dr. Gary Salyer's book, *Safe to Love Again*, he addresses the feelings we need for finding and maintaining healthy love. These feelings are Welcomed with Joy, Worthy and Nourished, Cherished and Protected, and Empowered with Choice. Dr. Gary has identified these as the foundations for finding lasting love. As I read this book, I realized in my own life that when we communicate or interact with people, we all want to feel welcomed into the conversation, worthy of being included, cherished and safe while expressing, and empowered with choice—even a choice as basic as whether or not to continue a conversation.

Imagine being single and looking for love—a safe love that allows you to envision a future. Understanding what you need from your relationship becomes even more intense, because honestly, who wants to spend a lifetime in a situation where they weren't welcomed from day one? We all want to feel welcomed, worthy, and heart-protected.

The feeling of Empowered with Choice stood out to me. It's a very important feeling when it comes to singles and relationships in this day and age. With phenomena like "ghosting," "cuffing," and "Netflix and chilling," where potential partners are leaving relationships without explanation, creating seasonal relationships, or spending time where sex is the ultimate and maybe only goal, there seems to be a propensity for people to think they don't have a choice. *Love should be a choice.* With whom you communicate should be a choice. More importantly, with whom you decide to spend a lifetime should be a choice YOU make. It shouldn't be because you feel you only have limited options to stay with the one who *didn't* ghost, cuff, or simply chill with you.

Dr. Gary's book really hit home to me as a matchmaker, husband, and father. I want every single one of my clients to read this book! This is the kind of self work you often see glorified in memes, but no one gives you the tools for how to do it in real life. And by work, I mean preparing to be a mate while you're still single! Singles who read this book will definitely walk into dates with a healthier checklist of the ways they want and need to be loved. They'll know when they're welcomed and nourished. They'll engage, knowing that they're worthy of love.

How will they know these things? They'll have done the work to reclaim their missing rights to love as identified by Dr. Gary. These rights can be missing due to childhood experiences, negative self talk, or even a few bad dates. You may not be able to feel authentically worthy, for example, until you work on the things from your past that make you feel unworthy. Dr. Gary shows you how.

As a married man, this book has added another pillar of support to the already wonderful seventeen years I've shared with my partner Jill. No matter where you are in your marital journey, it's always good to check in with your mate and make sure their feelings are being heard.

As Dr. Gary explains in *Safe to Love Again,* it's best to address any discord as soon as possible. As scary as the idea of divorce may be for you and your mate, staying in a marriage in which you don't feel overjoyed to be there, is even scarier. *Safe to Love Again* puts rhyme and reason to those feelings, and gives you directions for how you and your significant other can find answers, together or separately, to bring you closer together.

My biggest *"aha!"* while reading this book came as a father. My intention with my children has always been to build a legacy of love. In this way, I hope that they will know love in their own relationships, and therefore, their children will know love in theirs. *Safe to Love Again* showed me that our responsibility as parents is to raise adults who *feel* Welcomed with Joy, Worthy and Nourished, Cherished and Protected, and Empowered with Choice.

"If you *stay* ready, you don't have to *get* ready," is one of my favorite mantras. Teaching our children to know what kind of love to seek in their relationships, so they're ready when the time comes, is an important job for a parent. Modeling healthy love in my marriage has always been a priority for me. After reading *Safe to Love Again,* I realized that showing them *how* to love someone is rooted in how they show up for themselves when *looking for love.*

It's my job as a parent to teach them to love themselves first so they *can* love a partner and what they should expect to feel coming *from* a loving partner. They must understand what makes them feel nourished and protected. What makes them feel worthy? When do they feel Empowered with Choice? These are the questions I now ask as a parent after reading this book.

In every aspect of life, you need communication skills. When you feel *Safe to Love Again*—welcomed, worthy, cherished, protected, empowered—you're a better communicator. You'll make better impressions, better relationships, and even better keynote speeches to a hundred thousand people! You'll even talk to yourself in a more loving way. *And that can change everything.*

Knowing who and what makes you feel welcomed, worthy, nourished, protected, and empowered is an important conversation to have with yourself, and then with your loved ones. I'm thankful—and I'm confident that you will be too—that my friend, Dr. Gary Salyer, is starting that conversation. I'm glad you've joined us.

Wishing you love,
~Paul C. Brunson

Paul C. Brunson is a happily married husband to Jill, his loving wife, as well as a committed father, elite matchmaker, and celebrity television dating show host. In addition to mentoring thought leaders, Paul has hosted several television dating shows, including *Love Town, USA* (OWN), *Date Night Live* (Lifetime), and *Help! I Need Love* (ABC). He currently hosts the British television dating show, *Celebs Go Dating*. Paul's life purpose is to help people to live their best life.

One

The Question of Our Time: Am I Safe to Love Again?

If you've ever felt afraid to put your heart on the line for love again—whether you're a scared, frustrated single, or a hurt and disappointed partner—you've come to the right place. Love takes real risk. The trick for creating lasting love is to know how to release old hurts so you not only can feel *Safe to Love Again*, but to create the sort of love you wanted in the first place.

This book began years ago when a curious young boy looked out at his world and wondered why so many people were miserable and didn't feel loved. My mother and uncles drank deep into the night because that was the only way they could feel happy. Even then, I understood perfectly well that my aunts had taken up drinking because it was the only way they could deal with the pain of their absentee husbands. It was better to join them in their misery than to be left alone night after night.

As a child I swore to myself that I would be different than my family. Going to college, I enrolled as a psychology major to make *sure* my life would be different. Four years later, I received a huge shock; preparing for graduation, a professor gave me a personality test to see how *fit* I was for adult life. That's when he dropped a bomb on me, "The tests tell me that you have a 90 percent chance of being divorced." The words fell on my ears like a grenade. Within hours, I decided that if a double major in psychology and religion weren't enough, then perhaps a third would do the trick. I prolonged college for a fifth year to gain a third degree in marriage and family relations.

Imagine my surprise, when 12 years later my marriage was in flames. How could all that determination in *three* areas of study—each deliberately selected to stave off a divorce—have worked out so poorly? I was stymied. After years of therapy following my divorce, I finally pronounced myself ready to marry again. It was therefore devastating to me when my second marriage began to unravel after just a few months. Four years later, divorce came knocking on my door a second time. Confusion ruled the day. After all my studies and almost a decade of therapy between marriages, the test I took at 22 had proven to be accurate. Doubly so, even!

A part of me was now scared to death of love. After one painful breakup with a woman I absolutely adored, a soul level decision came to me. Tired of losing love, I dedicated my life to cracking the code to making love safe, lasting, and wonderful. While traditional therapy and psychology had done me much good, they did not change my core style of relating. Once I realized this, my new life's purpose was to unearth what truly changes a brain when it comes to someone's love style.

As a result, things began to shift deeply as I threw myself into discovering the secret to lasting love. My research focused on attachment theory, neuroscience, NLP (neuro-linguistic programming), and whatever else I thought might re-wire a brain to help create secure and lasting love. I soon added couples research into the mix. Eventually, from my own experience as well as what I had observed in my clients, I noticed there were *transformational gaps* in all of those areas. So, I added them to my list of things to figure out about love. Out of those insights, and above all what actually worked for my clients, this book was born. *Safe to Love Again* is a total theory of love—a unified field theory, if you will.

My life story and its lessons are all here in this book. Looking back, I can clearly see that my soul chose a lot of lessons. Yes, there were painful relationships, but at some level they were all *my* choices. *All* of it was in the service of learning the lessons that lay behind every page in this book—inviting you, the reader, to have a more fulfilling experience of lasting love—*this* is the ultimate promise behind this book.

If you long to create extraordinary and lasting love, I'm going to show you how it's done. If you're single, I'll show you how a well-trained brain attracts a true soulmate. If you're already part of a couple, I'll teach you how to *create, maintain, and keep* a soulmate connection. If you've lost that loving connection with your partner, you'll learn how to craft a calm, peaceful, endearing bond.

This book is about attracting and keeping the love you deserve, Because most singles don't want to stay single, and couples don't want to become single again.

In the hearts of both singles and couples is the burning desire to love and be loved well. As you will come to see, buried deep in your brain are permission slips for love which influence *everything*. From the perspective of neuroscience and relationship science, your *brain* creates *all* of your experience. While this book begins with singles and attraction, most of the book is going to deal with how your brain creates painful relationships, and what you can do to stop that. The middle section of the book will show you what your brain needs to create the wonderful, passionate, and lasting love that you deserve.

If you're like so many people, you've probably experienced the searing disappointment of a bad marriage, or perhaps multiple, hurtful breakups. Whether it's a string of painful breakups or a disillusioning divorce, the very relationship that you thought could be trusted can turn out to be like the burning of Atlanta scene in *Gone with the Wind*. After an excruciating breakup, our hearts will often turn towards Love and say, *"Frankly my dear, I don't give a damn!"* Who wants that to be their last word on love?

Who is This Book For?

You'll find this book life changing if you have one of the following concerns, which I often find smart, successful, and absolutely loveable people have—especially those who are hungry to find or create quality romantic love:

1. You're tired of being alone.

The side of the bed that's empty . . . it seems like a barren moonscape some nights, doesn't it? You wonder if the garden of love has been lost forever. All of those statistics about how the lack of love or a poor relationship can affect your health and welfare—with less vitality and length of years—secretly scare you. You worry that if you don't find or create a healthy relationship with a partner, it's going to cost you.

2. You're scared because you got burned in your marriage or last relationship, and you're not going there again.

This often results in a *once burned—twice shy* belief that a committed relationship is too risky. It's as if some part of you is saying, "Sure, I'd love to have someone who has my back, but the scar from being stabbed in it the last time just has me over a barrel." You worry that you'll wind up as some jaded version of yourself that you swore in high school you would never become. You want to rally for love, but don't quite know how to find a safe haven for your honest need for meaningful connection and lasting love.

3. You're afraid that all of the good ones are gone so it's hopeless.

This belief usually manifests as a lack of motivation. You sometimes hear a sad inner voice saying to you, "What's the point of trying if the game is so darn rigged?" You wonder why you should even bother getting *on* the road to love, if it just leads nowhere in the end. You wish you had a guide who could transport you across this chasm of despair and help you take a giant leap towards the love you yearn for.

4. You're worried that something is wrong with you and you don't really deserve love.

It's always been there—that nagging little feeling that you're flawed—that you're just not good enough somehow. You think that everyone can see it; especially your partner or date! You long to find someone who can help you find the wonderful person inside of you who has every right to be loved.

5. You're anxious that your relationships are so profoundly disappointing.

It gets bad some days. Sometimes you wonder if you've lost your mojo. All those Photoshopped pictures of happy couples on social media followed by awkward coffee dates at Starbucks, or painful breakups just when you start to fall in love or get serious makes you wonder if a soulmate even *exists* for you!

6. If you are currently in a relationship and you ask, "Why do we create the same frustrations or distancing moves every day?"

There are couples who have found each other and really seem to make each other happy. You've seen them strolling on the beach holding hands, or looking at each other with longing eyes over a romantic dinner. But it's always *other* couples who are close; not you and *your* soulmate. Deep down inside, you know you can't settle for this sort of love.

7. You remember being so much more in love and long to feel that way again.

Life happens. Children come along or we get involved in our careers, and before you know it, those long hours have taken a toll on your love life. The conversations across the table have become lackluster; the sex is tepid—or worse—nonexistent; the fire has somehow gone out. You *know* you love each other, yet behind the scenes you worry that you'll become the couple you once said you'd never be. You want your *loving* relationship back and are willing to fight for it. You're *down* to do the work to find a sense of *We* again. You just don't quite know where to start.

8. You're tired of fighting and yearn for peace and love.

Conflicts are washing over your relationship like a tsunami some days. When your mate walks in the door, you often think, "Here it comes!" If things don't change soon you know your relationship will end. For some reason, you seem to bring out the worst in each other. You could cut the tension and distance between you with a knife. And yet, there's still love beating in your hearts, and you know it. You want your marriage to work. So you think, "If only someone could show us how to calm things down, so we can get back to loving each other."

9. You just want your relationship to last.

The thought of your relationship ending is unbearable. You love this person deeply and have totally invested yourself in this relationship. At the beginning, you swore the two of you would never divorce or break up. *Yet*, there are signs all over the place that something isn't right. The feeling that one or both of you want to leave haunts you. All you ever wanted was for love not to go away. *Everyone deserves a love that lasts,* right? So you long for a guide to show you the door that leads to lasting love and the keys to unlock it.

10. You are in a good or great relationship, and want to make it better.

Better is stronger, right? Lasting couples are always looking for how they can make each other feel more loved. If that's you, you're in a great place to make your love even stronger.

If you can relate to any of these descriptions, then congratulations! What I'm going to show you is not only how to become safe in love, but more importantly, what makes love sizzle! When you're truly *Safe to Love Again,* your heart will only settle for the kind of love that oozes with passion, joy, intimacy, fun, peace, and so much more!

> Passion and joy are the hallmarks of a
> brain that is Safe to Love Again.
> Love can be easy and fun!

Ask How, Not Why

In my area of expertise—attachment theory—there's a lot of talk about people having a *secure attachment*. When you have a secure attachment your brain has learned it's okay to be in a loving, dependable relationship, and to be depended on by an equally loving partner. Moreover, a secure brain is skilled at attracting, maintaining, and keeping a healthy, loving, intimate, passionate, and safe relationship with a committed partner. I'm going to show you *how* a secure brain feels and thinks deep down inside, so that you can retrain *your* brain to feel and think differently. One thing I've learned is that we must *train our brains* to have the love we want.

Here's the question that's been uppermost in my mind for more than a decade: *How does the brain of someone who's created a loving, lasting relationship work deep down inside?* What are the *insider secrets* for getting a secure brain that just knows how to pick Mr. or Ms. Right, and then insures that the relationship lasts for a lifetime in a way that feels good? Conversely, what's happening inside the brains of those who are plagued by a lifetime of anxiety or fear? What's going on inside those who are constantly jeopardizing their relationships?

I've spent the last decade discovering *how* a brain creates all experiences of love. If you've spent time asking *why* you did what you did in your relationships, I've discovered that the *why* question is not enough to change your fate with love. Asking *how* your brain creates experience is the life-changing question.

So let's start with *how* instead. What I want to give you is a roadmap for *how* your brain is creating your experience in love, and also *how* you can retrain it to create the love you deserve. I'm going to describe the deep, inner, and mostly unobserved mental moves and emotional responses that stop lasting love in its tracks. More importantly, I want to unpack and unlock the inner moves and emotional responses of the masters of relationships so you know how they did it. Not just their *mindset,* but, more importantly, the *way* their brain creates that precious experience called *lasting love* at all levels. In other words, I'm going to track your brain in the act of creating love, so I can show you the *difference that makes the difference* in love.

You'll learn not just the *mental moves* of the brain, but the *deep feeling states* that you must have in order to feel *Safe to Love Again.* When you finish this book, you'll have the complete inner roadmap, both emotional and mental, for finding your way to the loving relationship you so want. Are you ready to upgrade your inner GPS for love? If so, read on!

What Is Love?

Love is a full body-based feeling that resonates in every cell of your body. When we feel securely and genuinely loved, we know deep in our bones that we have a homeport in the heart of that one special person. Moreover, love is the earthiest of experiences. It's waking up at 3:00 a.m. and feeling the warmth of your beloved's skin touching you as you drift back to dreamland. It's smelling the scent of their body and sensing the soothing familiarity of it all.

Genuine, secure love is sharing a host of little moments with each other as you go through your day. It's that lingering hug and kiss as you leave for work; it's getting a quick text message with a simple, silly red heart that says, "You matter so much to me." Love is seeing a smiling face or hearing a soothing voice as you walk through the door at the end of a harried day that says, "Welcome home, darling." It's stopping your life to listen when your beloved is overwhelmed or troubled; it's praising them for the smallest of achievements just because you take notice. Love is all of this and much, much more.

When we feel loved to our core, it's because we've been offered a host of *little moments* often, in caring, attuned ways that are always packaged in simple, earthy, daily, and grounded action. In its essence, love is the most natural of experiences composed of a thousand micro-moments that whisper to our hearts, "I am loved," or "I love them so much!"

This is what I want for you, my reader. My passion is to help people discover how they can have a loving partner lying beside them at night, rather than a lonely pillow or a frustrated, distant mate. I want to help you rewire your brain so that you can find a committed partner, or empower your existing relationship to support the intimacy you crave. I wish for you to feel *truly loved*.

Love's Big Questions

No matter where you go, from Los Angeles to New York or anywhere in between, people ask the same questions over and over again. Essentially, the questions singles ask revolve around two simple concerns: "Why am I still single?" and "How do I find and keep a lasting relationship?" If they're part of a couple, most of the questions revolve around issues like, "We've been together for a while . . . is there any way we can reignite the flame we once had?" or, "How do we get beyond our stalemate and become the soulmates we want to be?"

Some of these love seekers are very passionate about finding love; others are confused by the state of things, especially with the advent of the online world of dating. They want more from their relationships, yet don't know how to get there. Some part of them intuitively knows that endless texting, last minute cancellations, and senseless breakups cannot be the real story of love. Still others will complain about how difficult dating is or how strained their relationship has become. They want to find a way to make it easier, less frustrating, and mostly, just *fun* again. Some just want to know how to *connect* more with their partner. *Does any of that seem familiar to you?*

The key issue under all of those questions is, "How do I become *Safe to Love Again?*" How is it possible to find and keep the true love of one's life? For many singles (and couples as well), the royal road of relationships has been too painful. *Love* has been more than daunting—as a matter of experience, it's been found to be downright painful and lacking. As a result, we either run like the wind, or alternatively, fight to try and keep it. Unfortunately, neither of these tactics works so well for finding and keeping a soulmate. When your brain is in either fight or flight mode, how can it help you find and keep a lasting relationship?

These are the questions of our day.
How do we become Safe to Love Again?
How do I create the love I deserve?

From Lusting to Lasting

Let's start out by addressing singles. While speaking in Portland, I rediscovered something very significant about singles and love. At one point, there was a long discussion with the audience about how to *get* a date. The men were bitterly complaining about how difficult asking women out had become. One man in particular was turned off by how *entitled* he thought women had become. Of course, there were a lot of scoffs and heckles from the women who were listening. One woman countered that all you had to do was gain a few extra pounds and the game was off for men!

A lively, engaging discussion ensued on how to get a first date. Lots of fashion advice was given by one expert, to both the men and women, as to how they could *attract* potential mates better. The online dating coach suggested great tips for writing an appealing online profile. This went on for thirty minutes or so.

During this discussion, I noticed something; the debate wasn't touching the audience at a very deep level. You could see it in their eyes. Some people had a glazed-over look that basically said, "So, what's new?" Or was it disbelief that I was seeing on their faces? "Yes, it's all so very interesting," their faces seemed to be saying, "but . . . I've tried that before and it still didn't go well."

Then it hit me; this Portland crowd isn't interested in dating anymore—and it's not because they can't attract or flirt—that they could do in spades. The *real* truth was that they were *leery* of love. It wasn't a lack of first dates that was the problem; it was what happened to them at the two or three month mark, in their past relationships, that's when things turned painful. This crowd was *annoyed* with love.

With that realization, I stood up and said to the entire audience, "Let's raise the bar here for a moment. *How many of you are interested in a first date?*" I paused for a moment and took inventory. About seven hands went up in a crowd of almost 150 people. *Ah, there it is,* I thought to myself.

Then I asked a few deeper questions; "How many of you would rather have a frigging soulmate? I mean, a *true* soulmate—somebody who has your back, that you know will be there for you, who knows you inside and out and still loves you anyway? And how about one who knows just how to pleasure your body as well as engage your mind? How many of you want to find *that* kind of love?" After a brief pause, I polished it off with a single query, "*So, how many of you want to know how to go from lusting to lasting?*"

When I finished my thirty-second sound bite, the entire left side of the room—all of them women stood up in unison. I got a standing ovation. This was what they had come to hear. They didn't simply want a *date*; they wanted to find a good *candidate* for the love of their life. Simply put, they wanted a *soulmate*. What these women most deeply desired was to know how to go from *lusting to lasting*.

The Three Styles of Love

Why were so many people in that crowd annoyed with dating and love? What's going on that so many singles are finding it hard to find a special someone to fall in love with for a lifetime?

Here's the *first key* to becoming *Safe to Love Again*; we must understand how our brains work. The science of relationships tells us that people are wired for love in three primary ways. These attachment or love styles are—*secure, anxious,* and *avoidant*. However, only 50 percent of adults are *securely attached*. That's a fancy scientific term for when somebody feels really, really safe in a relationship. When somebody has a *secure attachment*, or what I call a *secure love style*, their systems are wired to pair up in healthy ways. They quite naturally and easily stay bonded with their partner. You often see such couples holding hands in restaurants and gazing into each other's eyes. They're masters of the *little moments often* strategy I spoke about earlier.

The other 50 percent of adults are scared of love at some level. They're what relationship science calls *insecurely attached*. That's the expert term for people who are not safe with love at a deep level. Of these adults, 25 percent will run from love. They have what is called an *avoidant attachment style*, or as I put it, an *avoidant love style*. These folks have a *flight* response and run like hell from intimate relationships—especially when it gets to the commitment stage. These are the people who are gone for a week on a business trip and say they miss you terribly. When they get home on Friday night they make passionate love to you, and promise to spend the weekend having fun with you. Then, magically, on Saturday afternoon something *urgent* comes up at the office. *Poof!* They're gone again.

Another 20 percent of adults have developed a *fight* response to managing their relationships. These folks have what is called an *anxious attachment* or *anxious love style*. They constantly worry that love will go away, and so tend to create a lot of drama around their relationships. They will often ask things like, "Where were you…?" or, "Do you still love me?" These types are the drama queens and kings of the dating world. They often drive their partners away due to the excessive tension they create around love.

The other 5 percent of adults split the difference and are both *avoidant* and *anxious* at the same time. Many of the people in the Portland audience that night were probably in the 50 percent of adults who, at some level, are scared of love and its commitments. (The fourth love style, disorganized, will be omitted as it is not a mainstream issue due to its limited, clinical nature.)

For many of us love is a kind of *boogieman*. The scariest thing for our generation is no longer the monster in the closet or the bad guy from the movies. These days, the *boogieman* for many adults is *love*. Most are scared to death of it, or mortified by its commitments. However, that *boogieman* that scares us is not what we think it is. Real, secure love is never the monster we feel, think, or fear it to be.

Marcos and His Dog

When anything disrupts the flow of our relationships, it spawns a profound, yawning pain. Because we were born to engage in significant, deep, and lasting relationships that are meant to empower *all* areas of our lives, our brains will not easily let go of our longing for love. I've seen this many times in my clients.

Marcos was the sort of *self-actualized* man whom you never could have imagined would have trouble with romance. He was in his late thirties, highly educated, and had a very successful career. When he first came to see me I couldn't help but notice his very expensive, dark gray, Italian silk suit that was tailored immaculately to match his perfect, masculine build. For a moment, I thought Pierce Brosnan had made an appointment. While he seemingly had it all, his love life was as barren as a moonscape. Marcos could attract women—that wasn't the problem—the problem was he was attracted to women who didn't truly love him. In other words, Marcos never felt worthy or cherished in any of his relationships.

I usually ask my clients this question during our first session; "So, what would you like? What if a variety of miracles happened and you suddenly had what you most want in your love life?" Marcos' first words were spoken firmly, yet with a tone of resignation. He looked me squarely in the eyes and said, "What I want more than anything is to be loved for being *Marcos* rather than the other *M* word—*money*. Women always seem to associate me right off the bat with my money." Then he asked me the most stunning question; "Why am I still single? *Why is the best relationship of my life the one I have with my dog?* How did I miss the love boat?"

I've heard many variations of Marcos' personal torment in my male and female clients' personal stories. Yet here's the bigger point of this story; because our brains evolved to create deep bonds with a loving partner, Marcos' brain knew that he was not safe being bonded merely to his dog. Although Americans spend 53 billion dollars a year on their beloved pets, they won't fill the bill for the deep-seated heart yearning for a human companion. Millions of years ago, evolution created a mammal brain that knew it needed strong bonds to survive. Nothing's going to change *that* fact anytime soon.

People often try to fill this need with something else, like tail wagging dogs or purring lap cats. But you really can't fool that part of your brain. It knows love's chicanery when it sees it. Great friends can't give you all that your heart longs for, either. Here's the kicker; all of the success or self-actualization in the world won't give your brain what it needs, if it knows it's not well bonded. Marcos had all the treasury bonds in the world, yet what his brain needed was to be loved and treasured for himself. Eyes like Marcos were what I had seen in the eyes of my Portland audience.

Wanted! Deep and Lasting Bonds

Fleeting dates and frustrating relationships are not the experiences for which human brains were designed. We are a species that was designed by millions of years of adaptation to create deep and lasting relationships as a way to survive. Everything about being human revolves around the bonds we create.

Some love experts say we shouldn't *need* relationships; rather, we're designed to be *fully actualized individuals*. It's like the Marlboro Man meets Match.com in some circles. However, as Dr. Sue Johnson points out, that idea is a myth. It started with the teachings of Abraham Maslow in the '40s and continued with famed therapist Carl Rogers in the '60s. That myth is *still* haunting us. The ideal of the *Fully Actualized Individual*, which has been rampant in much of pop psychology, is a fad that has outlived its usefulness. Here's the reality—such ideals are more of a fairytale created by the grand cultural scheme of *Radical American Individualism* than it is the actual human experience.

All *individual* potential is first and foremost grounded in a network of close, loving relationships. This begins before we're born and continues until the day we die. Moreover, every inner template that anyone has ever used for a full human experience was learned in their early relationships with significant others. Individuals do not actualize by themselves; it takes a web of deeply bonded relationships to create a self-actualized person. A fully actualized brain needs a lot of bonding and a great community. The top of Maslow's famed pyramid of needs should have been *fully actualized relationships*.

The top of the pyramid of self-actualization
is *fully actualized relationships.*

This overemphasis on the individual has created havoc and much confusion in the modern love and relationship scene. As Dr. John Gottman points out in his groundbreaking research on what makes love strong, Maslow and Rogers pointed an entire generation of therapists in the wrong direction when it came to couples. Until about ten years ago, the dirty little secret in therapist circles was that if couples were having problems, they had a better chance of staying together if they did nothing, than if they went to see the traditionally trained therapist. Marital therapy worked only 18 to 25 percent of the time! The reason was that you couldn't treat a couple using methods that emphasize the individual. Let me explain why that is so.

When two individuals, or two *I*s, come together in an intimate relationship, they don't stay individuals for long. What develops is an inevitable field of energy that stands between them like an invisible third party. That third party, what most of us call the *We*, is what everyone craves at the deepest levels of their hearts. This *We* is *emergent* because although it combines the two individuals, it's always more and different than either of them standing alone. You can think of it like the molecule for water. Hydrogen and oxygen are both gases with distinct properties. When you combine them into one molecule, you get water, and water doesn't look or act like either hydrogen or oxygen atoms when they're on their own.

Look for *Signs of the We*

That sense of *We* is the true goal for anyone seeking a great relationship. Maslow took an unfortunate step when he put *self-actualization* above the *We* that stands at the heart of all lasting relationships. I know when working with couples that the *We* is at least as important as the two *I*s. In fact, the *We* is my true client. When couples learn how to create a fulfilling *We*, they become an *extraordinary couple*. That's the goal of this book for you, too.

Learning how to spot someone who can create a great *We* is the ultimate goal for finding and creating a great relationship. Singles need to learn how the brain recognizes when another person is wired to create a lasting *We*. Likewise, you'll need to know that for yourself as well. Lasting love seeks the *Signs of the We*.

> To create a lasting *We*, the programming in each
> *I* must honor the *We-love* at its highest manifestation.

If we approach dating as two individuals simply *matching up* (as most online dating sites suggest), we are losing sight of the one thing humans are most deeply in search of—that emergent, created, dynamic sense of belonging and *We-ness* which is the signature of every great, lasting relationship. Long-term and short-term, your brain needs to be looking for *Signs of the We*, and whether or not a *We* is possible with someone. Training your brain to notice that will make you a far better and wiser dater if you're single. When a single person trains their brain to scan for what creates a great sense of *We-ness*, I call them *extraordinary singles*. If you're part of a couple, it's about training your brain to create an empowering and dependable sense of *We-ness* between you and your partner. Then you become an *extraordinary couple*.

Four Feelings Create Lasting Love

Here's the *second key* to becoming *Safe to Love Again*. What dominates the brain patterning of both extraordinary singles and couples is a persistent attention to four feelings that all masters of relationships create naturally. Those four feelings are:

- *Welcomed with Joy*
- *Worthy and Nourished*
- *Cherished and Protected*
- *Empowered with Choice*

A brain that is aligned with these four feelings easily creates a profound, intimate, deep, calming, and empowering *We*. From this *We* extraordinary couples are born, nurtured, and raised.

As you will soon discover in more depth, the presence or absence of these four feelings determines your love style. When a brain is wired and trained to give and receive only these four feelings in a relationship, we call that a secure love style. However, when your brain doesn't easily or consistently give and receive the four feelings of *Welcomed with Joy*, *Worthy and Nourished*, *Cherished and Protected*, and *Empowered with Choice*, the result is either an anxious or an avoidant love style. The key to restoring your brain's ability to attract and keep a great, lasting relationship is to train your brain to give and receive these feelings with regularity and ease.

Notice that becoming *Safe to Love Again* is an *active* process. You can train your brain to do this. Creating a great relationship is about *designing* your experience with love. Becoming *Safe to Love Again* at a very deep level is about creating a *designer experience* with love—*your very own* designer experience! There's no sit back and wait for the universe to toss a soulmate your way. As I'm prone to say, the universe is neither rewarding nor punishing. It's a mirroring universe. So, the more you train your brain to scan for the *Signs of the We*, and become aligned within yourself with *The Four Feelings* that create deeply fulfilling, lasting love, the more easily your soulmate will show up or your relationship will heal. To adapt a quote from R. Buckminster Fuller, "The best way to predict your future with love is to design it."

Safe to Love Again is an active experience through which you design your experience with love.

Love Depends Upon Six Rights

Here's the *third key* to becoming *Safe to Love Again*. Between the ages of 0–3 especially, but sometimes later in life, your brain gets wired *by* experience to create *future* experience. It downloads instructions for what experiences it's allowed to create in both life and love. Basically, your brain gets a series of *permission slips* from early relationships as to what kinds of loving experiences are allowable in the future.

I call these early permission slips for creating experience, *rights*. Essentially, you should get six *rights* or *permission slips* early in life:

- *The Right to Exist*
- *The Right to Have Your Needs Met*
- *The Right to Separate and Belong*
- *The Right to Create Your Own Experience*
- *The Right to Assert with Voice and Choice*
- *The Right to Love and Be Loved*

Moreover, whether or not we are actually *given* all of these rights, has a lot to do with whether we have a secure, anxious, or avoidant love style. You need all of these rights to love well.

As we shall see later on, these six rights are very much related to *The Four Feelings* of secure love. Each right gives you one of *The Four Feelings* as a *reference feeling* for love. A full *Right to Exist* naturally gives you a feeling of *Welcomed with Joy*. *The Right to Have Your Needs Met* allows you to feel *Worthy and Nourished*. When you have a balanced *Right to Separate and Belong*, you will feel *Cherished and Protected*. *The Right to Create Your Own Experience* and *The Right to Assert* give you the feeling of *Empowered with Choice*. Add these up and you get *The Right to Love and Be Loved*. Then you feel totally *Lovable*.

In other words, *The Four Feelings* and *The Six Rights* work in tandem to create your love style. The goal is to reclaim all six of these rights and to use *The Four Feelings* as your new GPS for love. Doing this will give you a secure love style. From there you can attract your soulmate, or heal your relationship if you're part of a couple.

The best way to attract your soulmate or to improve your relationship is to upgrade your *rights* so your brain has the full set of permission slips to create the love you deserve. Here's the truth about love: *we are always having the experience we feel we have the rights to have*. If you're having a painful, limited experience with love over and over again, you can rest assured that your brain was programmed with that exact permission slip for love. Nothing is actually wrong, though; nothing is wrong with you, either. Your early brain simply got a limited set of permission slips. You need only update them, so love goes well both now and in the future.

This is why mere relationship coaching often doesn't change things long-term. Giving people new tools and skills won't stick unless they have the rights for the new experience. When we give people new skills or advice without updating their rights, it's like giving somebody a ticket to a Norwegian Cruise but not giving them a passport. Because they don't have the rights to go, they eventually stay at home. If you've ever wondered why coaching advice doesn't work sometimes, this is the reason. You didn't have the rights to experience what the skill set would give you. What you needed was a deeper transformation. When you restore your missing rights, you get your passport to the love you want.

Look for Mr. or Ms. Rights

This is why I tell singles that come to my workshops and retreats that they should not look for *Mr. Right* or *Ms. Right*. Rather, who you are looking for is Mr. or Ms. *Rights!* A true soulmate is the person who reflects back your complete set of rights. He or she is the one who makes you feel safely, securely, completely, and passionately in love by reflecting back all of your rights. So, here's the secret to finding a soulmate; you need to restore all of your rights to their original factory settings. Give your brain a full set of permission slips to have a great relationship. When you have a complete set of rights, love goes better. You'll also naturally, without much coaching, stop attracting Mr. or Ms. Wrong. Instead, you'll start attracting much better partners who can become a soulmate.

Exchanging missing rights for full rights is part of what it takes to design your experience with love. Working with limiting beliefs is great. Yet, as I'll explain later, these rights are in play well before your brain can even make up a single sentence, let alone a belief. This emphasis on reclaiming your rights is what makes my approach very different. In this book, you'll discover what creates those missing beliefs in the first place. You'll also learn how to restore your missing rights so you can attract and keep the love you want.

Nobody Is Wrong

Whatever problems you're having with love, you came by it all naturally. In fact, there's absolutely nothing wrong with your brain! If you have either avoidant or anxious tendencies, nothing I'm saying is about guilt, judgment, or feeling bad. *Au contraire*, your brain simply took the best deal available at some earlier time. Therefore, all you really need to do is update your brain by giving it a better deal now. So no guilt trips here! It's all predictable, and actually quite good. These earlier adaptations kept you sane and on the planet! So, we like them, but we'd also like to update them so love works well for us *now*.

Nothing is wrong with you. Your brain once took the best deal possible. We want to give it a better deal.

Bonding with Your Brain

For love to go smoothly, we need a close bond with a partner or spouse. We also need a close bond with our *brain* to make that happen. Allow me to explain using a scene in the movie *Avatar*. Sometime in the future, humans are mining a faraway planet for an expensive ore. Inhabiting the planet is a race of humanoids called the *Na'vi*. The *Na'vi* is a hunter-gatherer society. The main character is Jake Sully. Using advanced technology, Jake's mind is beamed into a genetically reproduced *Na'vi* body as a way for humans to understand and communicate with the native people.

At one point, Jake is ready for his final training as a hunter. He is led to the den of a bunch of flying reptiles called *ikran*. Here he must find his own *ikran* to fly. Once chosen, an interesting game between an *ikran* and the *Na'vi* hunter ensues. For a hunter to fly with an *ikran*, a neural bond must be made between them. The two brains must work together as one for it to work. As Jake surveys the nest of *ikrans*, he's looking for the one who will choose him back. Eventually, one roars at him. Jake has been chosen.

At this point, the rodeo begins. Jake approaches the *ikran* and of course, the *ikran* tries to buck him. His teacher, Neytiri, who is the chief's daughter, yells at him *"Tsaheylu! Make the bond!"* But Jake doesn't, so it turns into a big fight. Eventually Neytiri forcefully reminds him, *"Make the bond, Jake!"*

Once he makes the bond with the ikran's brain, everything calms down. Their brains are now aligned. The drama ends. A lasting connection is made between Jake and his flying reptile. The first flight isn't exactly smooth, yet soon it all levels out and both are seen gliding on the wings of their great bond together. When their brains are calmly bonded, the flying is smooth. This sounds like a great relationship, doesn't it?

How does this story apply to us? Relationship pain comes from having two brains that are not aligned *within themselves* or with love. In order to bond well with another person, you must first have a working relationship with your brain and its need for *The Four Feelings* and the six rights below those feelings. When you restore your rights, things calm down and you get the love you want and deserve. I call this *getting in rapport* with your brain.

My Experience with Love

Okay, so what's the state of love in your life today? Let's start our journey together with a few simple questions.

1. List four things that you really want in a relationship with your soulmate or your partner.

These can be states (like fun or curiosity) or feelings like cherished or adored.

A. _____

B. _____

C. _____

D. _____

2. Now list four things, feelings, or states that scare or worry you the most about love.

These four things should be *repetitive*, painful experiences that always seem to show up in your relationships but don't work for you. Like the movie, *Groundhog Day*, they always seem to be a part of your experience with love. So, if something happened but it wasn't one of those "*Oh, no, here we go again!*" experiences, that's not what we're looking for here.

A. _____

B. _____

C. _____

D. _____

For the moment, simply notice your experience. Don't judge any of it; not one bit! It's all there for a good reason. The attitude I want you to take is more like, *"Hmmm . . . of all of the experiences I could have had with love, isn't it interesting that I usually have that one? I wonder how my brain is creating that experience with love."*

I promise you, the latter list will make perfect sense in a while. For now, you only need to get conscious of your typical patterns with love. Soon I'll tell you more about what these two lists are telling you about your brain's rules and rights for love. More importantly, you'll learn what you can do about it and how *it's all adjustable*!

Remember; It's all adjustable!

Only so much can be put in this book. However, I have prepared a digital workbook just for you. If you want guided exercises and additional resources, go to *www.garysalyer.com/lovemanual* and sign up for more supportive helps. Here you can also join the movement for secure love and be connected to others just like you. The guided exercise for the first chapter will help you get perfectly clear on what you truly want and deserve in your loving relationships. Together, we can begin the process of you *experiencing* the magic of a fully open heart that feels perfectly safe with love.

Two

A Generation Without a GPS for Love

Behind all the questions that singles and couples ask there is but one important question; *how do I know when I'm truly loved?* On this question, both singles and couples are in complete alignment, though many are confused. Let's begin by addressing the big question for everybody; how does your *brain* know when you're loved?

That question arises whenever a single person is *ghosted* by some would-be pursuer who just a few days ago was head over heels interested in them. Then, out of the blue, they're ditched without so much as a word; without even the common human courtesy of a caring phone call to break the news. All that passion and flirtation just a few days ago sure seemed like *love*, didn't it?

If you're part of a couple, you may be wondering why in the world your relationship feels so *off*. At one time, you both gazed into each other's eyes, promising to love each other enthusiastically with words like *cherish*, *honor*, and *protect*. Now there's a thin veil of conflict, disappointment, hopelessness, or distance that's constantly in the air. One thing's for sure; it doesn't *feel* like love. So you ask yourself, "What's missing here?" Or perhaps, "What does love even feel like?"

In this chapter, I'll answer all those questions. It's time to give you access to your brain's true GPS for love. For singles, knowing the answer will allow you to navigate online dating in far better ways. You'll understand clearly why so many find it frustrating, and what you can do about that. Dating is going to become a whole lot more exciting and easy. You'll also come to understand what really drives your love style and every relationship you've ever created. Finally, I'll show you how you can become a better couple by using *The Four Feelings* of secure love as a *barometer* for monitoring the *weather conditions* in your marital friendship. What you'll learn in this chapter will help you create better relationships in all areas of your life—including partners, children, family, and friends.

So here's what you need to know; your brain uses four specific *feelings* to know when it's loved. There's a natural strategy for finding true love that is simple, elegant, and not as complicated as many make it out to be. Understanding how your brain knows when it's loved is the first step to reclaiming a secure love style. So, are you ready for some high definition connection?

Rachel and *The List*

This is what the problem looks like if you don't understand how your brain knows when it's loved. The grandmaster of *the list* was a thirty-five year old client I'll call *Rachel*. Rachel was the consummate *Match.com* girl. She was an upwardly mobile, millennial generation professional woman who owned her own business. Rachel was a stunningly pretty brunette who had it all—Italian good looks, the tall, statuesque build of a *goddess*, and she was also very intelligent, funny, charming, and social to her core. She lacked nothing except the *family man* who would step into her dream of having a loving husband and children.

Rachel was an architect who designed homes for people. From her business experience, she *knew* that the key for client satisfaction was getting to know all of the specifics somebody wanted before you even got to the drafting board. Just so, she had honed her own mate specifics into a list that was quite extensive. In our first session together, she told me how distraught she was about online dating. You see, Rachel's list of qualities was fifty-four standard criteria that she plugged into the *Match.com* search engine. Somewhere in those fifty-four items was the man with whom she would have a family. Or so she assumed.

I asked her what some of those were. Of course, she shared them. After she went over about fifteen items on her list, Rachel's usually beaming eyes began to tear over. Her voice went low as she dropped her head while saying, "But on all of *Match.com*, there are only twenty-five such men spread all over the country. What's a girl to do about that?" I also noticed something else. Strikingly, there was a pattern in her list; there were only a few *feeling* words. It was almost all about the external attributes of the man, and not so much about the qualities of the relationship. If ever there was a strategy for pulling in futility and hopelessness, this was it.

Rachel met many men who were professional, tall, handsome, funny, and so on. Yet, most of those dates left her feeling a bit empty or unfulfilled. As Rachel put it during a session, "I'm meeting men who like what *starts* a family, but they aren't really into me or being a daddy." After a few months of this, Rachel was ready to find a different way to date. What Rachel needed was a different GPS system with which to find her soulmate.

If you're single, you hear a lot about *the list*. It's supposedly the key to finding a soulmate. *The list* takes up a lot of bandwidth for many people dating and looking for their life partner. Once you've created a list, if you want to attract your ideal partner, you'll have to visualize them too. Admittedly, there's a lot of truth to the visualization method.

Visualizations are useful when it comes to being motivated for specific goals. But when it comes to finding a lasting life partner or soulmate, it's missing something. Neuroscience knows that the brain absolutely needs a mental picture to find what it wants. What we call our *subconscious* mind is really a euphemism for the fact that every human on the planet has the brain of a reptile, early mammal, and great ape (primate) running beneath the *human* brain. Moreover, every animal needs a picture or sound to know what to *run* toward. However, our attachment system isn't running toward pictures or a list as much as it's seeking feelings; four of them, to be specific.

Dying for Love

Science has studied human bonding in a field called attachment theory. It's basically all about how your brain creates love. To understand what your brain is looking for, we'll have to go back all the way to the beginning, when attachment theory was first born.

Working in British orphanages after World War II, Dr. John Bowlby noticed that young children who lost their parents, yet were safely sheltered, warm, well fed, and who had sufficient *supervision* were unexpectedly dying for what seemed to be no good reason. According to the current understanding of the time, these children should have thrived. After all, they had everything on *the list* that current society believed children needed.

Dr. Bowlby came up with a daring and provocative explanation. These children were dying because of a lack of *secure attachment* with a parental figure. Without love, something was missing. So much so, that the human heart could not sustain life without that missing connection. These children were dying because humans need more than what's typically on our *lists*.

What all humans need is something deeply internal. As attachment expert Dr. Daniel Siegel points out, we need an inner map for love that says I'm *seen*, I'm *soothed*, I'm *safe*, and therefore I feel *securely loved*. This map, however, is not something visual in nature. Neither is it auditory. This map is an internalized set of *feelings* about oneself, others, and the world that says, "I'm safely connected to those who value and care about me, and therefore I can relax and feel safe." That's how a human knows they're loved.

You need an internal map that says I'm seen,
soothed and safe to feel securely loved.

So, you may be asking yourself, which feelings tell a person they are loved? After all, the English language has thousands of words devoted to describing feelings. There are a lot of feelings out there to experience. Surely, not all are equal. So what if you could pinpoint which feelings tell a brain it's loved? Then you would have the proper GPS to find a love that is actually safe, passionate, intimate, and lasting.

Early Feelings Create Love Styles

It was John Bowlby's student, Dr. Mary Ainsworth, who discovered something very interesting about humans. Dr. Bowlby could never quite quantify his insights. Then Dr. Ainsworth got the brilliant idea that if you separate a young child from his or her parent, you'll find out exactly what type of bond that child has with their parents. It's an experiment called *The Strange Situation*.

Dr. Ainsworth designed a situation where she would bring a mother and her toddler into a room with lots of toys. Next, a stranger would enter the room. The first thing they noticed was how the child reacted to a stranger. Did they run to mother? Did they ignore the stranger or look very nervous? Or did they keep playing? They would then ask the mother to depart from the room and leave the child alone. The reactions of the child told an even deeper story about the nature of their relationship with mom. Predictably, most children protested with crying, tears, and chasing after their mother. After a few minutes, the stranger would enter the room and try to calm and comfort the child. Again, as you probably guessed, this was one of those *no spaghetti* moments where most children were not soothed by the stranger.

Finally, the magical moment came when the mother re-entered the room. From the way the child reacted to the *reunion* with mom, attachment researchers discovered there were basically three ways that children reacted. They classified those reactions as *avoidant*, *anxious*, and *secure* attachment styles.

Most people are wired to have three types of recurring experiences with love—anxious, avoidant, or secure.

When love scientists like Drs. Alan Sroufe and Mary Main tracked these children for the next twenty to thirty years, those styles *persisted over time*. Unless there was an intervention, this early style of being with a parent would translate into how that child would be in later romantic relationships. In fact, it predicted how they would be in *all* relationships, beginning with school and extending all the way through professional, casual, and romantic relationships. Love wires us for *all* of life it seems. I'll discuss why this is so a little later.

One group of babies would treat the reunion like it was no big deal. They looked precociously independent and didn't reach out to mom for much attention or solace. Love scientists called that an *avoidant* style. Though they looked mature, something was off. When they tracked that baby as she or he grew up, they discovered that those with an avoidant style would become very dismissive of their partners in later relationships. They preferred emotional distance to actual closeness in any relationship, had difficulties being emotionally present to their significant others (or themselves), and often had problems committing. In a word, they didn't like depending on others or being depended upon. Those babies grew up to be Mr. or Ms. No Commitment.

Another group of babies turned the reunion into a drama filled ordeal. When mom re-entered the room, they would run and cling to her. There was all manner of crying and protesting as if to say, "I thought you'd never come back!" Yet something very interesting was also going on. In addition to their fear and very pronounced anxiety, these babies were extremely angry with their moms. When the love scientists tracked these babies, they discovered that those with an *anxious* attachment style grew up to be pre-occupied with the fear of love going away, being abandoned, or any sort of disruption in their relationships. In a word, their worst fear is being abandoned or their love partner going away. They want to lock down love at any cost. These types will worry if you haven't texted them back within ten minutes. *Where were you?* is a mantra. If you've ever dated or partnered with a Drama Queen or King, you've seen these babies as adults.

The third group of babies was what we call *secure*. Yes, mom left, but these babies were overjoyed when she returned. There was a joyous reunion.

Their systems took it all in stride. It was as if they were saying, "Sure, mom can leave. No, it doesn't feel good, but I'm sure she's coming back, and when she does I'm going to be there too!" When mom did return, it was as if nothing had happened. They calmed down easily and soon. When they tracked these babies into adult relationships, they acted free of undue anxiety or fear. Those with a secure love style naturally seek out people who will genuinely love and commit to them. As if by instinct, they just seem to know when someone truly loves them. They don't pick Mr. or Ms. Wrong very often. When they get in a relationship, they give neither *distance nor drama*, as I often put it to my clients.

So, our question is simple—*what tells these secure babies they are loved? And most importantly—what tells those babies as adults how to pick a partner who loves them so well?*

> Whatever tells a securely loved baby that she or
> he is safely loved also tells you when you are loved.

The Four Feelings of Secure Love

To answer that, let's step into the experience of a brain that is only one year old. By the time you were one year old, your brain, just like those of the babies in *The Strange Situation*, had already made a map of what love is, and had decided whether or not you were truly loved. Your *love style* has been running silently behind the scenes all of your life, just like it does for everyone else on the planet.

First off, we know from neuroscience that nothing logical or abstract is even remotely functioning at that time. The pre-frontal cortex, which handles those sorts of things, is like a tire sitting on the wall of a Goodyear Tires store; it's in a *deflated* state and is waiting to come online. The uniquely human part of your brain, the pre-frontal cortex, is totally offline.

That means the *human* part of the baby is just sitting there. There's no *list* running here, that's for sure. You can also forget anything that is abstract. Nothing like a sense of *me* or *my identity* is running either. The pre-frontal cortex is the part of the brain that tells the story of *me*. So it's not a story or belief that tells a one year old that they're loved either.

If you step into a mind at this age, you realize something is running the show that's *deeper than any limiting belief.* Most limiting beliefs come online starting at about age three to *explain* things that are *already* there. Limiting beliefs aren't the root cause of your love issues. If you're still dealing with your limited beliefs, you need to go deeper to change your fate with love.

Second, we know that conscious, explicit memory is also offline. The hippocampus, which gives us recall memory, won't come online until after 18 months—or just after the above experiment is over. Without recall memory, it's not about any story or conscious sense of what happened to me. What tells a secure baby that they're loved isn't located in logic, identity, story, beliefs, or even conscious memory.

If you take away all of that, you're left with only one thing that tells a baby that he or she is securely loved—*feelings*—just feelings! These feelings are stored in what we call implicit memory. Implicit memory is memory that cannot be consciously recalled. Or, as I like to say, it's memory that *you can't remember yet is unforgettable.* These feelings are like a soundtrack that plays beneath the *movie* of your life. That implicit memory and emotional soundtrack is housed in the amygdala rather than the hippocampus. If you've followed me this far, you're probably already asking the most important question you'll ever consider about love—*which feelings tell my brain it's loved and loveable?*

It just so happens, that *The Strange Situation* tests for four primary things. First, it tells you how a baby feels about being in close physical proximity to the mother, and whether it's seeking to maintain that physical proximity. Attachment theory calls this *proximity maintenance.* Second, you also learn a thing or two about how the baby feels about the mother as a *safe haven* who will be there to meet his or her needs. Third, you get a good sense of how the baby feels about the mother as a *secure base* that she or he can use as a touchstone as they explore their world. Finally, *The Strange Situation* tells us how a baby feels about separation, and whether they *manage anxiety* and choice well. This is a simple explanation, but it's useful for understanding how your brain computes *love equals safe.*

Here's the key thing—beneath each of these four experiences is a *baseline feeling* that's running the show. That's all the one-year old brain has to work with in order to know anything at this age—just feelings! As a result, there are basically four feelings that a secure baby must feel to have a positive experience of trust and safety in these four ways.

However, there's an even deeper reason *The Strange Situation* is testing for four feelings. We now know that love, as usually expressed in your early relationships, literally hardwires your brain to create more experiences that are just the same as the ones you experienced as a child. Neurons are actually created or purged in your brain depending on the amount and quality of loving relationship experience you receive from parents or caregivers. *Hardwired* literally refers to neurons in your brain and not something *mental* when it comes to how love tells your brain to actually physically shape itself. Love *literally* wires your brain.

These early experiences wire your brain for later relationships. I call such wiring, *rights*. Essentially, early brain wiring acts like a set of permission slips for creating love (or not). By the time a baby reaches the age of *The Strange Situation*, they have already received (or not) five of the six rights everyone gets between ages 0-3. Those first five rights are felt by the baby as a set of *reference feelings* for creating future relational experience, i.e., love.

Reference feelings and *rights* are like flip sides of a coin—they always go together. *Welcomed with Joy* is the flip side of the coin for *The Right to Exist*. *Worthy and Nourished* is the flip side of the coin for *The Right to Have Your Needs Met*, etc. Each has an inextricable connection to the other. As I see it, the feeling is the *cause* while the right is the *effect* of all that early learning by your brain. So, rights and reference feelings must always be seen together.

Later in the book we'll go into far more depth on these four feelings, and the rights underneath them. For now, it's important to know that in the first two months of life a baby is given a *Right to Exist*. That registers as the feeling of *Welcomed with Joy* if the parent has offered attuned attention, and has truly been delighted with the arrival of their little one. If they're not given a full welcome into life, babies will learn to feel unwelcomed, not special or sometimes hostility as their reference feeling for love and life.

From ages 2–6 months, babies are given the *Right to Have Your Needs Met*. If they're given lots and lots of attentive responses to their cries, they feel *Worthy and Nourished*. That feeling then becomes the second reference feeling for love. On the other hand, if they don't receive a lot of attuned attention to their needs, they'll feel unworthy or not good enough.

Beginning at six months to about one year the game changes. Babies learn to crawl and walk. At about eight months infants learn they are *separate* from mommy and daddy, and in fact are an individual *self* at a body based level. How parents navigate this budding experience of selfhood comes in as the *Right to Separate and Belong*. That means they get to be a *Me* and *also* belong to a protecting and empowering *We* at the same time. The reference feeling they get for all ensuing loving relationships is *Cherished and Protected*. If they didn't get a full permission slip to belong, they'll opt for feeling separate at the cost of the *We*. Or, if they were given too little right to separate, they'll feel enmeshed at the cost of the *Me*. These types will later feel as if either, "I have to do it on my own," or, "I can't be myself in a relationship."

Finally, between ages 12 and 24 months, babies are given two rights simultaneously. Those are the *Right to Create Your Own Experience* and the *Right to Assert* with voice and choice. When given a full set of rights, the baby learns that they can feel *Empowered with Choice* in loving relationships. Later, in the third year of life, the sixth right comes into play; the *Right to Love and Be Loved*. The baby's brain essentially adds up the math from the first four reference feelings. Based on their presence or absence, the brain deems them lovable, or not.

After the rights are put into place, starting at about age three the brain creates beliefs to explain why you didn't get a full set of rights. All limiting beliefs are *explanations for these previously missing rights*. They are *not* the causes of limiting experiences, but rather the explanation. Limiting beliefs come in three basic varieties—something's wrong with me, something's wrong with them, or something's wrong with the world. But here's the good news about limiting beliefs; if you restore the missing rights, limiting beliefs can easily be upgraded. However, if you don't restore the missing rights, the limiting beliefs will usually reset. You must first restore a missing right before you can modify the explaining belief.

The Strange Situation is actually testing for four feelings that baby brains associate with love. These four feelings, learned early in life, are your brain's natural GPS for knowing when you're loved. Let's get better acquainted with your inner GPS for love.

Beneath every love style is a positive or negative
baseline feeling running the show.

First, when a baby is held and cuddled, receiving the gift of physical closeness and *proximity*, he or she feels the first of the four feelings: *Welcomed with Joy*. When a baby feels securely loved, they have a sense that mom and dad are there and it's a good thing. Moreover, they're here too, and that's also a good thing! They feel that they're *Welcomed with Joy* into their parent's world. As University of California at Los Angeles researcher Dr. Allan Schores has noted, human bonding is different than other mammalian types of early bonding. What seems unique about humans is that we need a lot of highly positive initial emotions to bond properly. That primary bonding emotion is *joy*. Joy is the gateway to human bonding and love. When a parent is crazy about their child, a "*So glad you're here!*" kind of love welcomes them with joy. Let's call *Welcomed with Joy* our *secure north*, so to speak. It's the reason why love usually starts out with fun, playful times called *dates*.

Second, when a baby feels they can count on mom to meet their needs, they develop a sense of being worthy and deserving of having their needs met. Such babies naturally reach out to the parent as a *safe haven*. They don't *pull back* from asking for their needs to be attended to. The second feeling a securely attached brain uses to know it's loved is a full-bodied feeling of *Worthy and Nourished*. Worthy and nourished is the *secure south* of our inner love GPS.

Third, the secure baby has an inner sense that they're being watched over and can therefore explore their world safely. The child knows this when they can depend upon the parent to provide a *secure base* for all of their exploration and learning. When a baby knows they can depend on a parent to be a secure base, they feel *Cherished and Protected*. This is our *true east* on the compass, which links the love and exploration systems in our brain. The secure baby easily goes back to playing with its toys and can explore the entire room. They can take risks because they trust that someone has their back.

The fourth feeling comes from the baby's feeling that choice is both good and approved of. They have an inner freedom to choose without *anxiety*. Underneath the ability to separate without distress is the secure feeling of *Empowered with Choice*. When a baby feels securely loved, they know it's okay to make choices and have their own voice. They don't shut down or cling to the parent as an anxious baby might. Nor do they go away and play by themselves because they feel disconnected like an avoidant baby does. The *true west* for our brain's natural love compass is *Empowered with Choice*.

Here's your new GPS for finding real love:

Welcomed with Joy

N

Empowered
with Choice   **W**   **E**   Cherished
                                                     and Protected

S

Worthy and Nourished

Notice how different your brain's inner system for knowing whether or not you're loved is from *the list*! It's not complicated. In fact, Mother Nature usually prefers simplicity in such matters. In NLP circles, Richard Bandler and John Grinder called it the *Elegance Principle*. Albert Einstein told us, "Everything should be as simple as it can be, but not simpler." The problem with *the list* is that it makes things more complicated than they are. So, let's trust Albert's most sage advice when he cautioned scientists; "If you can't explain it simply, you don't understand it well enough." *The Four Feelings System* fits all the requirements of an elegance principle.

A New GPS for Online Dating

Here's the *first thing you need to know* when going online. When you use a *list*, you're using a mate selection system that your attachment system doesn't use. That's what's wrong with so much online dating these days. Asking people to select a bunch of criteria and basing matches on those selections (the *lists*, so to speak) is not how your brain deeply knows when you're loved. It also badly violates your brain's own elegance principle for love.

One of the dirty little secrets of online dating sites is that they have spent years developing algorithms for predicting great mate selection, sometimes referred to as *chemistry*. Yet, no matter how sophisticated the algorithm, the programmers for these sites now know after many years of tracking that who people actually go out and fall in love with is often unpredictable based on their *selections* and *preferences*. In other words, these dating site programmers are actually mystified about how to predict real love between any two people.

You can read all about this in Christian Rudder's peerless book, *Dataclysm*. He's the former president of the dating site *OKCupid*. It's truly a very interesting *tell all* about online dating. As Christian so honestly put it, "In short, people appear to be heavily preselecting for something that, once they sit down in person, doesn't seem important to them." That's because when they sit down, their attachment systems and love styles take over. While they're at their computers, their attachment system is mostly *offline* for many reasons, even though they're technically *online*. Ironic, right? Then when you're sitting in front of your date at Starbucks and talking over that first cup of shared coffee, the attachment part of your brain takes over the conversation. It's as if your brain is saying, "I'll take a cappuccino with a secure love style, please!"

The research by Dr. Ted Hudson at the University of Texas is also illuminating. Observing couples in a longitudinal study, Dr. Hudson discovered that *objective compatibility* such as you find on many dating sites predicts almost nothing about long-term marital happiness. Lastingly happy couples didn't accent their compatibility, but rather the quality of their relationship. It was the unhappy couples that blamed things on compatibility rather than attending to how well they got along with each other. In other words, compatibility is how couples explain a bad relationship when the actual problem resides in the ways they fail to attune and the *feelings* they give to each other. Relationship happiness is best predicted by the strength of a couple's commitment and the quality of their friendship rather than *compatibility*, per se.

Here's the bottom line; there's simply a difference between *date selection* or *compatibility* versus knowing when somebody has the capacity to securely love you. So, am I saying not to date online? No. I'm saying, know what it's good for and what it's not. Online is about introductions—it isn't true dating—dates happen *offline*. Moreover, offline is where your love style kicks in, big time!

To successfully date and find the soulmate you deserve, you'll need to get in touch with the emotional compass points that your brain has used to know when you're securely loved since you were one year old. Moreover, you'll need to feel them at your core. These four feelings must become your new *Secure Reference Emotions* for dating selection and relationship maintenance. When you use the feelings of *Welcomed with Joy, Worthy and Nourished, Cherished and Protected*, and *Empowered with Choice* as your new reference for mate selection, *everything* will change.

Your Brain Creates "Experience"

Let's go a little deeper into your brain here. The choices you make in your love relationships don't come out of the blue, nor do experiences with love *just happen*. All experience is actually *created* by your brain. There are no exceptions to this rule.

Perhaps the quintessential and most dramatic example of this rule can be seen in the case of Paul. Paul came to me trying to unravel why he was twice divorced. He wanted to figure out how he could stay married the next time. Paul had a certain *strategy* running in his brain when it came to his relationships. But it wasn't working.

By now you may be wondering what causes an anxious or avoidant love style. You may have even deduced that some form of parental neglect is the culprit. However, as much as that may be true, sometimes the reasons can be utterly surprising. This was the case with Paul. His family was nearly the perfect example of a secure love style. Mom and dad had a wonderful, loving marriage. At the time Paul came to me, they had been happily married for 53 years and counting. Both were model parents in every way by everyone's estimation. Even Paul said so. Paul's two siblings had a secure love style just like their parents. In fact, there hadn't been a divorce in the entire family for over three generations! Then there was Paul, with his two divorces. Nobody in his family could figure it out. He was "the family enigma" as Paul put it to me.

Paul had an anxious love style. In our first few sessions, what kept coming up like a mantra was the phrase, "When will love turn on me?" Time and time again, his brain kept looking out for the day love would *turn* against him. *Turn against me* was his constant refrain. Of course, this drove both of his wives crazy. Paul would often accuse them of turning against him at the slightest whim. As you might have guessed, neither of them wanted to stay in a relationship filled with such mistrust and anxiety. Paul himself lamented during one session, "The fact of the matter is I drove them both away. I created my own worst nightmare."

Indeed, that's the fate for most people with an anxious love style. Anxiety is always its own worst enemy when it comes to stabilizing long-term love. That's because anxiety puts a partner on high alert, and nobody associates that with love. Love and feeling safe always go together. If safety is not present, then bad things ensue for any relationship. Our brains expect love to be calm and safe.

Eventually, we tracked that feeling of *When does love turn against me?* to an incident around a campfire when he was four years old. One evening, as his family was hanging out together, his father *turned* on him for no reason. "He just *turned on me* and began beating and beating on me," recalled Paul. That was the moment his brain got the mantra, *When will love turn against me?* Here's the rub in the story as Paul remembered it; there was never a time before or after that such a thing even remotely occurred again. His dad was a model parent all but for this one incident. It happened only once. Yet his young brain made up a strategy to protect him in any loving relationship lest it ever occur again; *look out for the day that love turns against me.*

More revelations were to come however. A few months later, Paul attended one of my workshops with his securely married brother along for support. Paul raised his hand and began to tell his story about the night his father *turned on him*. As he was telling his story, I couldn't help but notice the look of utter incredulity on his brother's face. Eventually, his brother could not contain himself. The brother interrupted Paul with the sound of utter astonishment ringing through his every word. What came next was as shocking as it was heartbreaking. He said to Paul, "So, *that*—that's why you're *divorced*? That's why you have always been so *anxious*? My God, Paul—you got it *all wrong*. I was there. I was nine and you were four. You were playing too close to the campfire and your pant leg caught on fire! Dad grabbed you and beat on your legs to put the flames out! He wasn't *turning* on you! He was keeping you from becoming a *marshmallow!*"

You could have heard a pin drop in the room. Paul and his brother stared at each other in utter astonishment. I let that sink in for a moment and then said to everyone, "This is the perfect example of a real big truth about all of life. There's what happens to us, and then, there's the experience in our brains. Our *experience* is never a carbon copy of what happened. It's important to realize that your *experience* is a creation of your brain. Next time you think that life or love is such and such, just remember—that's *your* experience talking—it's not necessarily true about either love or life."

Paul's four-year old brain missed a few important things about the campfire being so close and his pant leg being on fire. Then it drew a horrible conclusion about his father and the nature of love. From that moment on, his brain created an *experience* from a life event, but a lot of things got deleted. Then his brain distorted it with a broad generalization that believed *love will always turn on you*.

Therefore, when the adult Paul got into any close relationship, his brain would unconsciously remember this picture of the campfire scene from hell. Associated with that picture was a *reference feeling* of anxiety. Tragically, his brain made one event more important than any other in his life. Why? We really don't know except that the human brain is hardly logical, especially at four. Paul's brain then used that reference feeling as a way to navigate every relationship in order to keep him *safe*. At least, that was the intended positive thing his brain wanted for Paul. We simply note the brain never does anything without an intended positive intention.

---

*Our experience is never a carbon copy of what happened.
Experience is a creation of your brain.*

How Reference Feelings Operate

Here's the big truth about your brain—it uses a specific reference emotion for every strategy it has. Together, these strategies create a whole range of experiences called *my life*. This is the big truth underneath Paul's story (and yours as well). Whatever feeling is associated with a strategy controls that strategy and its experience. These controlling feelings underneath any strategy we call *reference feelings*. So whatever feelings designed your strategies in the first place, and also keeps them in place, is actually in the driver's seat of your experience. These reference feelings even dictate your experience of *you*.

The reference feeling of anxiety created havoc for Paul's ability to create a lasting relationship. *Lasting love is a well-managed state of reference feelings and experiences.* Let that sink in for a moment. Neither an anxious nor an avoidant love style manages the secure feelings for love very well. Are the lights coming on?

To create lasting love in Paul's life, we had to exchange that reference feeling of anxiety for *The Four Feelings* of a secure love style. Just for the record, every anxious love style has either anxiety or a close relative as its primary reference feeling for love. In the same way, an avoidant love style usually has a primary feeling of fear or distance running somewhere in the background. Neither of these negative reference feelings will manage a loving relationship well. That's why it's so important to exchange them for the true reference feelings that will create and manage a lasting love.

Here's the *second thing you need to know* when going online. There's another reason why *the list* may be so popular. When so many people don't have secure reference feelings for love, wouldn't it feel better to exchange that underlying feeling of anxiety or fear for something a bit more external like a bunch of characteristics? Then you don't have to feel it so much! Yippee!!! Your brain is always looking for the most positive feeling it can get. If love equals anxiety or fear in your brain, the more positive feeling would be to run a strategy that gets you as far away as possible from that negative reference feeling. Helpless, hopeless, worthless, terrified, and grief are some of the more popular negative reference feelings people carry. These feelings can even feel like a pervasive, all encompassing, always present baseline state for many people.

A third thing to notice is that a long list also can serve the purpose of keeping us out of a relationship. When some part of you is running on anxiety or fear equals love, then a long list provides an ample number of deal breakers and excuses to exit and remain *safe*. Yes, the human part of you can be saying, "I want a relationship." Yet deep down, *the list* is in cahoots with a part of your brain that wants to keep you safely out of a relationship, because it never wants to feel that negative reference feeling again.

Here's my point. The real reason why *the list* is so important for many singles is that they've lost touch with their internal GPS for tracking real, secure love. Nature abhors a vacuum. We all know that. So, we'll substitute a list for the real GPS. That's also why many people will bolt from a good relationship.

Here's a key principle for becoming *Safe to Love Again*; you must retrain your brain to *replace any negative reference feelings* about love for the original, four feelings of a secure love style. When a reference feeling of anxiety or fear is exchanged for *Welcomed with Joy, Worthy and Nourished, Cherished and Protected*, and *Empowered with Choice* we change the valence and experience of love in our brains. That, in turn, changes even how you experience *you*. What controls your experience with love are reference feelings. It's imperative to have a brain with the right reference feelings. When you replace negative reference feelings for love with *The Four Secure Feelings*, scientists who study love call that an *earned* secure attachment or love style. Then the anxiety, fear, or distance goes away. Your relationship woes also go away.

> What controls your current experiences with love
> are the reference feelings you learned early in life.

Beyond "Chopped Liver" Partners

I was speaking in Phoenix at a singles event. One young woman on the left side of the room, about 28 to 32 years old, told a heartbreaking story. She shared how several boyfriends had broken up with her at about the two to three month period. These men told her they "weren't sure" and that perhaps, "there's someone better for me out there." "What's up with all of these break-ups?" she bitterly lamented. "I'm a quality woman who wants to find a man to settle down and raise a family with before I run out of time. I start to date these men. Things are going well, we're falling in love, and then he says, 'I think there's someone better out there.' What's all this stuff about looking for somebody better? What am I, chopped liver?"

I remember thinking that for a young woman this must be a living nightmare. Why did these men break up with her? Here's one possible answer—like many people, these men weren't in touch with their brain's real GPS for love. So instead of referencing *The Four Secure Feelings*, they had a negative reference feeling for love that was pre-programmed to fire off when things got *serious*, which was usually about 2-3 months into her typical dating relationships. That's the real deal usually running beneath Mr. or Ms. Unavailable.

So here's the *fourth thing you need to know*; there's yet another reason why you want a brain that feels the four secure reference feelings for love. Our brains are always seeking similarity in order to feel safe. When you have a brain running *The Four Feelings* of a secure love style, it naturally picks up whether those feelings are present in prospective dates. Then things go much better for love.

Once your reference feelings for love are *Welcomed with Joy, Worthy and Nourished, Cherished and Protected*, and *Empowered with Choice* your brain will start being attracted to others who have the same reference feelings for love. That is why those with a secure love style almost never pick someone who gives them any BS. This is the neurological explanation for the *law of attraction*. It's primed into our very neurology.

If you want to avoid ghosting, simmering, icing, and all those other antics going on in the dating world today, you'll want a brain that can sense when somebody has secure reference feelings for love. Such a brain will only be attracted to those who can truly love them.

Adam Attracts Better Dates

Adam was one such example. I can still remember the day he called me after our eighth session. We had worked for about 5 months replacing his old anxious love style with a more secure love style. He knew *The Four Feelings System* for finding real love. Adam was now fully conscious when his brain was feeling them in a relationship. Moreover, we had rewired his brain to *accept only* these four feelings for feeling loved at an unconscious level. No longer was *anxiety* his brain's reference feeling for love. Adam's brain was now properly aligned with his inner GPS system for love.

One day, the call came. Adam exclaimed, "Gary, something totally new is going on. I'm no longer attracting the drama queens. And I'm no longer going out with 19–21 year olds. It's strange, but the woman I'm seeing now is the first woman I can remember who isn't into drama. She actually predicts my needs ahead of time! I'm just attracted to different people now. Honestly, I'm attracting a type of woman I've never attracted before. I can't believe it, but I'm actually attracting a way better quality of woman! This feels so much better to me." Yes, that woman was near his age!

That's the power of working with your brain's natural GPS for love. When you work with that GPS, you naturally and effortlessly start attracting people with a more secure love style. Adam didn't have to think about it anymore. Ms. Wrong was no longer showing up. His unconscious brain had been updated. It was selecting and attracting women who could actually love him. For the first time, Adam felt safe in his relationships.

That's the secret to feeling *Safe to Love Again*. It's about getting your brain to accept only *The Four Feelings* as acceptable from a potential or current love partner, and to give only these feelings as well. When you have full access to your brain's natural GPS for love and are using *The Four Secure Feelings* as your new reference for knowing if someone is right for you (or whether your current partner really loves you if you're part of a couple), that's when the game of love becomes safe again.

The secret behind Safe to Love Again is retraining your brain to feel The Four Feelings as references for love.

Maximizing Choices, Minimizing Feelings

Those with anxious or avoidant love styles never have full access to this beautiful compass in our brains. They're not accessing their true reference feelings for secure love. Fear and anxiety often block their access. Or else they're following our culture's advice to maximize their *full potential* rather than listening to their true feelings. Either way, it's making love much more difficult these days. The problem for the modern love and relationship scene is that we've become a generation without a GPS for love. Or, as attachment theory calls it, we don't have a secure love style.

For instance, Lori Gottlieb, author of the New York Times best seller, *Marry Him: The Case for Settling for Mr. Good Enough* tells one rather paradigmatic and heartbreaking story about a woman who was so loved. Her boyfriend of two years adored her and was totally committed and *there* for her. He finally convinces her that she's really a great gal. What does this particular woman do with that love? She consults her *list* and says to her girlfriend, "If I'm really all he says I am, then I can do a lot better." She then breaks up with him because *the list* has persuaded her to change course. Predictably, she crashes the relationship.

That's what a non-secure love style usually gets you; more pain for everyone. In turn, this makes love feel unsafe for an entire generation. According to Tracy McMillan, fear of missing out (FOMO) often presents itself in women more along the lines of *"Hmmm . . . I know he's got a stable job, but maybe I can find a millionaire out there."* Anxious and avoidant love styles often give you a false indicator light when it comes to landing your relationship on the tarmac of commitment. That's why so many relationships are crashing and burning these days!

The Paradox of Choice Revisited

Here's a *fifth problem* with online search criteria. When those sites encourage making a list, while they may be helping women and men find a date, they're actually exacerbating the problem of how to find and create *lasting* love. That online dating site checklist can give you some rather harsh and painful false indicator lights down the road. Too much *list* is not a great way to begin or continue a lasting relationship.

As Barry Schwartz points out in his book, *The Paradox of Choice*, people will often consult the list to see if they're *maximizing* their choices. They do this rather than listen to the feelings of their inner GPS system. Because online dating offers so many choices today, it can actually cause people to create *less* satisfaction in their lives. Rather quickly, a missing item on the list will take precedence over whether they feel *Welcomed with Joy, Worthy and Nourished, Cherished and Protected,* and *Empowered with Choice*. Love can't win with such criteria.

The title of Lori Gottlieb's book, *Marry Him: The Case for Settling for Mr. Good Enough,* seems to suggest that women should accept a compromise regarding who she marries. However, Lori points out women often pass on men who were in reality, way better than their list allowed them to see. These women's *definitions* of love were off about what creates lasting love. Lori is very clear about that.

So let's talk about that sense of *definition* and what it means. I too want to be perfectly clear here. Your brain's natural GPS for love isn't into compromise either. What I'm talking about is hardly about *compromise*; it's about recalibration. Secure love is about marrying Mr. or Ms. Four Feelings.

To put this in perspective, it's like going out and buying a TV. Mr. Good Enough sounds like you're purchasing some small, basic standard definition TV with most of the features you need, yet it's not quite top of the line. However, when you go with your brain's natural GPS for love, it's never, ever about lowering your standards. *Au contraire*, this is about raising your standards, but in a different way. Secure love is always about hi-definition connection. When you get in touch with your inner GPS for love, it's like discovering what HDTV looks like for the first time.

Then you think, "OMG, I never knew it could look and feel this good!" That's because when you get in touch with your brain's natural GPS for love *you will be feeling hi-definition connection for the first time.*

Let's get very clear here; a secure love style has nothing to do with compromise. It's about recalibration to the best emotional clarity and definition you have ever known in terms of real, abiding, lasting, fulfilling and soul-stirring love. Then you'll see life and love the way it's always been meant to be seen and felt. In turn, you'll see the men and women you date differently. If you're already coupled, you'll experience your partner in much deeper ways. Mostly, you'll feel love's possibilities in an entirely different way.

When you access your brain's inner GPS for love,
you will feel hi-definition connection for the first time.

GPS for a Better Partnership

Couples must also learn to use *The Four Feelings* as a way to navigate their relationships. When couples come in to see me, I usually take inventory on how strongly (or not) both partners are experiencing each of the four feelings of secure love. The couple research of Dr. John Gottman has shown that the key for all lasting couples is the quality of the marital friendship. Whenever I learn that more than one of the four secure feelings is missing, I know the friendship between them is suffering terribly.

The secret to improving their relationship is to enable the feelings of *Welcomed with Joy, Worthy and Nourished, Cherished and Protected,* and *Empowered with Choice* to flow easily as a natural part of their daily interactions with each other. The key is to work with the couple so that both partners have full access to all of their rights, as well as the secure reference feelings that go with each right. Only after they've restored their rights to a better relationship can the marital friendship be healed.

For instance, let's say that the feeling of *Welcomed with Joy* is missing. First, a couple must do the deep work so that both partners have a proper *Right to Exist* (and any other missing rights that may be affecting their relationship.) Then, and only then, do we work on specific skills like turning toward their partner when they make a bid for connection, attention, or support. They must be taught to turn toward each other positively rather than turn against or away from each other in some negative way.

When couples learn to welcome each other with joy as a way to say, "I'm here . . . so glad you are too," that's when the magic begins to return to their friendship. I'll explore all of this in the upcoming chapters. For now, however, just notice which feelings you give each other on a regular basis. Also notice the feelings you would like to have in your relationship that are missing. *The Four Feelings* should become your constant barometer for understanding the *weather conditions* in your relationship. *The Four Feelings* are not just a new GPS for dating, but for mating as well.

Discovering My Love Style

Here's how you can begin to reclaim *The Four Secure Feelings* as your brain's GPS for love. It starts by figuring out your love style. You'll also need to figure out your current reference feeling for love. Here's a little quiz to get you started.

Circle the description that best describes you:

A: I'm to some extent uncomfortable being close to others. I find it difficult to trust them completely, and so I find it hard to allow myself to depend on them. I'm nervous when anyone gets too close. Often, love partners want me to be more intimate than I feel comfortable being. I can only offer so much.

B: Being close to others I love is simple and uncomplicated. I'm relaxed. Depending on them and letting my partner depend on me feels good. In fact, I expect it. I don't worry about getting dumped or deserted much. Someone getting close to me is usually okay and feels good.

C: I'm sometimes disappointed that others are hesitant or unwilling to get as close as I would like. I'm often concerned that my beloved doesn't love me like I love them, or isn't as committed as I am. I want complete and total intimacy with my romantic partners. Yet my need for closeness can sometimes scare my partners away.

If you thought <u>A</u> best fits you, then you have an *Avoidant Love Style.* If you found <u>B</u> to feel right, you have a *Secure Love Style.* If you resonated with <u>C</u> then you have an *Anxious Love Style.*

Don't worry about labeling yourself. *Each of these love styles at one time was the best deal available.* This is the main point. It's your love style (a.k.a. attachment style) that's driving the bus concerning everything you're creating or experiencing in love (and if we were honest, in other areas as well, such as success, money, or business.)

Now ask: *What feeling is underneath your love style?*

As I said, your brain is running a certain reference feeling about love. You might want to answer this question:

I feel _____ when I think about dating, getting into a relationship, or being in a committed relationship.

(For instance: Fear, Anxiety, Angry, Happy, Sad, Insecure, Distant, Peaceful, Powerful, Joyful, Confused, Humiliated, Depressed, Hurt, Rejected, Interested, Excited, etc.)

If nothing is coming to you, simply imagine that *Love* is sitting in a chair across the room. Notice what feelings come up when you place *Love* in a chair as if it were a person. That feeling is probably your reference feeling for love.

Finally, ask yourself this: *Which of the secure reference feelings would you like to feel first, or the most?*

- *Welcomed with Joy*
- *Worthy and Nourished*
- *Cherished and Protected*
- *Empowered with Choice*

If you go to *www.garysalyer.com/lovemanual,* you'll find a digital workbook with more resources. There you'll find a guided exercise that will help you know which rights and secure feelings need restored so you can begin your way back to secure love.

Safe to Love Again Assessment:
How's My GPS for Love?

Let's take a few minutes to see how your brain is doing using *The Four Feelings* of a secure relationship as its GPS for love. As you know by now, your brain uses the feelings of *Welcomed*, *Worthy*, *Cherished*, and *Empowered* to know when it's securely loved. Your brain has been using these four feelings since you were a year old.

Take a few moments and look at the following questions. If you're in a relationship use that as your reference. If you're dating, think about what you typically feel when you're on a date. Or, what have you felt in past significant relationships?

With "1" being the lowest and "10" being the highest, how are *The Four Feelings* showing up in your relationships? Rank the overall feeling, not the individual bullet point examples.

What does Welcomed with Joy look like in your relationship(s)?
On a scale of 1-10, does/did your sweetheart...

    1   5   10

- Light up with joy when they see you?
- Turn toward you when you ask for attention or support?
- Make you feel cozy in your body?
- Stay in the *now* with you?
- Are consistently there for you when you need it?

What does Worthy and Nourished look like in your relationship(s)?
On a scale of 1-10, does/did your sweetheart...

    1   5   10

- Acknowledge that your needs are valid?
- Make accurate *love maps* of what you need, want, and like?
- Assure you that you can count on them when the chips are down? (Or just *whenever*.)
- Give and take in ways that feels balanced and good?
- Provide the support you need physically and emotionally?

What does Cherished and Protected look like in your relationship(s?)
On a scale of 1-10, does/did your sweetheart...

1	5	10

- Allow you to have your own life, yet provide a safety net beneath you?
- Include you in most aspects of their life?
- Support the risks it might take to become your best, fullest self?
- Always have your back?
- Look for ways to make you feel special and important?

What does Empowered with Choice look like in your relationship(s)?
On a scale of 1-10, does/did your sweetheart...

1	5	10

- Encourage you to create your own positive life experiences?
- Willingly accept the privilege to design a great *We* experience with you?
- Communicate that they're okay with your weaknesses as well as your strengths?
- Share influence on major decisions so you can both feel empowered?
- Open up a world of choice and possibilities by supporting your highest self?

Generally speaking, if one of those feelings is typically missing, then you're probably thinking it's a good relationship but needs a little work. Something, but nothing major, is a little (or sometimes more) off. If two of those feelings are usually missing, then it's a problem relationship. You're probably thinking you need to talk to a therapist, couples counselor, or take a course together. If three or four of those feelings are missing, you're in a toxic relationship that needs a major course adjustment. Failing that, you need to get out.

Add up the total points you gave your relationship(s). Here's how to score your responses:

34-40 points: Your GPS is working great and only needs a little fine tuning. There are probably little things you can tweak in your relationship. Read the rest of the book to see how you can go on to create an extraordinary relationship.

23-33 points: Your GPS needs some tuning. Generally speaking, you're probably in an *okay* relationship that needs some work. Read the rest of the book to learn how your brain is creating that experience. Remember, it's all adjustable.

12-22 points: Your GPS needs some definite work. Your relationships tend to be on the low side of what's possible. Read the rest of the book to look carefully at what's going on inside of you. Find out why you've picked that person or persons. If you are in a relationship, it's almost assuredly a toxic relationship, or it's getting close. You probably need a professional who can help you rework your relationship as a couple.

1-11 points: Your GPS needs a radical upgrade. Don't judge yourself, however. It's just that your brain is using a lot of out of date security protocols to create this experience. Nothing is wrong with you, or your brain. Read the rest of the book with the goal in mind to find a therapist or coach who can help you do the work that most *jumps out* at you. You deserve a lot more in life and love than your brain is allowing you. Don't ever forget that. It's just time to do the deep work.

If you want to take this inventory to an even more insightful place, allow someone who truly cares for you, like a friend, family member, teacher, or co-worker who has intimate knowledge of you and your relationships, to fill out this questionnaire for you. This is a way of gaining independent feedback. Make sure if it's a friend, they're not the jaded type.

If there are any variations between your scoring and theirs, find out why they see your relationships differently than you do.

Hint: If you can find a good friend who's in a *good, secure relationship*, that's even better. Sometimes our friends and family can see things that we can't. Remember, there's no such thing as failure, only feedback. Have fun!

Three

Love Is the Operating System

Experience; everyone has it, yet few understand what creates it, or even that it was created in the first place. Many mistake their *experience* for life or love itself. Most people believe that *my experience* is actually what happened or is happening. But as you're now becoming aware of, that's hardly how it works in a human brain. Our brains are not *life recorders.* Rather, they're *experience generating machines* that have more than a few bugs. That was the lesson we learned from Paul in Chapter Two.

Tracking our experience can be difficult or elusive. It takes a true observer's position to get a handle on it. Unfortunately, none of us have complete access to such a position. Therefore, it takes more perspective and skill to create the experience in love and life that you want. If there's anything I want you to get, it's that *your experience with love is open to serious negotiation and may not be your truth.*

Just because you had an experience with love
or with a specific person doesn't mean that's your truth.

Cookie Cutter Experience

Over the years, I noticed that *attachment* issues rarely stayed in a nice, tidy little corner of our life called *love*. If I worked with someone on their relationships, over the course of time they would almost invariably discern that the same missing right was also stopping them in their business, was affecting their success, showing up in their money patterns, or even their health. The reverse was also true. If a client came to unravel a business problem, it was almost always showing up in their relationships too.

Daniel came to me because he was feeling isolated from his wife of fifteen years. Things weren't terrible, but they sure weren't great either. Daniel was also an IT professional in his late thirties, holding down a not so glimmering middle management position in a large corporation. His uncertainty about himself was apparent from the first handshake as I greeted him.

In his first session, Daniel explained his situation; "I feel lonely in my marriage. The love we once had is now just lukewarm. We each do our own things, deal with the kids, pay the mortgage, and talk nicely to each other. But the passion isn't there anymore." As I listened to him describe his relationship with his wife, my first impression was that here was a man who was not happy in several areas of his life.

"Traffic was just wretched," Daniel muttered as he arrived only a few minutes late to our next session. "It was a parking lot all the way to your exit. But this one guy just pissed me off. He must have *cut me off* a good five times before I laid down the horn on him. Then another idiot *cut me off*, nearly taking off my left front fender. I kept on getting *cut off*."

I've learned over the years that client *small talk* is rarely unconnected to what they need to work on that day. As I listened, Daniel extrapolated, "I've been *cut off* my entire life. Last night I got *cut off* from an important conference call. At work, I'm always being *cut off*. Every time there's a promotion, somebody else gets the prize. I'm even getting *cut off* by my wife at home. I can't remember the last time we had sex." When key words like *cut off* are all over a person's life, there's a reason. It was like every area of his life was shaped by the same cookie cutter. *Every* part of his life resonated with the frequency of *cut off*. What Daniel needed most was a new cookie cutter for creating his life.

The cookie cutter for Daniel's life was set at age three, when his younger brother was born. I asked him about that, and received a very telling response. "I was the eldest of three children. Those first few years it was just mom and me. Then Mike was born. Now, all of the attention went to him. I felt *cut off* and alone. There was nothing I could do about it. Mom just told me, 'Your baby brother needs me more than you do. You're a big boy now.' Later, whenever I asked for attention, mom would give me the look that said, 'Don't ask now.' My brother was now the worthy one. I spent a lot of time wondering why I wasn't worthy of the attention I so wanted anymore."

The cookie cutter, or template, Daniel got from love was, "I'm not worthy to have my needs met or have the attention I deserve." He therefore chose a partner and created a marriage that would give him that exact flavor of being *cut off*. Just like at three, when Daniel hinted he wanted to make love, she would give him a look that said to him, "Don't ask now." So Daniel stopped asking for his needs to be met. He couldn't recall the last time he asked for something from her.

Out of curiosity, I inquired, "So, did you ever ask for a promotion at work?" As you may have guessed, the answer was *No*. The template of *not worthy* was running all over his life. Daniel had a missing *Right to Have Your Needs Met*. He couldn't reach out to his wife to get his needs met. Moreover, that missing right in his love style had grown legs and walked all over his life.

This pattern happens a lot. Many begin with a good enough *right to their needs,* only to have it yanked away when a younger sibling comes along. We worked with restoring his feelings of *worthy* and *deserving.* Eventually, we created a better skill set for him so he could properly ask for his needs. Daniel soon discovered that his wife was overjoyed to make love more often. Later on, I suggested he ask for a well deserved raise at work. Turned out, his boss agreed.

What we learn from early relationships, always affects other areas of our lives. In other words, *our love style affects our lifestyle*. Nearly every client who wants to work on their relationships, if they're an entrepreneur or a business owner, invariably asks to work on the same issue in success, money, or business too. Contrarily, when a client works on success, they realize at some point after careful guidance, "That missing right is limiting my relationship, isn't it?" Our love styles do not stay isolated in our brains. They affect our experiences in success, business, money, and health as well.

Our love styles do not stay isolated in our brains. They affect experiences in other areas of our life.

So, here's my big question. Why do the templates for experience we learn from early loving relationships spread to the rest of our lives? Just how does one *program* in the brain (called *love*) affect so much else? On your computer, Microsoft Word doesn't dictate how Excel performs, now does it? There's only one answer to that question. *Love isn't a program in your brain. It's the operating system itself.* So how do we understand that?

This chapter will expand attachment theory beyond anything you may have read in the field. By the end, you'll be given an absolutely panoramic way of viewing love. You'll learn why love impacts nearly *every area* of your life. You'll discover how early experiences create your *love style*, which in turn tells your brain how to create experience *across the board* in your life, ranging from business to health to success. You'll also learn much more about how *rights* work in your brain. Finally, you'll be shown how missing rights create a *false self*. And most importantly, you'll discover how to reclaim your original, authentic, loving self.

The Molecule of Secure Love

One December, *all* of my clients asked me the *very same question;* "What creates a secure love style?" Another requested, "Can you create a workshop that would give us a secure relationship in a weekend?" I can remember thinking, "That's a tall order for a weekend workshop!" Yet that was the beginning of the *Safe to Love Again Workshop* and the *Extraordinary Singles and Couples Retreats* that I offer (found at www.garysalyer.com.) Although I can't tell you that it's possible to attain an earned secure love style in just a few days, it *is* possible to rewire your brain for secure love with the right mentor in less time than you might think.

To have a secure love style you first need to understand what goes into one. We can think of a secure love style as if it were a molecule in the world of chemistry. Every molecule is composed of atoms. If you change any of the atoms, you change the molecule. Then you no longer have the same *substance*.

The *atoms* in this analogy are certain engrained *experiences* and resulting *brain patterns* which I call *rights*. When we're not given all of the experiences and rights needed to create a secure love style, it changes our love style. Your once secure brain begins acting like a molecule that's missing a few atoms. If your brain wasn't given all of the *atoms* or *rights* that create secure love, then your love style becomes either anxious or avoidant.

So, what specific *atoms* are needed to create the *molecule* of a secure love style? A love style in its depths is all about inner experience. It takes a certain combination of experiences to produce a secure love style. Just like water is a substance we all enjoy, without both of the hydrogen and oxygen atoms we wouldn't have the substance we all depend upon. Secure love acts the same way.

To understand the molecule of secure love,
you need to understand its atoms and what binds them together.

What make up the *molecule* of a secure love style are six specific love *rights*. Between the ages zero to three, your brain needs to be given six rights that produce a secure love style. As in organic chemistry, just as there are six atoms that create most life giving molecules on earth, so there are six rights that underlie your attachment style. Later in life your brain will use these early love rights, which are learned from early relationships, to create other experiences in your life.

Again, the six rights underneath a secure love style are:

- The Right to Exist
- The Right to Have Your Needs Met
- The Right to Separate and Belong
- The Right to Create Your Own Experience
- The Right to Assert
- The Right to Love and Be Loved

Like any molecule, a secure love style has its own distinctive *properties*. We experience these properties as *The Four Feelings of Secure Love* your brain uses as its GPS for love. When you have a full *Right to Exist*, you feel *Welcomed with Joy*. A full *Right to Have Your Needs Met* allows you to feel *Worthy and Nourished*. *The Right to Separate and Belong* makes you feel *Cherished and Protected*. Finally, the *Right to Create Your Own Experience* and the *Right to Assert* create a feeling of *Empowered with Choice*.

The Right to Love and Be Loved comes on board after these first five rights. If you get all six rights, you feel fully *Loved and Loveable*. Your brain has the complete *molecule* of a secure love style. You'll feel these feelings in the core of your being. In turn, these four feelings will influence *everything* you do.

A secure love style is composed of six rights
that give The Four Feelings of secure love.

What Is A Right?

What do I mean by a *right*? A right is set of neurologically engrained experiences within our brains that, in turn, tell our brain how to create future experience. Early experiences between the ages of zero to three essentially create neural mockups that dictate how your brain goes about seeking and creating more experience in the future. In other words, early experience in love gives you six *templates* (or *cookie cutters*) for creating secure experiences in your relationships. Your brain then uses these templates from love to create experience in other areas of your life such as business, success, health, career, etc. This is why I say that love is the operating system.

You may also see these rights as *permission slips* in your brain. Some people have a full set of permission slips that enable them to create full, lasting relationships. Others don't have a full set of permission slips when it comes to love and life. When there are incomplete rights or missing permission slips, the results are often painful, limiting, and sometimes even tragic. Missing rights will invariably result in an anxious or avoidant attachment style. A full set of rights creates a secure love style. You can look at the magical *molecule* of a secure love style like this:

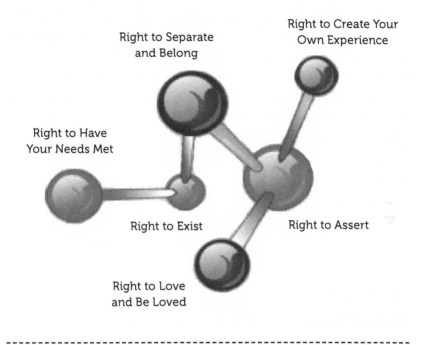

Right to Create Your
Own Experience

Right to Separate
and Belong

Right to Have
Your Needs Met

Right to Exist

Right to Assert

Right to Love
and Be Loved

Rights are templates and permission slips to create
secure experience in your relationships and life.

Rights Are Fully Embodied

A very useful way of understanding how the brain creates these rights can be found in Neo-Reichian developmental psychology. Dr. Wilhelm Reich was a psychiatrist in Vienna who was trained by Freud himself. However, he differed from his contemporaries like Freud, Jung, and Adler on how *character* was manifested in his patients. Reich noticed that what showed up from the subconscious in his patients was *blocked energy flow in their minds and body*. Breaking from his contemporaries, he began to observe that experience was a matter of *bio-energetics*. That meant it was no longer necessary to depend solely upon free association (Freud) or dreams (Jung) to understand unconscious impulses or resistances. The body would show you. So too would their general life patterns.

According to Reich, *the brain expresses its energy in the body as well as in the mind.* He was keen to observe what Dr. Daniel Siegel often reminds us of, that the *mind* is an energy that is both embodied and relational. Reich also noticed there was a deep correlation between this bio-energetic resonance in our bodies and our capacity to love, the conditions we set up for loving, the impulses that control our experience, and the ways we set out to achieve a loving relationship.

Love's energy is both embodied and relational.
Your love style has a predictable body expression.

The real genius latent within the Neo-Reichian tradition was given full expression by the career works of Drs. Robert Hilton and Stephen M. Johnson. Johnson combines the insights of Reich and Dr. Alexander Lowen with the developmental psychology of Dr. Margaret Mahler and object relations theory. Hilton was the first to call the brain's embedded bio-energetic templates, *rights*.

Rights in the Neo-Reichian tradition are considered to be *organismic*. Every living organism possesses them simply as a result of having the gift of life. You too have these rights, simply because you're alive. These rights are inalienable and come naturally with the *gift of life*. They're your natural birthright on this planet. You don't have to earn them.

When these rights are properly expressed in the mind and body, there's a natural energetic expansion and contraction, such as you see in breathing, walking, reaching and taking, etc. The Neo-Reichians call this natural flow of energy, *original organismic self-expression.* (OOSE) A full set of rights has a natural *ease* when it comes to reaching out for its needs, taking in what it needs, and releasing energy. Your energy must flow and be unblocked for you to have a good relationship with life and love.

As Dr. Daniel Siegel points out, when our energy is blocked, it shows up as either rigidity or chaos, such as we see in avoidant and anxious love styles, respectively. Your love style is therefore a bio-energetic gestalt that affects the *whole* of your being and life. Early experience creates templates for love that function as an *operating system* for both your brain *and* body.

Your love style is a bio-energetic gestalt that affects the whole of your being and life. Love is the operating system for your brain and body.

For instance, if a child doesn't have their needs properly responded to, they'll stop reaching out for their needs to be met. To *protect* themselves from the frustration of not being properly nurtured, the muscles in their shoulders will tense up and prevent them from reaching out easily. If they do reach out, it can feel painful or uncomfortable. Limiting body musculature is not limited to just the *Right to Have Your Needs Met*. There's a specific limitation of movement for every missing right. If you've ever seen anybody who looks *up-tight*, you've intuitively observed how a missing *Right to Love and Be Loved* shows up as a state of mind and body.

So, where do you hold tension in your body that seems to have always been there?

Your love style's impact goes well beyond musculature. Dr. Gabor Maté is a physician who integrates attachment theory and medicine. In his book, *When Your Body Says No*, he points out that when women are both stressed and socially isolated, it increases their chances of breast cancer by a factor of nine. It takes *both* factors to increase those chances. When a woman is stressed but a loving partner holds her hand, that comforting touch lowers cortisol levels, allowing her immune system to reset. However, if she's isolated and there's no one to care for her, her immune system remains disabled, allowing cancer cells to get the upper hand in her body.

As Dr. Maté points out, cancer is not a disease of the individual. Cancer is impacted by attachment issues. Our relationships affect our bodies in ways we're just beginning to understand fully. Your love style affects more than your brain. It interacts with *all* of the systems in your body, making your love style a wholly embodied experience.

When your attachment needs are not met, it can become the source of disease and pathology. Reclaiming a secure love style, therefore, is about the healthiest thing you can do.

Your love style affects every system in your body.
Reclaiming a secure love style is a healthy thing to do.

Neurons and Missing Rights

When a child is first born, only 28 to 40 percent of the brain has developed. In order to complete its development, the genes depend on experience to guide them. Your brain comes with *experience expectant* wiring, meaning that your brain expects to receive certain experiences, like being held, smiled at, nurtured, protected, etc. Here's the rub in that arrangement; if your brain doesn't receive the expected experience, it will disable the circuits which would support that experience. Neurons that are dedicated to supporting love develop in conjunction with secure, loving experience. If your brain doesn't receive the appropriate caring experience early on, those neurons and dedicated circuits will die off or be pruned down. When that happens, it creates a *missing right*.

We can see how this works in a Nobel Prize winning experiment by Drs. David Hubel and Torsten Wiesel on the effects of visual deprivation in cats. Very young kittens were placed in boxes where they could see either only vertical or horizontal stripes. Cats that *experienced* only vertical lines developed vision which could only *see* vertical lines. Likewise, cats that only *experienced* horizontal lines could only *see* horizontal lines. Like humans, developmental windows were in play; the developmental window for all of this was around the twenty-eighth day of their life. If these two cats were your pets, one would only see the top of your dining room table while the other would see just the legs. One would constantly be walking into the table legs while the other would never be able to jump on the couch.

Hubel and Wiesel found only neurons dedicated to either horizontal or vertical lines in these cats' brains. The brain that could see only vertical lines purged itself of the neurons dedicated to seeing horizontal lines, and vice versa for the brain that saw horizontal lines. Early experience had modified their brains. These cats no longer had full access to their brain's original visual abilities.

This can happen to human babies as well. If a new born child is kept in a completely darkened room for 3 to 4 weeks, their brain will turn off the vision circuitry. Though its eyes are normal, that child will never see. Their brain needs to *experience* light in order to properly develop its vision circuitry. If the brain's natural circuitry is not activated by the proper, expected experience, it will often turn those neural circuits off or prune them back. Babies need the experience of caring, attuned responses to develop a brain wired for secure love.

Babies need the experience of caring, attuned
responses to develop a brain wired for secure love.

If you're afraid that your love style is terminal, don't worry; your brain is gifted with something called *neuroplasticity*. That means it adapts with each new experience and can actually restore most circuits it pruned earlier in life. Whatever got wired early in life can be rewired and restored. It's all still adjustable. Even this level of wiring can be adjusted and a secure love style reclaimed.

All Access Pass for Life

Your brain's capacity for creating future experiences is fashioned and shaped by early caring experiences. Just like those kittens, there are specific developmental windows where certain capacities are targeted by the brain for either priming or pruning. Each of your rights is forged in a particular developmental window. Your love style is the result of how early experience either turned on or off your brain's neural pathways which support natural relationship capacities during those windows. We call those capacities, *rights*.

As with the cats with limited vision, parental love determined how your brain developed at the level of neurons and synapses. Early loving (or not so loving) experience created the brain wiring which underlies your love style. In the first three years, the most important thing getting wired is your love style. The six rights wired into your brain and love style during these windows then determines what experiences you may have in other areas of your life.

Your love style is, in essence, the total effect of your neural wiring and firing patterns which developed in response to your experiences during six developmental periods in your life between birth and age three. This wiring becomes the neurological basis for the *rights* that underlie nearly all of your experiences in life.

So, when I say that love is the operating system, I mean it at the most basic level of how neurons are either encouraged to grow or be pruned. That brain wiring then either allows you to have a certain experience or not. Just like those cats that could only see horizontal or vertical lines, you may only see others' needs rather than your own. Or, perhaps, you may only have the right to love others, but not truly be loved yourself. When your brain doesn't get the early loving experience which turns on its full relationship capacities, you won't be able to have a full experience with either *love* or *life*. If you want to change *any* area of your life, start with your love style. It's the basis of nearly everything.

> Love is the operating system. It provides the master
> templates for every other experience in life such
> as success, business, money, health, and more.

Mirror, Mirror in My Staff

Several seven-figure entrepreneurs have worked on their love lives with me. One asked me early in our work together, "How can I have a secure attachment rather than this polarizing attachment I have lived with my whole life?" In each of their cases, they didn't feel like their boyfriends or spouses were particularly supportive.

Stephanie was a seven-figure business coach. Her past several boyfriends were all the sort of men who conveniently disappeared whenever there was an emergency or a deadline. As she shared, "It feels like I'll never find a man who'll have my back. I'm there for him, yet when I ask him to do something simple during crunch time, suddenly he goes home. He disappears and only reappears when the crunch is over. I'm sick of having no support in my life!"

Stephanie's mother, who suffered from mental illness, could never welcome her daughter into life. At age six, she was given to aunts and uncles, who then raised her. Unfortunately, nobody ever truly took her into their hearts. By the age of sixteen, she left the domestic mayhem of her family to start life *afresh* and "on my own." From the day she was first floated to a well-meaning aunt, her mantra was, "I'll Make It on My Own." That's the mantra of anybody with a missing *Right to Exist* and more rights to separate than belong.

Missing rights induced Stephanie to be attracted to men who never fully supported her. Not a one had ever given her the gift of belonging. Once we cleared that up, she broke up with a man with whom she was pitifully mismatched. We reclaimed her *Right to Exist* and restored the natural balance of a *Right to Separate and Belong*.

One day, Stephanie confided to me, "You know, I think I've hired a support staff that mirrors the men I've dated. My web developer just took off without warning for a week while I'm in the midst of a huge project. That got me thinking. I realized that of my seven staff members, only one or two really have my back. Is it possible that my missing rights are also playing out in my business?"

With that awareness and her missing rights restored, within a few months Stephanie had replaced almost everyone on her staff. I suggested that she seek staff members with a more secure love style so they would be naturally predisposed to support her. We even had a session in which I taught her what to look for whether a new staff member had a secure attachment style or not.

With many of my seven-figure clients, I've had virtually the same conversation about their *unsupportive* staffs. Many of them had few rights to be supported. Here's the really interesting thing; once they had the rights to a more supportive intimate partner, their brains *automatically took the new right to other areas of their life*. I didn't know anything about their staffs. They noticed it. This is the great thing about working with rights. When you restore the secure rights that tell the *operating system* how to go about its love *business*, other aspects of life *naturally change along with their love life.*

If I had just concentrated on Stephanie's limiting belief for relationships, which was, "If I'm supported, love will turn against me someday," her brain might never have made the connection. However, when you do the deep work of restoring your rights, you naturally upgrade your entire operating system. Just like on your home computer, this changes everything. If you want the best *results*, find somebody who knows how to restore your *rights*. That old saying *love is the answer* is pretty close to the truth.

> If you want deep change, find someone who can
> restore your rights and upgrade your operating system.

Losing Your Authentic Loving Self

Every child on the planet begins life by asserting their *natural self.* Rights allow us to express our unique, authentic human experience in the world. When we get negative responses from our environment, we naturally suppress various aspects of our original, authentic essence. We'll restrain our life force, give up our needs, deny our desire for support, limit the experience we want, choose what we don't want, or settle for less than being *truly* loved.

Whenever that happens, your brain makes an adjustment. It stops expressing its natural self and begins to create a *false self.* That adopted false self is the true pain in any missing right. If someone isn't welcomed into the world, they will flee from their own existence. Deep down, they adopt a sense of self that floats above life. They feel disconnected to even themselves. Then they adopt a sense of self that believes, "I can only connect to the world through my ideas." A good many intellectuals fall into this category.

Or, say they aren't given a full *Right to Have Your Needs Met.* In order to rise above the vulnerability they felt at a tender age, they'll stop reaching out for their needs to be met; then they turn the tables. They'll adopt a false self that says, "I'm the helper who needs no help." In order to feel safe, we adopt an identity that's wrapped around a contracted sense of our true essence and rights. Behind any painful or limiting identity are missing rights.

While this false self feels safer, it's actually an *illusion* of security. If a person with a contracted, false self is actually offered an experience that honors their full rights, *they will usually reject it.* Deep down, it will feel like they're dying, or have been threatened.

However, that sense of safety and the false self that's built upon it is just an illusion. We won't die if we reclaim our rights. Our false self isn't the haven we think it is. That threatening feeling comes from feelings buried deep within your brain. Those feelings are never the truth of you. So, are you ready to discover the rights and feelings that will allow you to express your most authentic self?

The false self is the true pain in any missing right.

What's My False Self?

Here are some false selves people employ as a protection against a missing right. You may resonate with more than one. Say them out loud slowly. Feel into each one. If any feel like the current version of you, notice in your body where you feel the false self and mark it.

- ❏ I'm the Special One because I'm so Smart or Spiritual (1)
- ❏ I'm the Distant One or the Marlboro Mate (1)
- ❏ I'm the One Who Connects through Ideas and Ideals (1)
- ❏ I'm the Helper (2)
- ❏ I'm the One Without Needs (2)
- ❏ I'm the One Who Can't Be Given To (2)
- ❏ I'm the Independent One Without Support (3)
- ❏ I'm the Loyal One (3)
- ❏ I'm the Responsible One (3)
- ❏ I'm the Perfect One who has No Faults (4)

- ❑ I'm the Great One (4)
- ❑ I'm Who You Need Me to Be (4)
- ❑ I'm the Good One (5)
- ❑ I'm the Powerless One (5)
- ❑ I'm the Victim (5)
- ❑ I'm the Attractive One (6)
- ❑ I'm the Accomplished One (6)
- ❑ I'm the Committed One in My Relationship (6)

Do any of these identities feel familiar? If so, take a few minutes to journal about each false version of you. See if you can locate the missing right underneath each false self. Notice, you may have more than one false self and missing right. Check any that apply:

- ❑ If you circled any item marked with a (1) - you may have a missing *Right to Exist.*
- ❑ If you circled any item marked with a (2) - you may have a missing *Right to Have Your Needs Met.*
- ❑ If you circled any item marked with a (3) - you may have a split *Right to Separate and Belong* with proper support.
- ❑ If you circled any item marked with a (4) - you may have a missing *Right to Create Your Own Experience.*
- ❑ If you circled any item marked with a (5) - you may have a missing *Right to Assert* your voice and choice and have your wins in life.
- ❑ If you circled any item marked with a (6) - you may have a split *Right to Love and Be Loved.*

Ask yourself who you would be if you restored these missing rights? Journal for a while about your *True Self* that's just below the surface, waiting to come out and play. Take your time! It might just be the first time you've ever met your true, authentic, natural self.

When you restore your rights, you're actually reclaiming your original essence and truest authentic self. That's the bonus right you get when you recover all of your rights and true self. You get to be the fullest version of *you* that you've ever imagined. Are you ready to reclaim your secure love style?

> When you restore your rights, you reclaim your
> original essence and truest, most authentic self.

Speaking of claiming things, you can download more resources to love including an exercise that will help you to access your truest, highest, and most loving self at *www.garysalyer.com/lovemanual*. You can begin to expand your current self and start reclaiming your original secure love style today.

Four

Welcomed with Joy

Joy. It's an underestimated emotion when it comes to feeling securely loved. Have you ever wondered what makes a person feel charismatic to you? You know . . . the ones that can just light up a room with nothing but their *smile*? Is it really the smile? Or is it the joy they greet you with that makes you feel so warm and fuzzy toward them? If you think about it, it's the warm, welcoming joy they beam that makes your heart light up with delight and trust.

Dr. Allan Schore, an attachment researcher at UCLA, observes that unlike other animals, human babies need *positive* emotions, like joy, to bond to their parents or caretakers. Without the experience of utter joy on their parents' faces, babies will feel unloved. What jumpstarts a baby's attachment system are joy, smiles, fun, and laughter. It's also what jumpstarts your love style as an adult, too.

Animals don't need as much joy to bond. However, joy is the primary feeling for humans that create our first moments of bonded feelings as we enter life. For a human baby's first year, by "en-*joy*-ing" the child, the parent and baby are creating high levels of positive emotions in each other. Joy tells our brains we are loved. That's why the first secure feeling is *Welcomed with Joy.* It's the gateway feeling when it comes to feeling well-loved. From crib to couple, our brains are always looking for joy in another's eyes which says, "You are welcomed and your presence delights me."

Elusive Second Dates

However, not every child is welcomed into life by their parents. Jason was a very bright, middle-aged man who worked in the high tech industry. In our first session, I asked him what he wanted most of all. Jason gathered himself. With more than a disappointed look on his face, he lamented, "I'm on a bunch of dating sites. But only three or four times, out of seventy-plus dates, have the women I've gone out with agreed to a second date. I want to figure out why I can't get past a first date." It took a lot of courage and honesty to be that truthful.

With Jason, I noticed the *usual* things were in order; he was attractive, fit, made great money, and had done quite a bit in the personal transformation community. I largely suspected that what lay beneath his daunting dating experience was an avoidant love style with a missing *Right to Exist*. His father was a world class rageaholic whose anger was always directed at Jason from the day he was born. Jason could do no right. As a child, his father would purposely pick fights with him. Then followed the merciless, humiliating beatings out back where mom wouldn't see it.

Jason was the result of an unwanted pregnancy. His father resented the new financial responsibilities, while his mother felt obligated to marry a man she didn't love. The problem with unwanted pregnancies is the feeling of *unwanted* often transfers to the child. When I suggested he had a missing *Right to Exist*, Jason reflected, "All that existed in my family was my dad's rage. In my crib, he would take my bottle if I cried too much. The only way to survive was to neither be seen nor heard. I decided very early, 'I will just disappear so I won't upset you.' My mom wasn't present either. She never made me feel wanted or calm. I think she resented me." That's how a missing *Right to Exist* feels. The Neo-Reichians refer to those with a missing *Right to Exist* as the *hated child*.

As a result of this early hatred and anger, Jason's brain was constantly fending off bears in the woods. With a lifelong, disengaged, social engagement system, one could totally understand how women often didn't receive the clues that would tell them, "Here's a possible keeper." Nothing less than an *attachment makeover* was necessary to get Jason to that second date more often.

In this chapter, you'll experience what it feels like to be securely *Welcomed with Joy*. You'll also learn how important the *Right to Exist* is for everyone's love style. It's the foundation for all love. I'll show you how this right is lost, and the ways in which it can be reclaimed. Going deeper, you will recognize the common relationship patterns that come from a missing *Right to Exist*. This will allow singles to date in smarter ways, and for couples to understand what's underneath the *disconnect* in their relationships. You'll also discover how the *We* in your relationship absolutely needs a *Right to Exist* too. Lastly, I'll teach you specific skills that allow both singles and couples to give the feeling of *Welcomed with Joy* to their beloved.

Welcome, Dear Reader, to your *Right to Exist*!

Recognizing Counterfeit Love

I want you to have a bright, brilliant, glowing, if not stunning, description of the emotional state that each right gives you. My goal in this and the following chapters is to describe the positive reference feeling for each right. Then I'll make sure you're clear as a bell on what the restored right feels and looks like. After all, we want those positive emotions running our love styles rather than the existing ones. Then love shows up differently.

A long time ago, before technology made counterfeit money a true science, the government had a very interesting training program in the counterfeit division of the FBI. It didn't start with an overview of all the ways that fake money could be created. Nor did it begin with how you would determine if a bill was the real thing or not by the minute details of its design. Rather, potential agents were placed in rooms where for one week all they did was touch, count, and feel real money running through their hands.

On the last day, counterfeit bills were circulated among the authentic bills. Almost immediately, as if by magic, each agent would *easily* recognize the counterfeit bills. Once they touched them, they just *knew* something was different and wrong. The reason was that once their brains had acquired enough experience with real money to understand what genuine currency *felt* like in their hands, it recognized a fake bill within seconds. With that stellar insight in mind, I'm going to introduce the *experience* that a full right offers you. After you get a *feel* for the authentic right that's underneath a secure love style, only then will I tell you about the missing right.

Once you know the positive feelings for each right,
you will automatically recognize what fake love feels like.

The Fully Embodied Self

The first right that creates a secure love style is the *Right to Exist*. When you fully have that right, you naturally feel *Welcomed with Joy*. It's the first *atom* that creates the *molecule* of secure love. *Welcomed with Joy* is the reference feeling this right gives to a secure love style. It's the *true north* for your inner *GPS for Love*.

A *fully embodied connection* with both self and body comes from the *Right to Exist*. This link creates the foundation for every secure connection you will ever experience. *Welcomed with Joy* is how we know we have a place in the world, and indeed, in any relationship. When a mother allows the warmth and joy in her body to radiate into her baby, the little one experiences the full wonder and pleasure of being in their own body. From there, they feel at home in their body. In other words, they have been given the full *Right to Exist*. This grants them permission to be fully embodied and connected to life, others, and themselves. The resulting feeling of calm gives them full permission to feel into things with *both* their mind and body.

A connection to your body is incredibly important for emotionally connecting to others later down the line. Our very ability to feel into another human being and to create a deep bond starts with a strong connection to our body. We often think that we feel with our brains. However, neuroscience now knows that *feelings are a complete body-mind unity of experience.*

Your brain creates empathy and a lasting bond with others via mirror neurons housed in the pre-frontal cortex. Mirror neurons are specialized neurons in the front of your brain that allow you to understand the intentions and interior states of others. They permit you to understand what's in the *mind* of someone else.

Empathy and lasting connections with others start with your mirror neurons. The right side of your brain is also very important as it's more connected to your body than the left side. Your right brain takes in most of the *contextual cues* from the environment. It's the one that takes in all the non-verbal communication like tone of voice, body posturing, the look in someone's eyes, etc. Access to those cues is important because they constitute 93% of all communication. Deep, enduring relationships need partners with access to their right brains.

For your mirror neurons to properly feel into another person, they must have a firm connection with your body. Here's how your brain creates empathy. For you to empathize with someone, your mirror neurons must see a situation that tells them, "Something intentional is going on with that person." If an action or gesture signals an intention, your mirror neurons fire off, and a signal then goes to your body. Your body checks in with the signal to see if it can determine from its own remembered experiences what that other person may be feeling in their body. From this, you *know* what they're feeling. Empathy comes from *you* and your *body* working as a team. Neurologically, empathy is always a team effort with your body.

At that point, your body and brain have collaborated to create an inner map of what your partner may be feeling, experiencing, or desiring. Without a connection to your body, your mirror neurons will never be able to finish their job. They need the stored references of life experiences from your body to figure things out. If you don't have a great connection to your body, then your ability to create empathy and deep connections with others will be compromised or severely minimized.

A fully embodied connection with self and body creates the foundation for secure relationships.

What's underneath the feeling of *Welcomed with Joy* is the *right to exist in a body that can connect with others*. We need that right to make a connection with our body, which in turn enables us to connect with others in a meaningful, intimate way. Seen in this way, a missing *Right to Exist* is like having a computer that can't connect to the internet. Let's say you have data files that have been stored in an online storage site. Without an internet connection, your computer won't have the data to complete the project at hand. A full *Right to Exist* gives you the *internet connection* to your body's internal *database* of experiences. It allows your body and mind to communicate with each other like a well-connected Wi-Fi network.

When you have this deeply embodied connection between your brain and your body, you *feel at home* with your feelings and gut sensations as much as you do your thoughts. In turn, you *settle into your body* as well as you do your mind. It feels as if *the world is your oyster*, and that your body is a *warm, comfy sanctuary* for life. This is how it feels when you have been *Welcomed with Joy*; *life feels cozy*. Your body feels like a *healthy haven* for your personal journey through life. Because you feel so well-connected to your body, your body feels like your *teammate* in all things. You *feel at one* with all of you. This fully embodied connection with all of you allows you to *access and affirm* the embodied fullness of those you love. Then *everyone* feels loved!

Lost Right to Connect

When I spoke to Jason in our early sessions, he couldn't focus on me for long. His eyes would dart around the room when I talked. It was pretty apparent after a few sessions how his missing *Right to Exist* was playing havoc with his relationships. Few women want to try and connect with such *disconnection*. It takes eye contact, deep listening, and a few other things to welcome anybody on a first date. However, I knew that Jason had come by all of this naturally. We just had to convince his brain it was okay to be in his body, and to be present in the here and now with both himself and his lady.

Jason was not *Welcomed with Joy* by his parents. Neither did mom or dad ever step into his emotional states. Jason's young brain wasn't taught how to calm down, or ways he could connect to himself. As he shared with me, "My parents didn't talk to me much as a child. They were usually yelling at me for something. It was easier to look away than to engage them, lest they get upset and beat me. To be honest, I never wanted to feel my emotions. They all seemed so confusing to me. I've never understood all the hub-hub about them. I'd just rather stick to the facts in my relationships."

You can imagine how that strategy went over with most of his dates. But we can also understand how his brain was trained by early experience to not make eye contact with people. That was about the last thing that little Jason needed back then. His avoidant love style was Jason's brain taking the best deal available—forty years earlier.

Often, when there's no parental *emotion coaching* the result will be an avoidant love style. Jason had that in spades. It took a few sessions to restore his *Right to Exist*. We had to bring a lot of *safety* and *welcome* back to the little version of Jason. Eventually, we trained his brain that keeping eye contact with someone was survivable. Once that was accomplished, new dating skills and eventually couple skills were added. Jason's brain needed a few restored rights, emotion coaching, and new couple skills. We also had to reconnect him to his body. Jason successfully married some years later. It was an amazing transformation to witness.

When there is no parental emotion coaching
the result will be an avoidant love style.

Welcome Wires Our Brain

Let's try to understand what naturally happens to a brain in the first few months after birth, and how it might affect the *Right to Exist*. From the last trimester of pregnancy through the second year of life our brains more than double in size. Initially, what's maturing is your limbic system that houses your GPS for love. In order for the genes to spin out these neurons, certain experiences are needed to activate those genes. If the parent and baby enjoy a positive, joy filled relationship then the full potential of the genes will be implemented. Thus the neurological foundations for a secure love style are laid down during the first two months when the *Right to Exist* is coming online.

This is why the feeling of *Welcomed with Joy* is so important for creating a secure love style. When there's joy, the mother and baby's endorphin systems regulate each other. Neuroscience now knows that endorphins positively regulate genes and encourage the production of their full potential. However, the opposite is also true. Negative, stressful emotions will release cortisol in both mother and child. Cortisol also regulates genes, although in a negative manner. Stress and negative emotions impede the full potential of the genes. The bond between mother and baby is directly regulating the genome and how the genes will encode the brain development of the baby. Joy and calm are the great stimulators of your brain's full potential.

> The bond between mother and baby tells the genes
> how to spin out the brain of a baby. Joy and calm
> are the first great stimulators of our brain's full potential.

Although the Reichians say the *Right to Exist* is put into play during the first two months, we should also add the last trimester of pregnancy. We now know our brains are picking up on whether or not we're wanted in the womb. Neuroscience accepts that *imprints* or deep memories can happen before birth. So, the updated period where we get the *Right to Exist* is the window from two months before until two months after birth. During this time, all of the higher cortical functioning of the brain is offline. In fact, most of your higher brain hasn't been spun out from the genes yet.

With all that cognitive functioning waiting for later development, *a baby's brain isn't developed enough to make a distinction between internal experiences and those outside in the environment.* Not until the eighth month will the brain develop to the point where they know that *me* does not equal *mommy* or *daddy*. And so it also goes for the young brain when it faces parental rejection. A young baby's brain can't handle the experience by saying as we would, "It looks like mom and dad are having a bad day." Instead, it experiences that rejection as *their actual existence*. For the newborn, parental hatred is *me*. It's encoded as an *internal* experience rather than something coming from *outside* of them.

A newborn has no cognitive *shields* to protect them against any rejection they experience from mom or dad. Everything gets *inside* them in a way that it becomes their internal experience. *If they experience anything from a parent, that experience becomes me.* For the newborn brain, any such hatred, hostility or rejection becomes about *me* and *my existence*. Imagine how that must feel to a newborn.

The result is most unfortunate; the parental hatred, hostility or rejection is experienced in their body and mind as *me*. Then, the young brain of an unwelcomed newborn makes a fatal deduction—*my life threatens my life*. If your own life is a threat, the solution is to tone your life and existence down so you can exist. It's ironic.

The brain without a *Right to Exist* will tone down its existence by fleeing to the left brain and its logic, away from the right brain and its deeper connections to both emotions and the body. In other words, the *Right to Exist* becomes the *Right to Exit* from life. This flight *left* manages the pain, yet sets these babies up with less of an ability to connect to life, their body, feelings, their true self, and others. The unwelcomed child withdraws from life, because who would want to experience such *un-welcome-ness* at the core of their being? This is the primary feeling that's running deep in their implicit memory as the soundtrack for life and love.

The young brain of an unwelcomed newborn makes a fatal deduction—my life threatens my life. The solution is to tone your life and existence down so you can exist.

Re-Bonding with Life

I know something about the feeling running through the core of a missing *Right to Exist*. This was my missing right, or I should say, the one that had the deepest impact on my life. My mother was bitterly disappointed I wasn't a girl. She refused to even name me until three weeks into my life. Add in that she resented me because I looked like the man she once loved, and you get a perfect recipe for rejection. I never got much of a feeling of *Welcomed with Joy* with all that going on. Luckily for me, my grandmother gave me a lot of care and attention to compensate for her troubled daughter. So too did a few uncles and their wives. I got just enough to survive.

Underneath every missing *Right to Exist* is a strange cocktail of rage, depression, powerlessness, and annihilation. There's also a high degree of abject terror. I can still access from implicit memory those feelings, though they bounce off my identity as *insignificant* these days. Still, I totally get why anybody with a missing *Right to Exist* flees from that feeling into their left brain and its logic. To linger there is more than unbearable. One would lose their mind if they stayed with that inexorable feeling all the time.

If you're reading this and you begin to feel that old helpless and hopeless feeling again, I'm here to tell you a new truth. That feeling is nothing but an illusion waiting to liberate you into a completely new life. It's just an old sensation that's not your truth; i.e., it's a mirage. Moreover, it's been waiting all these years to be released by doing the deep work. I know, because I did that work myself.

In one session with my NLP mentor, after about fifteen minutes of experiencing the worst terror of my life, my brain learned it could survive that early experience. The feeling dissipated as my brain discovered that this horrible feeling was no longer true. In truth, I had *survived* that experience many years ago. We simply had to update the part of my brain that still thought I was two months old. I came out of that re-imprinting session knowing I have a full *Right to Exist* at the core of my being. In the process, I re-bonded with life and existence. Now, I feel that rightful connection to life in every cell of my body—so does Jason—and so can you.

Relationship Patterns

Those with a missing *Right to Exist* never attached to their parents. Later in life, if there's a bond between them and another person, it's rarely very intimate. Not all those with an avoidant love style remain single, though. Some can be in a committed relationship. However, a bond with them can feel like your partner is always in the next room. You'll never feel closeness on a regular basis with someone who has a missing *Right to Exist*. The most common complaint by a partner is that they are *not present*. Singles complain they are *unavailable*.

Those with this missing right often seek to validate their existence by being *special*. Given that they sought refuge in their left, logically oriented brain means they're prone to proving their worth intellectually, or sometimes spiritually. If you threaten, disagree, or refute their ideas it becomes a threat to them. They can become most aggressive during any argument that challenges their specialness. The reason is that when you dispute their ideas, it's a threat to how they validate themselves. Therefore, the argument becomes a danger to their very existence and value. As a result of trying to authenticate themselves in this way, those with a missing *Right to Exist* will often float above life as the intellectual or spiritual one.

The desire to *live above life* often results in a flight into the realms of spirituality. Those without a *Right to Exist* can appear so very, very spiritual. The logic is that if my parents didn't love me, I'll find a Heavenly Parent who will. While they may love humanity, they don't want to dirty their hands with real, committed love.

Loretta's Spiritual Man

Loretta had such a boyfriend. For five years, she was dating a *very spiritual* man who looked like her dream man. Loretta was still looking for a ring on her finger. She came to me seeking some answers. As Loretta reflected during one session, "Chad seemed so grounded and spiritual. I mean, he meditates and does Tai Chi every day. He just radiates gratitude and wisdom. Our conversations are so deep! Yet each time Chad and I get close, he goes to India for three months to visit some new ashram. I can't get him to commit. It feels like I'm always competing with the angels. Why can't I get him to love me the way he does his spiritual guides?"

The answer is that her *dream man* had a missing *Right to Exist*. It's a lot easier to love an angelic guide or God than a real life, flesh-and-blood woman. When I reveal this pattern, that's when the lights come on for women like Loretta. They finally get it. Marriage would commit their man to a real, embodied experience with a woman. Such boyfriends flee to the angels, guides, or to God where they can be special and remain uncommitted for the best of reasons.

When someone pursues spirituality at the expense of commitment, that's your first clue you may be with an avoidant. It's called a *spiritual bypass*. Those with a missing *Right to Exist* fill their inner void with strong pursuits that allow them to float above life, such as work, career, success, money, degrees, hobbies, electronic games or even spiritual *journeys*. Many workaholics are missing this right. They seek to be special in some way to compensate for their missing right.

Those with a missing Right to Exist often choose a
flight into spirituality. It's a lot easier to love an
angelic guide or god than a real life partner.

Here's a second clue that you or your partner may have a missing *Right to Exist*. The hatred and abandonment they received will often be given to those they love. If you're with someone with a missing *Right to Exist*, just know they'll pay forward the abandonment that they received. That abandonment may come in many forms. They may be *in their head*, making them emotionally obtuse or just not present. Some will be very uncomfortable with physical touch or hugging. Others may be prone to seek distance or become dismissive when they feel closeness. Some will never commit.

A third clue hints at the rage these people felt as babies. When they exit a relationship or somebody breaks up with them, that's when you may see the rage just beneath their usually calm, collected self. Those with a missing *Right to Exist* may seek vengeance in ways that seem far beyond what's needed. The punishment never fits the crime because they were given such a harsh sentence by life themselves. Any kind of *spiritual divorce* or *compassionate uncoupling* will be difficult if your partner has a missing *Right to Exist*.

It's Not Always So Dramatic

The last thing I want you to think, however, is that a missing *Right to Exist* always displays itself in dramatic ways like you see in Jason's or my story. In real life, there's a continuum for most things. Not everybody with a missing *Right to Exist* tries to create a dystopia based on a distancing intellect. You can actually have one operating and still have quite a bit of social skills. *The Right to Exist is about your ability to connect in a fully relational, emotional and embodied way.*

Ellen and I had been working for some time on her business issues, specifically the levels of anxiety she faced in professional situations. She was a very successful woman who had immaculate sales and leadership skills. Ellen had risen to the very top echelon of her company, to the point where she was now mentoring the promising young professionals entering the company. If you were to meet Ellen at a networking event, you'd be met with warmth, lightness, and an infectious smile. She was a stellar corporate success.

It had been 25 years since the love of her life, Mark, had passed. Ellen was still grieving the loss of that strong connection. There was a loneliness that stalked her below the surface of an otherwise socially active life. In one session, Ellen made this stunning insight; "I've always been social to the max. And yet, there are no real friendships there. I've had the right to *network*, but no right to *connect*! All those years, I thought I was so connected. But now, I realize it was just *business networking*." We sat with that insight for a bit. Shallow connections were all that Ellen had a right to experience. Sometimes, a missing *Right to Exist* can function socially, yet not in a deeply intimate way.

Ellen's missing *Right to Exist* stemmed from an emotionally absent mother. A well-known attachment research experiment, *The Still Face Experiment*, conducted by Dr. Edward Tronick at the University of Massachusetts Boston, explains the effects. A mother is asked to look at and interact with her baby as she would normally. The pair are typically smiling, gazing into each other's eyes, pointing, and doing the things that accompany the expected, coordinated interactions between moms and babies. Then, the mother is asked to hold a "still face" without any of the usual emotional, facial, or bodily responses she would typically offer her child. It's a bit like *The Strange Situation* except here, the mother is asked to *emotionally disappear* rather than to physically leave the room.

The baby notices right away that mom has *disappeared*. Immediately, the little one will try to get mom *back*. They'll smile, touch, point to mom's face or something else in the room. When this doesn't work, the protest behaviors start up. If those don't work, they will screech as if to say, "What's going on here?" Soon a sense of depression, hopelessness, and powerlessness enters the baby's world. The baby will turn away, withdraw, and cease smiling or responding. Stress hormones like cortisol rage inside their body. Unable to affect their mother, they lose any sense of empowerment.

Our brains are always looking for reciprocal responses from each other. We cannot bear a still face response.

In due course, the child turns inward, losing their sense of connectedness to not only their mother, but also themselves. In this experiment, the mother is asked to respond to their baby again after only a few minutes. If the mother's still face were experienced long enough, the baby's brain would make a permanent adaptation. Mom offers a repair as she responds again emotionally. At this *reunion* the baby expresses joy. You can watch this experiment for yourself on *YouTube*. It's the perfect example of what our attachment systems are seeking by being *Welcomed with Joy*.

Ellen had gotten a *still face* from her own mom for most of her childhood. I once asked her about the dominant feeling she felt as a child. Ellen paused just a moment before answering, "Oh, that's easy. I'm a *nuisance*. Mom is not going to be there for me. I'm alone, and no one is ever going to be there for me." Ellen's mother had lost her husband when he committed suicide just before she was born. That left her mother to care for four young children while also learning how to provide financially for her family. The pressure was on. Her emotional support system was exploded, leaving her overwhelmed. No doubt, Ellen's mother was a very depressed woman who no longer had the emotional resources to respond to her newborn child. These depressed "still face moments" were the memories at the bottom of Ellen's loneliness and disconnection.

Ellen got lucky in her marriage to Mark. Studies have shown that about 11 percent of children with a non-secure love style will recover a secure love style if they are given the right circumstances later on. When Ellen married Mark, her system learned to connect again. However, the loss of her husband re-opened an old wound that was never truly healed. Being social was how Ellen avoided feeling disconnected. Yet in the midst of all those connections, she always felt alone. In order to deal with her husband's death, Ellen's system went back to the old defensive posturing of, "I won't truly connect."

Even though no one would ever have confused Ellen's social skills with those of Jason's, in their own unique ways both had a profound inability to connect with life and themselves. You can have an avoidant love style that may commit, yet in disconnected ways. A missing *Right to Exist* doesn't always look nerdy or intellectual.

A missing Right to Exist doesn't always look
nerdy or intellectual. It's not always dramatic.

Notice that neglect or lack of an attuned response can be just as debilitating to our rights as abuse. In our digital age, we can do this to our children and loved ones by tuning into our cell phones, game boxes, or computers rather than to the ones we love. It's the modern version of *The Still Face Experiment*. If you're holding your child while preoccupied with an electronic device, you're probably not responding in a secure, attuned way. Couples also do this to each other. Have you ever seen a couple having dinner, yet both are locked into their cell phones rather than each other? Don't let your digital self replace your secure self. Turn off the device and attune to your loved ones. It's an attachment lesson our generation will need to learn quickly, or else the next generation may be far more likely to have an avoidant love style.

Rights of the *We*

The rights underneath your love style were never meant to be just about the *individual*. Every right is meant to create an individual *who can bond and create a We*. I know that's counter to almost everything you've ever heard from a therapist, the human potential movement, or the transformational community. Ever since Abraham Maslow and Carl Rogers, personal growth has been about the *individual* reaching their highest potential. The Reichians also see the rights in individual terms. It's typically been all about the *I* with the result being you think a couple is just two *individual*s coming together. So what about the *couple* reaching its full potential? Why hasn't that been addressed?

Once you step into a human brain that's wired for deep attachment, you realize that such a point of view is at odds with the grand overall purpose of your attachment system. Its goal is to help you create a lasting bond with a deep sense of *We*. *Every right in your brain is about giving you a full permission slip to connect fully to another person in a loving relationship.*

Every right in your brain is about giving you a
full permission slip to connect fully to another person.

All of these *I right*s must have access to a corresponding *We right*. Couples are meant to be bonded as individuals within a *We*. By a *We*, I mean the bond that makes two partners a team. They live their lives thinking of the other. Both partners feel each other's inner life. They want to play with each other and build a life together that's fully aligned. And so much more! Individual rights are meant to forge such a bond from the perspective of your attachment system. Any other perspective will be quite at odds with your attachment system's ultimate purposes and aims. Now, I'm not saying that being single is wrong; I *am* saying, however, that we need to see these rights within the broader perspective of your attachment system. Individual rights are the *atoms* that make up the larger molecule of secure love. We *must see their expanded attachment function* within this bigger context to understand them fully.

Sometimes the most distressed couples are those who've done the most personal transformation work on themselves as individuals. That seems ironic, doesn't it? When a couple works exclusively or mostly on their individual growth as two *I*s, invariably what you get is a *war*, not a *We*; and that's no way to create lasting love.

Simply put, the *We* has rights too. Each personal right is embedded within your attachment system and anticipates the needs of the *We*. Every right is meant to support a *We*. A couple must balance their individual *I* rights with the *We* rights if they want to create a lasting bond. Recall in Chapter One that old school marital therapy worked only 18 to 25 percent of the time. This is why. If the therapist doesn't treat the *We* as a fully accepted member of the couple with its own rights, the *We* will be starved until it collapses. This is why I make the *We* the primary focus when I work with couples. The *We* must be given a *Right to Exist*.

The *We* has rights too.

The *We* also has a *Right to Exist* in your relationship. For some couples, the *We* is a foreign concept. When I first begin to talk about it, it's like they've never thought of it. It's new territory because no one ever told them the *We* is their essence as a couple, let alone that the *We* has a separate *Right to Exist*. Two *I*s masquerading as a *We* is like the individual who, without a *Right to Exist*, splits themselves off from their body. Except in this case, the split occurs between the partners.

Neuroscience knows that this *split* in the couple often happened well before they got together, when one or both partner's brains fled into the "safety" of the left brain. A missing *Right to Exist* is damning to the formation of a *We* in any couple. As Dr. Daniel Siegel points out, the left and right brains are wired differently. The left side is great at dissecting. It thinks in a linear, logical, and linguistic way. Your left brain is great at analysis, breaking things down into its parts and making lists. It also tends to be very literal about things.

The right brain, however, is always looking for the bigger picture and the *whole* of things. It doesn't do words, but it picks up on all the non-verbal cues that constitute most of our communication. When recalling events, the left brain will tell you what the memory *means* while the right brain brings up the *feelings*.

Imagine what happens to the *We* when there's a left brain dominated partner stemming from a missing *Right to Exist* and an avoidant love style. A wife says, "Honey, I'm cooking and need something from the store. Would you run an errand for me?" Her left-leaning husband doesn't answer her. The cell phone has his attention. She's getting the *still face* treatment. So she asks again. His brain's mirror neurons still aren't picking up her intention. So he says, "Oh, I don't really need any garlic on the roast. I'm fine without it." She heads for the door saying tersely, "*Fine!* I'm going to the store, *Stewart!*" His left brain isn't picking up the context, but only the words. Stewart only knows she's going to the store. In his mind, she's even feeling fine. When it's time for dinner, he's confused as to why there's no plate set on the table for him. That's a typical communication mismatch brought courtesy of a left brain.

If Stewart had been listening with only his right brain instead, he would have known she was angry; however, he wouldn't be sure where she went. That's how an anxious love style, that has *leaned right* and created an overly active right brain, would have heard this conversation. Then Stewart would feel abandoned, and perhaps even more fearful. But if he had a brain with a *Right to Exist*, his two brains would have communicated with each other. He would have picked up on her intention and offered a more attuned response.

It's easy to see why a functional brain needs both its hemispheres to be securely connected. Above all, notice how a flight to the left radically affects a brain's ability to even see, let alone understand, join, or create a *We* in an intimate relationship. The left brain excels at dissection, differences, analyses, and breaking things down. Those things, however, won't create a *We*. In fact, they'll do the exact opposite, creating opposition rather than partnership.

To create a *We* you need the holistic knowing of the right brain. A *We* is all about the bigger picture between two partners. It's always built upon more similarities than differences. This is the deep loss that a missing *Right to Exist* inflicts on someone with a left-leaning brain.

It strips them of their ability to understand or create the oneness that every great relationship is built on.

In order to create a great bond with your partner, you'll therefore need to have your left and right brains create a bond with each other. Dr. Siegel calls this *bi-lateral brain integration*. My NLP mentor, Dr. Carl Buchheit, refers to this as having *rapport* with your brain. I use the metaphor of making a *bond* with your brain.

> Your left and right brain must create a
> bond with each other to create a *We*.

Here's what happens when a *We* is not created between you and your partner; just as the individual *flees from life itself* when there's no *Right to Exist*, so the couple *flees from their common life together* when the *We* has no *Right to Exist*. Your brain will eventually reject such a union because it doesn't feel bonded.

The *We* must be *joyously invited* into the relationship by *each partner*. A baby is invited into life by the mother's joy. In the same way, a couple must *joyously welcome* the *We* into their lives together. Secure couples give the *We* a *Right to Exist* by *consciously inviting* it into their mutual realities. *Welcomed with Joy* always has the feeling of invitation to it. So let there be an inner resonance of *invitation* which permeates your entire existence as a couple.

This allows your *We* a full *Right to Exist*, and you'll feel it in every interaction with your partner. Your every thought, attitude, and intention tells the *We* that it too belongs. Celebrate the *We* in both the common and the special, the little and the big things in life. Above all, let the relationship be a safe place for each other's unique individuality without a sense of *competing* identities.

The goal of the *securely* attached *We* is to allow for your full potential; *never* to limit it. A secure *We* is always about expansion and growth. Its greatest intention is nothing less than the fully embodied, relational celebration of your unique incarnations together as a sacred partnership for mutual self-actualization. The *We* is the doorway to the next stage of your evolution as a couple, *and* as individuals. Allow it to exist as you would your own body.

The *Right to Exist*, in its pure *We* form, is the ineffable and uncompromised feeling of having been invited into a partnership with life and love through partnership with your beloved. This is the feeling that secure couples naturally give to each other. So joyously celebrate the *We*. Allow it to breathe and exist between you. Walk hand in hand with the *We* as if you were on a journey together. Allow the *We* to be fully embodied in ways that aren't just sexual. The ties between the two of you must be emotional, mental, spiritual, and embodied. Above all, joyously celebrate the *We* in the *small* moments of connection, as well as the big moments like *anniversaries*. From this place of the *We*, a couple welcomes each other into the greatest place of personal growth imaginable.

Welcoming with Joy Skill Set

How does a couple welcome each other with joy, *practically* speaking? From the research of Dr. John Gottman, the first thing a couple must practice is *turning toward* each other. That means positively responding to your partner's bids for attention or support. Remember the protests of the baby in *The Still Face Experiment*? Partners who get a *still face* will do the same thing as that baby.

When somebody doesn't respond to us, we protest. We'll ask things like, "Are you listening?" "Are you with me?" "Are we even a couple?" If that doesn't get a response, drama ensues. Then, just like the baby from *The Still Face Experiment*, we'll turn away. Walls go up on both sides. It no longer feels like you're a couple. One or both partners will melt down as a sense of panic or insecurity invades the relationship. To avoid this, you must *turn toward* your partner with *joy* when they make a bid for attention or support.

Research shows that secure couples will turn toward each other when such bids are made about 86 percent of the time. The "disasters," as Dr. Gottman calls them, will turn toward each other only about 33 percent of the time. Our brain wants to know we're connected *most* of the time to feel safe. Millions of years ago, if someone was paying attention to you only 33 percent of the time, you wouldn't be alive for long. Nobody wants their partner to *turn away* from them by not responding. Our attachment system expects attuned responses.

Imagine that your partner sees a bird and says, "Look, there, at that beautiful cardinal!" If you want to welcome them with joy, you'll turn toward them and say something to acknowledge them like, "Yep, it's a pretty bird." That's a low level turn toward. You could respond even more positively by encouraging conversation, "Yes, that bird sure is pretty. Does it mean something to you?" Another great response might be something like, "Oh, my God! That cardinal looks just like the one that was outside the bedroom on our honeymoon! Do you remember that morning? It was the best morning of my life." When we turn toward our partner in positive ways, we're welcoming them with joy into our hearts.

When we turn toward our honey in positive ways,
we're welcoming them with joy into our hearts.

On the other hand, there are two ways that *don't* welcome our partners with joy. The first is to turn away, and the second is to turn against. Imagine again that your partner sees a bird and says, "Look, there, at that beautiful cardinal!" You might say nothing, or simply grunt. That's not an attuned response. Partners *turn away* by not responding. Or you might continue looking at your cell phone or computer tablet like their remark was never said. Here we value our digital relationships more than our relationship with our darling partner. That's giving our beloved a *still face*.

The other way that distressed couples may respond is by *turning against* their partner. Here, you get snarky responses that engage criticism, or sometimes contempt. You may say something like, "Yeah, but I'd love it if you would notice *me* sometimes, Mr. Attentiveness!" Or, "Oh, yeah, a bird for a bird brain!" These are not the responses that welcome with joy. Dismissive or contemptuous responses must be eliminated from a couple's interactions.

The second way that secure couples welcome each other with joy is to offer and accept repairs. Everyone blows it at times. Nobody's perfect. Did you notice in *The Still Face Experiment* the joy that the baby experienced when the mother offered a repair? Or the joy the mother felt when her baby accepted the repair? The same thing is true for couples.

All secure couples have a natural ebb and flow of connection that includes connection, disconnection, repair, and reconnection. The trick is to offer a repair without pushing for a response with anger, drama, or by pulling away. It's important that both partners offer *and* accept each other's repairs. Not accepting a legitimate repair attempt is just as deadly as not offering one. Secure couples re-welcome each other with joy by offering and accepting repairs.

The key to effective turning toward your partner is to listen well. Listening to *understand* your partner, rather than seeking to *persuade* them about the rightness of your position, is a key skill. So often we let the inner chatter within us distract us from the conversation. This leaves our partner feeling unheard, devalued, or unloved. Periodically, at least once a day, we should reach out to our beloved to just listen without any other agenda but to care and develop real intimacy with them.

There are four steps to listening well. First, *seek them out* or *schedule a time to hear about their day* or whatever is on their mind. Second, *clear your mind* of *self-interest*. Shift your attention from yourself and your concerns to your partner. Remind yourself this is your partner's time. Third, *attune to your partner while listening*. Truly listen between the lines for both the expressed and unexpressed feelings. Above all, don't try to fix anything. Just feel along with them and reflect back their feelings so they feel *felt*, not *fixed*. Fourth, *ask open ended questions* about their experience by saying, "Tell me more about that . . ." or, "What did that mean to you?" or, "Is there a story behind this?"

When listening to your partner, remain accepting. Don't judge or become critical. Don't take sides with the enemy. Remain on their side, as if to say, "I'm in your corner." Let them know you're hearing what they say. You can respond with, "Gosh, that must feel so sad," or, "I hear you saying that you're really upset about that." Here, you reflect back their feelings without offering advice, problem solving, or trying to fix them. Remain their friend and ally. Dr. John Gottman calls this a *stress relieving conversation*. This is how you stay *present* with your partner if you have a left-leaning brain or an avoidant style.

If you both want to discuss something important and you have different values or positions, you should listen by *taking turns* expressing your position. Here, you postpone *persuasion* or *rebuttal* by taking turns deeply listening to each other. *The key is to listen without any rebuttals whatsoever until you can repeat back to your partner what they are saying to their satisfaction.* Only after they communicate that you've fully understood their position should it be your turn to talk. When they feel heard and understood, then it's time for them to listen to you without rebuttals or persuasion.

Another key point here is that the speakers cannot engage in criticism and contempt. Both must speak using "I" language rather than "you" language. Simply say, "I feel X about Y, and I need Z." Nobody can listen to criticism without feeling defensive. If you can listen and talk like this to each other regularly, both of you will feel the *Right to Exist* and you'll connect in wonderful ways.

Dr. Gottman advocates such listening based on what he learned from political theorist Dr. Anatol Rapoport. Dr. Rapoport was a master at understanding successful international treaty negotiations. He discovered when both sides at the negotiation table suspended rebuttals and persuasive tactics until they could summarize the other side's position first, and *waited until the other side had acknowledged that they understood their side of things*, that the negotiations ceased being gridlocked. As it turns out, the same magic happens for couples when they suspend persuasion in order to listen. Give it a try sometime. It will do wonders for your relationship if you *listen with joy* to your partner.

Welcoming with Joy on a Date

Many people go on their first dates with a list of necessary requirements forefront in their minds. The *Tinder Generation* has reduced dating to something akin to ordering off a menu at a restaurant. And nobody likes to feel like the special of the day. Few feel safe and welcome on those first dates. As long as our brains need a feeling of *welcome* to make a bond, this will not make dating any easier.

When someone is invited into a house for dinner with a friend, they'll enter the home and notice things they like and appreciate. However, if that person were to enter the same house with a real estate agent in tow, a very different attitude and conversation would evolve. Instead of appreciating the good things about the house, they would notice anything *off* or that needed fixing.

When we approach dating like a *buyer*, it's no wonder that negativity soon fills the dating scene. Nobody wants to feel like a house for sale! That feels horrible to our relationship brain. The problem with the *buyer mentality* is that it immediately biases the entire process into a fear-based proposition. This can tell our brains to flee from the dating process. If we aren't careful, this may result in generational avoidant love styles.

Approach a first date with more of a sense of inviting a friend into your home for dinner rather than someone about to purchase a piece of real estate. Avoid having a *buyer* mentality; instead offer more of an, *I'll see the beauty in you* approach. When you meet them, notice there's a real soul sitting in front of you. Remember, *couple* dynamics start on the first date.

Take the opportunity to see what insights or lessons you might learn from your encounter with this person, even if they're not *right* for you. If you treat them like a soul, there's a greater chance you'll see the possible soulmate in them. Above all, just notice how appreciation and offering a feeling of *welcome* automatically opens up the chances of meeting your soulmate! At the very least, if singles started treating each other with the attitude, "I'm here!" and, "So glad you are too!" then a lot of the anxiety and dismay whirling around the singles dating scene would naturally dissipate.

Bring more appreciation and less expectation on a date.

My Right to Feel Welcome

Here's a way to see if you have a missing *Right to Exist*. Find someone who knows you well. Then say to them, "I have a full *Right to Exist*." Notice in your body if you can say it with ease, or whether it just doesn't feel right or there's a hesitation. Have your friend or partner notice whether you can say it with a congruent look on your face and in your voice.

To confirm this, say it *negatively* to feel the missing right. Repeat the above exercise with your friend or partner by saying, "I do *not* have a full *Right to Exist*." Notice what comes up. If you feel yourself pulling back, lowering your voice, losing the color in your face, or you stop breathing for a moment, you may have a missing *Right to Exist*.

If you have a missing *Right to Exist*, you'll want to find a professional who understands these rights and can help you reset that missing right. In the meantime, you may want to create a new perceptual filter for yourself. On an index card, write the following:

Ways I Can Feel Welcome and Worthy to Be Here

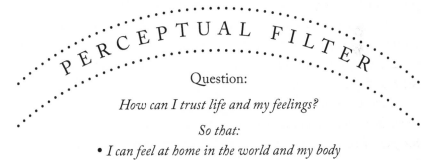

PERCEPTUAL FILTER

Question:

How can I trust life and my feelings?

So that:

• *I can feel at home in the world and my body*

For a few weeks, read this card two to four times a day. Read it in the morning and just before you fall asleep. You might notice that life has already welcomed you with air, water, and a planet that supports you naturally. Don't be surprised by what you have already taken for granted. Notice any people who already accept you just as you are. Feel into your body! Look into the mirror and say, "I am here. I'm so glad I am." While this isn't the deep work that I do with my clients by any means, it's a good start.

If you would like to begin reclaiming your *Right to Exist*, go to *www. garysalyer.com/lovemanual.* Here you can download additional, customized filters designed to help you create a more personalized experience with this right. Each filter is intended to help your brain start generating new possibilities for love. Life is full of love if you can notice it! I've even created a video to explain how these filters work to create more possibilities for love in your life. It's all in the digital workbook I've prepared for you!

Five

Worthy and Nourished

A baby reaches out their arms. Instinctively, the loving mother or father reaches back. That reach back is so important. Children are always asking for a comforting response that says mom and dad value me. Babies are discovering something very important when parents respond to them. They are learning to feel *worthy*. When we reach back to them, infants are given the *Right to Have Your Needs Met*. From that feeling of *Worthy and Nourished*, everyone is given a permission slip to reach out again and again to get their needs met.

Every response to a baby's request for attention is a love letter from the parents. Babies who are given lots of timely, receptive, and attuned responses are being taught that they're worthy and deserving of being nourished. It's like in those famous MasterCard commercials; the baby feels utterly and completely *priceless*. Emotionally, the baby hears, "Blanky—twenty dollars; Binky—ten dollars; Bottle of milk—three dollars; Smile on my baby's face—priceless." *Worthy* means they have an inherent, intrinsic value and importance. *Nourished* means they can feel the abundance of life in every cell of their body. People who feel *Worthy and Nourished* have the power to get their needs met.

Paying for Love

Again, not every child is responded to so well. Gwen was such a person. A tall, attractive, African American woman in her late thirties, Gwen came to the game of love with a missing *Right to Have Your Needs Met*. She had a nice life as a financial planner, but wasn't exactly enthralled with it. While her job paid for the basics, it was never lucrative. Her love life wasn't so hot either. Single her entire life, Gwen had been in many, many relationships, and yet none ever worked out. She compared them to some of the poorer investments done for her clients, calling them *low performers*.

Gwen was quite clear on her issue, "I usually give men what they *want* even on a first date. However, once I've given it to them, I want out. With longer relationships, I usually give and give until I feel resentful. By the time I start getting any of *my* needs met, I'm already tired of feeling like I'm *paying* for love." She paused and then summed it up, "I'm screwed with love. It's either resent them for *giving it up* too early or disdain them for giving too much. What I'd like is to be able to take care of myself better in a relationship."

It struck me that at no time did Gwen actually ask for a man to meet her needs. All she could imagine was simply not giving too much. Being able to receive properly from a man was out of her field of awareness. Gwen didn't even think to ask for it. That's typically the case for those with a missing *Right to Have Your Needs Met*.

In this chapter, you'll experience what it means to feel *Worthy and Nourished*. In the process, you'll discover how having a *Right to Have Your Needs Met* creates a secure love style. I'll show you how the right is lost, but more importantly, ways you can reclaim it. You'll learn to discern the common relationship patterns that stem from a missing *Right to Have Your Needs Met*. No one need ever feel unworthy on a date or in a relationship again! Couples can get beyond their debilitating resentment. You'll also learn how to nourish the *We* and give it a *Right to Have Your Needs Met* too. Finally, I'll teach you specific skills so that both you and your partner can feel wonderfully and lavishly supported.

Are you ready to meet the *Right to Have Your Needs Met*?

The Right to Feel Worthy

Feeling *nourished* is a birthright given from Life itself. Millions of years of evolution have given baby brains natural reflexes and instincts so they can reach out for their needs. In other words, *reaching out,* whether by a cry or a smile, came as a factory setting in our brains and bodies. That's because getting one's needs met is in fact another one of those inalienable rights we talked about.

Worthy and nourished means you feel the abundance of life in every cell of your body and emotional being.

Underneath the secure feeling of *Worthy and Nourished* is the *Right to Have Your Needs Met.* It's the second right for creating secure, loving experiences. The feeling of *Worthy and Nourished* is the *South Pole* for your brain's inner compass or GPS for love. If you didn't resonate with this baby who reached out for their needs, or you feel slighted, or even a bit resentful that your parents didn't reach back like those parents did, this just may be a missing right for you. It will be especially important then to understand this missing reference feeling for secure love, and how you can reclaim your natural birthright. This is the second *atom* in the molecule of secure love. Let's see what it contributes to your love style!

The Right to Reach Out

Feeling *Worthy and Nourished* is how we know we have a *right to reach out for our needs* in the world and in our significant relationships. Think back to a time when you tried to contact somebody and they didn't respond. You might have reached out by writing an email or sending an important text message. You get no response. How did that make you feel? Did you feel worthy and deserving? Do you trust your connection with them? Probably not.

Now, replay that text or email scenario again. This time, a response is in your inbox. Immediately, you get a hit of dopamine or even oxytocin if the person is close to you. Dopamine is the neurotransmitter that tells you to expect a reward. Oxytocin tells you, "Yes, we're still connected and I matter!" Consequently, your brain just might give you a little hit of serotonin to say, "I have some influence over whether my environment and close ones will respond to me." As Dr. Loretta Breuning observes, these are your brain's *happy* chemicals. Serotonin gives you the calm feeling that you can get your needs met. When you put together the trusting, well-bonded feeling of oxytocin, with the sensation of mastery and influence from serotonin, your brain adds up the hormonal *math*. You feel *Worthy and Nourished*, neurologically speaking.

Babies experience the same thing when parents respond to their needs. Every attuned response feels like they just got a text message from mom and dad saying, "You are so *valuable*, of course, I'll meet your needs." For the newborn, *Worthy and Nourished* is the sensation you get when warm milk hits your stomach and you feel yummy inside. The Universe then feels like one big *Yes!* That's the feeling of worthy and nourished. Life is one big, fat *Yes!*

The Universe feels like one big Yes. That's the feeling of worthy and nourished. Life is one big, fat *Yes!*

When you have a full *Right to Have Your Needs Met*, you feel *esteemed* and *deserving*. For some it registers as being *appreciated* and *valuable*. There's also a feeling of *agency* in play as well. You just know, without having to think about it, that you can reach out for the *abundance* that's always there. This empowers you to ask for your needs. It's like *you* are the cause of *celebration* in your beloved's eyes. Moreover, you expect that celebration to be clothed in joyful, caring responses to your requests for support or attention.

When a woman feels the *Right to Have Your Needs Met*, she will often say, "My man always makes me feel like I'm the *prize*." When a man feels worthy and deserving in his relationship, he will say, "She just makes me feel *special* and wants to be there for me. She's got my back." There's a *calm* feeling that comes from knowing you'll be taken care of when you ask for your needs. Women often feel most *Worthy and Nourished* when they can share their emotions with a caring partner, knowing they will attentively listen without trying to *fix* anything. If you're a man, I cannot underestimate the needs of women to have their *feelings* heard. When she reaches out to you, *feel* into her. It's the quickest way to create a bond with your woman's heart. Nothing makes a woman feel as nourished as when we understand her emotional state, and she *feels felt*.

For the woman who is partnered with a more conscious man, understanding our sentiments and moods is as important as our need to feel *respected* and *appreciated*. We need our partners to get that we too have unique emotional needs just like they do. While we don't *live* in our emotions as much as women do, the conscious man is quite aware that he has feelings, and that they're important to understanding him. Helping couples to *feel felt* is my priority. Lasting relationships come from deep emotional understanding.

The Abundant Self

When you have a *Right to Have Your Needs Met*, you experience nothing less than an abundant self. Life becomes a possibility sung in the key of abundance; *actually having* replaces *manifesting*. Rather than *hoping* your needs will be met, you experience the healthy *satisfaction* of your needs. *Have* replaces *hope* as the structure of your life. *Gratitude* replaces *grievances*. Scarcity thinking recedes. It feels good to reach out for your needs without hesitation. You calmly expect a loved one to support your requests. There's no sense of a pull back. *Anticipation* replaces *uncertainty*.

Your relationships become fuller, plentiful, and more generous than you ever imagined. If somebody does offer you the minimum requirements for any aspect of life, your system is wired to simply say, "No thanks. I deserve much better than that." This is what *Worthy and Nourished* feels and acts like. As a result, rarely does somebody with a full *Right to Have Your Needs Met* feel as if they must resort to demands. *Demanding* only happens when someone without a full *Right to Have Your Needs Met* partners up wrongly. An abundant self is rarely put in a position of demanding. That's because an abundant self chooses partners who reflect back that bounty without resorting to things like demands.

It cannot be underestimated how important it is for you to feel worthy. However, you must also make sure to give that feeling as well. The mature right is a *reciprocal right* once we become adults. Someone with a secure *Right to Have Your Needs Met* expects to receive and give the same level of support and giving. The full right will make you a master of both taking and giving.

As children, our job is to receive—that's the rule in life—parents give and children take. Later, such taking allows us to give as adults. When it's fully developed, the *Right to Have Your Needs Met* allows for the natural expansion and contraction of our being that characterizes all biological processes. We take and we give. Then we take some more and give some more. Love needs *balanced giving and taking* to thrive. Every couple intuitively knows this. What is not so often known is how this cycle may be disrupted and how to restore it.

Worthy to Be The Other Woman

Gwen was poorly cared for by her parents. Her father was something of a *runner* as she put it. Reflecting upon the sadness she felt in childhood, Gwen poignantly summed up her early years, "Mom never wanted to be the caretaker for anybody. If I asked for anything, she would scold me by saying, 'It's not all about you, honey. Stop being so *selfish*!' It was the same way for my father, too. Looking back, he was just trying to escape the continual demands my mother would make on him. When dad finally left my mom, I felt like I had to *pay* for my father abandoning her. I gave up my life to *atone* for him leaving my mom." One thing is noteworthy here. Notice how the word *pay* is a refrain in Gwen's experience.

From her mother, Gwen got the message, "Don't have needs. It's never about you." So, Gwen stopped reaching out for her needs. The belief her young brain made from her mother's selfishness was *If I don't take, I get to belong*. Based on that belief, and the missing right underneath it, reaching out for her needs felt *toxic* to her. As Gwen explained, "I always want to be the one who takes care of others. Looking back, I have tended to date broken men and the walking wounded who would need way too much from me. However, whenever I have dated a man who had his act together, it felt wrong and shameful to me. If a man provides for me, it somehow feels toxic." That's how a missing *Right to Have Your Needs Met* feels. Taking becomes toxic while giving becomes excessive.

Taking becomes toxic while giving becomes excessive
for those with a missing Right to Have Your Needs Met.

Gwen's father also played a more subtle role. Because of his own missing right to his needs, he married a woman who would never meet his emotional desires. We're always having the experience for which we have the rights. Without being aware of it, her father sought to meet some of those missing emotional needs by making Gwen a *Daddy's girl*. Nothing inappropriate was going on, other than the little one becoming an emotional substitute for his wife.

Going deeper, Gwen's pattern was to date men who were married. In spite of her best efforts, Gwen often chose or was fooled into being the *other* woman. While it's subtle to perceive, the mold for her future relationships was forged in those early years as *Daddy's girl*. Gwen's brain was primed to feel she only had the right to be number two in a relationship. While not every *Daddy's girl* feels this way, this was the experience her brain made of being an emotional substitute for mommy. In her first template for love, another woman gets to be number one. This dynamic became the cookie cutter her brain used to create intimate relationships with men as an adult. Gwen learned she had to be a sort of *third wheel*, or even a *substitute* in a relationship. There was also a split *Right to Love and Be Loved* which also shows this type of patterning.

We explored why Gwen either chose or was fooled into being the other woman. She waxed solemnly one day, "I have no idea how I find these men. I *swear* I'm so *over* dating married men! Then I fall in love with a new guy. At first it's always great. Then I'll begin to notice things are off. He'll just disappear like married men do. Eventually, I'll confront him, and sure enough, he's married! Fooled *again*! Some part of me just seems to *sense* when a man is married. It's so *frustrating*!"

Pausing for a moment, Gwen began to cry huge tears, "I'm *always* the *substitute*—the *other* woman (said with an unmistakable undertone of deep sadness and lingering contempt for herself). I'm *never enough* to be number *one* in a man's life. I always *settle* for being number *two*. It gets even weirder though; I can only express myself when I'm filling in for another woman. It feels like I'm *paying off* some kind of *debt*."

"*Paying off a debt.*" The words slid off her tongue as if they'd always been there. They rolled like an echo through a canyon. I wondered from where such an echo came. How could the little one have incurred such a debt? After a while, we discovered that Gwen didn't stay a *Daddy's girl* forever. Her father divorced her mom when she was seven. That's when Gwen incurred her *debt*.

After the divorce, Gwen was visiting one weekend with her father. They were walking down a busy street when she spotted an ice cream shop. Quite naturally, she asked her daddy if they could get an ice cream cone together. That's when her father's grievance against his ex-wife raised its hoary head. Her father turned to his precious nine year old daughter while pulling a roll of hundred dollar bills from his pocket. He sternly and angrily said, "*This* is a thousand dollars. *This* is what you *cost* me every month." Obviously to me, he had staged this one.

Gwen was stunned and utterly silenced by her father's display of anger. Without another word between them, the two walked past the ice cream store. "That was the day I learned to never ask a man for anything I wanted or needed. Being taken care of felt like someone was *paying* for you. It felt like I was incurring a *debt*. I've worked my entire life to *pay off* the *debt* that I cost my father." In his post-divorce bitterness, her father despised his childcare payments. In this tragic moment, *Daddy's girl* was given one more lesson in what unworthiness feels like. That's another problem with grievances; they rarely stay inside our minds. Children often incur the biggest damage from parental grievances against each other.

Gwen wasn't an evil woman looking to break up anybody's marriage. What she had was a severely limited *Right to Have Your Needs Met*. Early on, Gwen learned she was *not enough* to deserve the place of honor that a wife deserves. She had to settle for number two. Gwen never felt like *enough* to be the *one true love* in a man's life. Gwen was often the *other* woman because she didn't feel deserving to receive the honor that comes from being a treasured wife. Here we learn how important the feeling of worthy and nourished is in shaping our futures with love. A missing *Right to Have Your Needs Met* can affect our relationships in ways that aren't always obvious.

If you hear someone say "I'm not enough," you can rest assured there's a missing Right to Have Your Needs Met.

Worthy Wires Our Brain

The *Right to Have Your Needs Met* is first programmed into our brains between the third and sixth month after birth, though later experience can also affect it. The original template learned by a newborn is often what most affects our brain's wiring for later experience. From the third month on, the template that's being wired into your brain centers on the *Right to Have Your Needs Met.* The focus changes in terms of attachment to the child learning that she or he has a *safe haven.* At this time, children learn they can depend upon sensitive, timely, and attuned responses to their needs. We never outgrow our need for a safe haven. Dr. John Bowlby observed that all humans are happiest when we can depend upon the safe haven of a loved one.

Newborns learn that their parents can be trusted to soothe them when they're upset, fearful, or anxious. That's also part of having a safe haven. Infants intuitively know they need a calm brain to grow into their fullest, most loving self. The newborn brain has no real ability to calm itself. All such functioning has yet to be spun out by the genes. Infants reach out to parents to calm and soothe themselves.

Sometimes, life will gracefully and naturally give you this right later if you missed it as an infant. My fondest memories come from the times Grandma and I made banana ice cream together. On a hot summer day, she would fetch me away from playing on the swings. She would say, "Do you want anything, Gary?" She knew exactly what I wanted. "Banana ice cream!" I would gleefully blurt out. We would break out the bananas and the mixing bowls, and then get to work. Sometimes, she would offer me strawberry ice cream instead. Never forget the power of a grandparent!

I'm quite sure I got the *Right to Have Your Needs Met* from her. Thank you, Grandma!

Just as for the *Right to Exist*, a baby's brain cannot distinguish between their internal experiences and those outside in the environment. At this time, almost all of the higher, more *cortical* functioning is still offline. If you step into the mind of a two or three month old infant, any external experience becomes *them*. Neo-Reichian developmental psychology calls those with a missing *Right to Have Your Needs Met*, the *abandoned child*.

Unlike those with a missing *Right to Exist*, these babies did indeed have a bond with their parents. There was an *attachment*. However, a child may be welcomed into the world and wanted, yet not given the care they need for many reasons. A mother could be negligent or self-centered, as with Gwen. Another instance is the *good enough* mother who had the resources to deal with her first two children. However, the third child was simply overwhelming. Perhaps she was unfortunate enough to lose her husband by tragedy, or worse, was abandoned or divorced by him during pregnancy.

Sometimes, a parental illness or an accident might be the cause of a missing *Right to Have Your Needs Met*. Carolyn was a client who wanted to get to the bottom of her anxious attachment. To the amazement of everyone in her secure family, Carolyn was the *insecure one*. Her mother and father were wonderful people who gave everything they had to their children. She was stymied as to why love always felt so *evasive* and *unreliable*. Carolyn's mother was a world class mom in every sense of the word. She gave birth to four children, three of whom had a secure love style with lasting marriages to prove it.

However, there was one huge difference between Carolyn and her three siblings. When Carolyn was two and half months old, her mother was in a horrific car accident. She had to be placed in a body cast with two broken legs, a broken back, and a fractured arm. For the next nine months, mom recovered in a hospital room, removed from her daughter. A woman in traction can hardly attend to a newborn baby. Her father and immediate family did the best they could to deal with the loss of her mother.

While her father and aunts gave it a noble try, the result was that Carolyn didn't have the same timely, caring, and attuned responses at this critical time that her brothers and sisters did. The patchwork child care wasn't as consistent. When her mother recovered, she did a fabulous job being a dutiful, loving, attuned mom. However, the imprint of *intermittent responses* had already been given to Carolyn's young brain in the key developmental period. Sometimes, well-meaning, loving mothers come by their limitations naturally.

Since young babies can't distinguish between themselves and those who won't or can't respond to its needs, the abandoned child perceives those hunger sensations as the *enemy*. If the environment rejects or ignores their needs, that rejection or abandonment is internalized as being the nature of having creaturely needs. The baby's needs are therefore perceived as *a threat to them*. As with any *enemy* of the state, the issue then becomes, how do we diminish that threat? For the newborn, the way one does that is clear; *we tone down our needs and dissociate from our natural hungers*. If our needs come across as a threat, then the solution is to give up our needs so that the despair or helplessness can be lessened to a *tolerable* or *controllable* level. The child tones down their needs to gain control over their raging sense of deprivation. It's a great short-term solution, but with long-term, devastating results.

Those states of anxiety, abandonment, or deprivation then become the *cookie cutter* for love. Those with a missing *Right to Have Your Needs Met* most often, though not always, turn out to have an anxious love style. What you typically get is an attachment, plus an underlying feeling of constant anxiety, with just the hint of a *Paradise Lost* quality to it. The typical underlying emotional state for those with a missing *Right to Have Your Needs Met* is a feeling of insatiable need or contempt. Their partners may experience this inner state as an insatiable neediness with an attitude of anger or contempt.

The underlying emotion for those with a missing
Right to Have Your Needs Met is insatiable need or contempt.

A great *Right to Have Your Needs Met* is created by receiving *contingent responses*. These contingent responses must be given in a *timely* fashion to create a feeling of worthy and nourished. One of the most detrimental doctrines to ever cross the modern parental scene was the idea that *coddling* an infant would *spoil* them. As a result, parents were instructed to let their babies "cry it out" and learn to be sufficient, autonomous, and "self-soothing." These babies were essentially forced to grow up too soon.

Attachment theory and neuroscience now know that children don't have the cognitive ability to self-soothe until they're four years old or older. All *crying it out* did was raise the cortisol levels in these children, which does nothing but inhibit proper brain development. These disquieted babies naturally acquired an anxious or avoidant love style. A good many anxious or avoidant babies came from the *cry it out* advice of previous generations.

What does a missing *Right to Have Your Needs Met* feel like? It can feel like you have a real inability to feel fully satisfied in any relationship. It seems wrong to reach for your needs. You feel like a caretaker who must always give until the point of exhaustion and *resentment*; that last feeling is the tell-tale sign of a career giver. Often, you wait and wait for someone to notice your needs rather than straightforwardly asking for them to be met. There can be a deep feeling of dependency or even co-dependency. Once someone reaches back, you may notice you feel clingy or desperate to make sure they don't go away. This underlying feeling of neediness can drive away the people you love. That only deepens the feeling that you're not enough, and never will be.

Resentment is the tell-tale sign of a career giver.
It's a clear marker of a missing Right to Have Your Needs Met.

One of my clients described a missing *Right to Have Your Needs Met* as a sort of "electronic dog collar." Stacy explained the feeling so well, "Whenever my dog gets too close to my property line, the collar gives her an unpleasant feeling. Then the dog stops. Sometimes I feel just like my dog. Whenever I think of reaching out for my needs, I get this horrible, unpleasant feeling. So I stop asking." That's how a reference feeling of *unworthy* shows up; it stops you right in your tracks. In fact, every negative reference feeling acts like an electronic dog collar for some right. When you don't have a *Right to Have Your Needs Met*, requesting or reaching out is strictly out of bounds. You don't have the permission slip to go beyond the limit you learned long ago. Your brain sends out an unpleasant feeling that stops you from reaching out. If you manage to reach out, it's like you're stretching out with short, little alligator arms. You reach out only a bit.

However, you can take off your electronic collar by restoring the *Right to Have Your Needs Met*. Then you'll feel like you're *enough* at last! You can shake off your little alligator arms and begin to reach for the stars in terms of what you really want. That being said, reaching out for the full expression of your needs may need a stair step approach in real time. Few people who have this missing right possess the skills to make effective requests at first. Reaching out for one's needs takes a variety of skills, including things like timing, manner of request, building rapport, and sometimes, tact. Give yourself some time to build this skill set. Your first attempts will undoubtedly operate as a *starter set* of rights. When you first reach out for your needs, you might want to begin with those who are the easiest and most cooperative in your life, before moving on to the more challenging ones.

Relationship Patterns

Typically, those with a missing *Right to Have Your Needs Met* live a deprived life that leads to depressed moods. As Dr. Robert Johnson put it, they choose a *depressed life over an expressed life*. These people limit their life force as a way to be found acceptable. The early experience of deprivation was so devastating they have fled from any sense of need to control the pain.

Those who never felt worthy tend to idealize any new relationship. They're apt to see the new person as their savior who will make it all right. For singles, this is especially important to notice. However, *most* people don't *want* to be a savior. Such neediness tends to drive a potential life partner away. This inevitably sets them up for a life of anxiety. The fear of love leaving is a constant preoccupation for those seeking a savior. So they tend to hang on to their beloved in a suffocating way. Their great fear is being alone or abandoned.

Spending their entire life energy defending against having a need, they end up frustrated and scared. The belief running underneath all of this seems to be, "If I don't have a need, I won't be rejected, hurt, or, frustrated." That belief is nothing but a self-fulfilling prophecy. In an attempt to avoid frustration and abandonment, they invite the very thing they fear. Sometimes, you encounter the *people pleaser* belief, "If I don't have a need, I won't disappoint or hurt anyone." The end result is that you inevitably disappoint yourself.

More than anything else, those with a missing *Right to Have Your Needs Met* tend to be *the resentful giver*. Their template for creating balanced giving and taking is radically skewed. They take *or* give, rather than give *and* take. Their deepest need is to *reach out* to life and others for their needs, to *take* the required sustenance, and to *allow* themselves to be nourished in the ways that they need.

If those without a *Right to Exist* reach upward or inward, those with a missing *Right to Have Your Needs Met* are afraid to reach at all. They won't reach out to life, to others, or to love. Instead, they're filled with trepidation when it comes to asking for what they want. If given something, they will not keep their *grasp* on it. They'll let it go. Or alternatively, they'll find some way to not appreciate the gift nor let it in. Deep down, gratitude is a toxic state for those who must give.

Those with a missing *Right to Have Your Needs Met* must understand that they actually can't give to others without taking in the emotional and physical nutrients they need. When we don't have a proper bond with our needs, we can't meet our loved ones' needs either.

When we don't have a proper bond with our needs,
rarely can we meet our loved ones' needs.

Partners of those with this missing right often complain of being the victims of *controlling helpfulness* or *manipulative giving*. First, those with this missing right tend to give from a position of wanting and neediness rather than from fullness. Their partners therefore suspect that *something is up* with their gifts. Second, everyone has a primate brain that's interested in balanced giving. If someone gives and gives and gives but won't allow reciprocal giving, it causes their partner to feel guilty. This in turn produces resentment in the spouse; no one wants to feel guilty.

Too often, the controlling impulse underneath their giving comes out when they say, "I've *sacrificed* so much for you. Why can't you do this little thing for me?" That's when they drop the hammer of controlling guilt on the relationship. Others, because of their constant giving, will complain that they lose themselves in a relationship. Some will get angry if you give to them because it messes with their controlling interests.

Sexually, those with a missing *Right to Have Your Needs Met* tend to want more touching and snuggling than actual sexual contact. In their need for contact comfort, their propensity for wanting cuddles will often feel clingy to their mate. This tends to erode the natural eroticism and attraction between them and their mate.

The Grandiose Right

There is a second major way that a missing *Right to Have Your Needs Met* presents itself. Sometimes, the right gets *flipped* and it goes the other way. The person becomes a taker who cannot easily give. Dr. Alexander Lowen, a principal Neo-Reichian theorist, refers to this *flipping* of the right as *the world owes me a living syndrome*. Here the insatiable neediness comes across as a demanding taker. The original baseline feeling of contempt rolls into a neglect or even disdain of others' needs. That flip may appear as an obvious need for attention and praise. Giving is mostly a one way street with them. If they say, "I love you," it may *really* mean, "I want you to love *me*." Or it may feel as if they're giving only to take from you later. You feel manipulated by their giving. If you do take from them, you may silently wonder what this *gift* is going to cost you later.

This type of behavior and attitude typically goes under the rubric of *grandiosity*. As couple therapist Terry Real observes, a "common defense" against the experience of deflated value or worth is to inflate one's value. When the feeling of *unworthy* or *not enough* gets flipped; *the rightful feeling of worthy gets over inflated into a deep sense of entitlement.*

For couples, eventually what develops is a warped sense of partnership. The giving partner eventually realizes the taking partner is never truly going to be an equal partner or have their back in any real way. Divorces are often the result.

A common defense against the experience of deflated value or worth is to inflate one's value. Then the rightful feeling of worthy becomes entitled taking.

Grandiose taking can be a way of masking the shame of feeling unworthy that runs underneath a missing *Right to Have Your Needs Met*. When *not enough* gets flipped, the other partner will complain, "I can't give *enough* to them." If you're feeling this way in a relationship, your partner may be someone with a grandiose *Right to Have Your Needs Met*. However, if you look more closely, it just might have been your own missing right that chose this experience, because giving is all the right you believe you have in a relationship.

As a couple, you may have a dueling set of missing rights playing out in your relationship. You *both* may have a missing *Right to Have Your Needs Met*. This common ground can become a way to dialogue and understand each other. Then you can move into reciprocal giving.

Sometimes a child is given a sense of over inflated *worthiness* by a well-meaning parent. Pia Mellody observes there are two kinds of childhood abuse; disempowering abuse and false empowerment. A false sense of worthiness may lie behind grandiose receiving. Imagine if Gwen had been treated as a *little princess* by a stage mother? What if she had been the overly indulged *Daddy's Girl* who was not only given an ice cream cone, but gifted a shopping spree at Nordstrom's as well? In this scenario, she would have been given *too* much worthiness. Believe it or not, that's just as big of a problem later on when *balanced* giving and taking is expected. Grandiose taking never works in secure love.

Pam had been the consummate *Daddy's Girl* who was given and given and given to by her father. She and her husband had a business together. Bright and funny, my first thought was, "What a treat for her clients she must be." Married for eight years, things were fine at first.

During the courtship, Brad treated Pam like a princess. "He was such a giver," Pam told me. Brad totally supported Pam while she finished her degree. During those early years, he seemed selfless and loving. All that changed when the kids came along. Brad seemed stressed by the new responsibilities of being a dad. Pam sensed resentment from Brad and felt as if she had become a *responsibility*. She then resented him for his resentment.

When children come along, there's often a predictable drop in marital happiness for 67 percent of couples in the first three years, so says the research of Dr. John Gottman. Crying babies have enormous needs that are huge stressors on relationships. However, there was much more underneath this crisis for Pam and Brad.

When Brad came in, I learned how his missing *Right to Have Your Needs Met* and Pam's *grandiose right* were playing out. "She's not there for me," he began. "At first, while we were dating, I kind of noticed but it didn't bother me. I gave more to her but I just loved it when her face lit up. Then the kids came along. That's when I learned that Pam's just not up to giving most of the time. She expects me to give and give with hardly a thing coming back. She's never really pulled her weight in the business. She's great with the clients but she stiffs me with all the boring details of running it. What sort of business partner is *that*?" We talked some more but his *grievance* wasn't over yet.

"Parenting overloads me without a real partner," Brad continued in a low voice. "Being a parent has broken the camel's back for me. It's like everyone needs to support her. I feel so depleted. Now, I'm pissed and resentful. I feel like I'm on a see-saw of giving. When you see children play on a see-saw, one pushes off while the other gets lifted. Then it reverses and the other gets to push off and give a lift. There's a balance going on. Both are giving a lift. I never get a lift from Pam. How do I get her to play a balanced game of see-saw with me?" Indeed, that was the question.

That's what a grandiose missing *Right to Have Your Needs Met* feels like to a partner. Every couple needs balanced giving on the energetic, emotional, and financial levels to thrive. Often, it's the woman who comes with these feelings. Pam and Brad role reversed.

The problem for those with a flipped right is that this grandiose tactic is working for them. They usually don't see it as a problem. This was true for Pam, too. Many with a grandiose *Right to Have Your Needs Met* can have a degree of empathy deficit in their relationships. So much taking dulls the mirror neurons that create understanding.

Eventually, Pam got why Brad was dissatisfied with all of this imbalanced giving and taking. She began to connect the dots between her early years and how she was acting now. Being *Daddy's Little Princess* tweaked her *Right to Have Your Needs Met* into something very dysfunctional. From the time Pam was three or four, daddy gave her everything. She got a fine right to her needs as a newborn. It was later experience that tweaked that right into something unhealthy. Once Pam understood why she was asking too much of Brad, something shifted.

After some huge initial protests regarding how she deserved all Brad's support, Pam finally got why her father's over-giving was a poor template to put on other men, especially her husband. In a later session, Pam confided, "I can see how this affects my marriage now. My father never asked me to do a thing. I was given everything. Then I made a big assumption that women were the ones who were given to and supported. I can see that's a child's view now. It's funny. I never really noticed that mom was giving to dad too. In the future, I need to give to Brad like my mom gave to my dad."

Pam and Brad were the perfect example of how *dueling rights* can erode a once bright love. His missing *Right to Have Your Needs Met* perfectly matched her *grandiose* right. Brad was the *giver* whose missing right needed a *taker* to give him the only experience for which he had the rights. Both of them signed up for some deep soul lessons with each other. Restoring balanced giving was the key for Pam and Brad to experience the joys of a secure relationship.

When this balance was restored, magic occurred. The resentment and resistance to each other ceased. They found a level of connection and partnership that neither thought possible. Pam learned to appreciate the pleasure of giving and Brad discovered the joy of receiving. She took over more of the business responsibilities from Brad. They even made more money that way. Childcare was experienced as a partnership. Calmness replaced calamity. The children were happier. Both finally experienced the deep intimacy and partnership that comes with balanced giving and taking. Without the resentment and resistance, their hearts soared. It's amazing what a little balanced giving and taking can do for some couples. A complete and balanced *Right to Have Your Needs Met* is so essential for couples to thrive.

Conscious Giving

These days, men and women are looking more and more for conscious partnership. Men in particular still love to be the provider, the same as they did when they were hunters and women were gatherers. However, the modern notion of marriage isn't based on these strict roles any more. *Men are now looking to provide within a context of mutual partnership.* The conscious man is looking to provide financially, emotionally, and energetically, even as his conscious mate is providing financially, emotionally and energetically. Balanced giving is now broadened to including giving and taking in ways that used to be divided along strict gender lines.

Men must also create more emotional bonds with their partners. Once society moved from the extended family into the nuclear family, men and women were isolated from the broader support of their clan or extended family. That sense of isolation has changed things forever. In the new rules of marriage, men must understand that women often feel isolated from their circle of female friends. For thousands of years, women survived in a hunter-gather society by cultivating a large circle of supportive women. They got lots of emotional support for daily responsibilities. Many women today no longer feel adequate emotional support and connection; above all from their men. This is especially the case if they work outside the home or have professional careers where they must compete.

While that might seem strange to many men, the competitive world of work doesn't give women the emotional connections they need. Unlike men, women don't connect through competitive experiences. Indeed, studies have shown that competition stresses them out. What will soothe them are co-operative activities. When they come home, women now need from their man the emotional giving they once got from their circle of female friends. If they don't have this connection, a woman's dissatisfaction will evolve into quarrels with her mate. Whenever a couple complains of habitual conflict, I always look for where the emotional contact has been missing.

In the new rules of marriage, men must create more emotional bonds with their leading ladies.

On the other hand, men need women to have their financial backs, the same way they expected other men on the hunt to have their back so long ago. We're going out alone into the world, providing with no sense of anyone having our back. That's not natural for the hunter in any man. Today, in the absence of the larger family, we're looking for women to provide and give financially. Men want to know we're worthy of support from a woman in the same way women want to feel worthy to have our hearts and feelings open to them. Looking at the new rules for marriage, that's what I see. Today, more conscious women and men are seeking balanced financial and emotional giving, i.e., a financial and emotional *We*.

Rights of the *We*

As I've said, every individual right exists within a brain geared for attachment and loving bonds. Each right is meant to serve your lifelong need for connection and love. Individual rights were originally designed to create a well-bonded *We*. They were never put in place to advance just the growth and potential of the *I*. Thus the *We* has a right to its needs too.

The biggest need for the *We* is a steady diet of *positive* communication and energy. You simply can't offer each other attuned responses within a field of negative energy. As the Gottman couple research shows, 94 percent of the time that couples actively nourish a positive "spin" on the story they tell about their relationship and their partner, they will create a happy future with each other. To feel worthy, both partners will need to tell a secure, positive story about each other and the relationship.

The biggest need for the *We* is a steady diet of positive communication and energy. You can't offer each other attuned responses within a field of negative energy.

The preferred diet of a *We* consists of *fondness and admiration. Keep it positive* is the first need of the *We*. Dr. Gottman's research has shown you need a 5:1 ratio of positive responses for every negative response to create an aura of positivity for your *We*. That's the key ratio for making your loved one feel *Worthy and Nourished*. So track your attuned responses and notice when any negativity has crept into the *We*. Contrarily, unsuccessful relationships respond to each other in about equally positive and negative ways. Unfortunately, your bonding brain will never feel worthy with a 1:1 ratio of positive to negative responses.

A second need of the *We* is the gift of *prioritization*. Too many couples starve the *We* for the kids, to advance their careers, for the sake of their egos, or even for the benefit of friends and family. We must allow the *We* to take and bountifully receive what it most needs. One of the greatest hindrances to the *We* getting its rightful needs met is when one or both partners are committed to being *self-sufficient*. This can be a real problem if someone is devoted to relying only on themselves so as to never be dependent on another person (for instance a man, if you are woman). Such independence can stop the natural receiving that love needs right in its tracks. As one husband described it, "How do I give to this woman I love when she *thinks* she needs *nothing*?"

While I understand this attitude and where it comes from, too much independence can hinder the flow of worthy and nourished energy in a couple. In actuality, this is not independence; it is counter dependence and resistance. Remember, the *Right to Have Your Needs Met* is always about balanced receiving and giving. For that to happen, you both must be *willing to receive* and *to give* generously.

What destroys a *We* is pulling away, refusing to give, or resisting taking from the other. This happens most often when there's been a deep hurt. If there's any resistance to fully receiving one another, or in giving to one's partner, it will wreak havoc on the *We*. In a secure relationship, giving is a high stakes game where we're either all in or not. Couples construct a *We* only when they reach out and receive each other fully and freely. If you're not allowing each other into your heart and soul, the *We* will not feel nourished.

In a secure relationship, giving is a high
stakes game where we're either all in or not.

For couples with children, those caring for elderly parents, sick family members, or the like, I cannot overestimate the necessity to not sacrifice your *We-ness* for anyone's sake. Many couples make precisely this mistake. You must make the *We* your top priority; even above your children. Children need to see what a healthy *We* looks like in order for them to grow into securely attached adults. The best gift you can give your child is to show them that your *We* is of paramount importance. Don't show them the undernourished *We* of an overly taxed and undernourished couple who haven't felt close in years. The best way to teach your children about love is to show them a well nurtured *We*. That means you need a regular date night. Vacations without the kids are also appropriate. Setting boundaries with friends and relatives is also a good idea. They'll get over it.

Third, the *We* needs you to *monitor the flow of energy* between you. Most couples work *side by side* in order to face the challenges of the day. Those challenges include work, career, children, paying the mortgage, and so forth. Children take an enormous amount of side by side energy. However, the true sanctuary of the couple's *We* is the *face to face* energy they share together. *All couples must balance the side by side energy with face to face time together.* A great *We* needs ample face to face time. This is the key to keeping the *We* positive. Quality time is the key love language of any *We*.

All couples must balance their side by side energy with face to face time together.

The fourth need of the *We* is to *keep it real*. Do not make the *We* too romantic. An ironic thing happens when one or both partners are more interested in being a *couple* than they are a true *We*. Some singles rush into becoming a part of a *couple*. Yet once they get there, they act as if it were all about *their* dream of being in a relationship. It's as if they're in love with being in love, rather than being truly in love with their sweetheart.

The *We* is way more than a *couple*—simply because you're monogamous, have become *exclusive* or even married, doesn't mean you're a *We*. The *We* is a deep space of unity and alignment between your minds, hearts, souls, and bodies. *You can be a couple and not have a We*. Lasting love is not about being a couple; it's about being co-identified with each other so your separate *I*s create a unified identity between you. Where there's a *We*, there's a connection based on solidarity.

Every happy couple acts like a well-oiled machine for the important things. They check in with each other often. Decisions are made with the other in mind. They share influence. Whatever they set their minds to do, they often work together. You don't see unilateral decisions or secretive behavior. This doesn't mean that great couples never create as individuals. That would be a violation of the *Right to Separate and Belong*, which we'll discuss next. However, the *We* is a unified field where the secure couple *co-creates* with each other. It's a core energetic place between them that is sacred, protected, and consecrated to their togetherness.

So, are you noticing, tracking, and responding to the needs of the *We*? Not just your partner, mind you, but the *We* that's between you? Remember, the *We* needs you to notice it as you would your partner, children, friends, and other loved ones. When might be the last time you sat down with your partner and asked, "How's the *We* going between us?"

Here's one way to feed the *We*. Take a relationship inventory on a weekly basis. First, ask each other on Sunday evenings, "On a scale of 1 to 10, how is the *We* going between us?" Next, ask the second question of the *We* check-in. "On a scale of 1 to 10, how have I been as a partner who met your needs this week?" If the answer is less than a nine for either of those questions, ask the follow-up question. "What would make it a ten?" Explore together how the *bonded couple* energy between you unfolded this week. Remember, the *We* is about the energy that's *between* you.

A *We* is more than just saying you're a couple.
It's the energetic third partner in your relationship.

Sometimes, the *We* makes a bid or a request of us, but we aren't listening. That happens to all of us. There are seasons in a relationship. The needs of the *We* can change over the course of time. If there's been a crisis, the *We* may be crying out for a little extra attention. Or perhaps intimacy has become routine between the two of you. In that instance, the *We* may need more diversity of encounters or experience. It may be asking for more fun. On the other hand, it may need something more serious if it's starved for depth between you. So, start attuning to the *We* too.

Here's a quick way to remember what feeds the *We*. To create and keep a lasting *We*, you'll need to *PREP* it. That means:

Positive energy that leads to fondness and adoration
Real expectations that move you from couple to a true *We*
Energetically track if you have sufficient face to face intimacy
Prioritize the *We* above the competing things that starve it

If you can PREP your *We* on a continual basis, it will pay big dividends to you and your beloved. So start PREP-ping the *We*!

Worthy and Nourished Skill Set

The *We* is more than a skill set. It's actually an emergent mentality and consciousness that runs between you. However, there's a skill set that helps create a positive, well bonded *We*. The first big skill is to build up what Dr. John Gottman calls *detailed love maps*. An attuned response is based on having a mental catalogue of your beloved's needs, preferences, and deepest desires. This means you must observe your partner with empathy and understanding. More to the point, you must step into their inner experience in a deep way. Offering an attuned response is more than just noticing that your partner loves a Venti-sized, skinny Caramel Macchiato with coconut milk and two extra pumps of espresso at Starbucks. It's about understanding them at a very deep level.

You need to know what's important for your partner's *inner reality*. Who are their friends? Why do they value those friends? Are there any important events coming up? What are their current hopes, dreams, fears, and worries? Do you understand how their childhood or past relationships shaped them? You get the point.

The key tool here is to ask a lot of *open-ended questions* that cannot be answered with a simple *Yes* or *No*. When you ask these sorts of questions, listen with all of your interest, power, and ability. Ask for clarity on what their key words mean. Imagine they say something like, "I had a *disappointing* freshman year in college." That's when you ask, "What do you mean by *disappointing*?" When you ask about the meaning of a key word it tells them you're interested and curious. That does wonders for making them feel worthy.

Another important thing to note is *do you know how they create their experience*? Do they tend to run toward their dreams or away from their pain? What motivates them? Do they experience safety by running their cherished procedures and routines, or do they feel most secure when there are options on the board? Do they want it all spelled out, or do they simply want the bottom line and bullet points? When they want something, do they tend to be proactive, or do they wait until they must respond to a situation? Every relationship has its rules. Do they have rules for themselves, yet allow you to have your own rules, or do they impose their rules of life onto you? Why?

These are the deeper ways in which I teach couples to step into the experience of their beloved. I give them tools to make a three dimensional map of how they create experience as a couple. When you understand not only what your beloved is experiencing, but also *notice how they create their experience*, that's the day you create deeper intimacy with each other.

- -

The truly attuned mate knows *how* their
beloved creates their experience.

- -

At this deep level of making each other feel worthy you'll need to move beyond your personal *self* map and onto their map. When somebody listens to another person but references their own inner map too much, I call this *self-awareness* or *self-mode* of knowing your mate. If a person is in the self-mode of knowing, they know the other from the vantage point of their own feelings and point of view. The partner is seen almost entirely based on their own experience.

Have you ever talked to somebody who habitually responds by saying, "That reminds me of the time *I* _____ (fill in the blank)"? Or they never ask any questions at all? Everything you say must be translated through their personal experiences. This is a sure sign of too much *self-mode*.

True intimacy needs *switch-awareness* or *switch-mode* to know the other. Switch-awareness happens when we step fully into the other person, leaving our own experience behind. Here, we experience our self as the other person. We get a *hit* of their feelings, i.e. their state of being in a pure form. As we *switch* into them, we get *into their* feelings. Our head is out of the way.

It's like we become the other person for a moment. This is the awareness that allows the other to *feel felt*. In all secure relationships, both partners *feel felt* because they have *switched into* each other. This is a higher game of empathy, courtesy of your right brain and mirror neurons.

If you're single, *dating is about setting up the parameters of a worthy relationship.* That means noticing how well your date engages you with a great skill set. Observe how the people you date step into attuned resonance and empathy with you. Do they develop detailed love maps about you? How well do they make you feel worthy and nourished? Do they naturally practice a secure skill set? If they're a bit lacking, are they willing to work on a new skill set?

My Right to Feel Worthy

Here's a way to see if you have a missing *Right to Have Your Needs Met*. Find someone who knows you well. Then say to them out loud, "I have a full *Right to Have My Needs Met*." Notice in your body if you can say it with ease, or whether it just doesn't feel right or there's a hesitation. Have your friend or partner notice whether you can say it with a congruent look on your face and in your voice. To confirm this, say it *negatively* in order to feel the missing right. Repeat the above exercise with your friend or partner by saying, "I do *not* have a full *Right to Have My Needs Met*." Notice what comes up. If you feel yourself pulling back, lowering your voice, the color going out of your face, or that you've stopped breathing for a moment, you may have a missing *Right to Have Your Needs Met*.

If you have a missing *Right to Have Your Needs Met*, find a professional who can help you reset that missing right. In the meantime, create a new perceptual filter for yourself. On a 4 by 6 index card, write the following:

Ways I Can Feel OK to Have My Needs Met

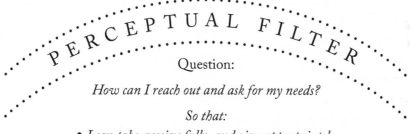

PERCEPTUAL FILTER

Question:

How can I reach out and ask for my needs?

So that:

* *I can take, receive fully, and give appropriately*

For the next few weeks, read this card two to four times a day. Read it in the morning and just before you fall asleep at night. Notice any ways that you're being nourished by life.

If you would like to begin reclaiming your *Right to Have Your Needs Met*, go to *www.garysalyer.com/lovemanual* where you can download additional, customized filters. Each filter is offered so you can choose a more personalized experience with this right.

Six

Cherished and Protected

Wheels; do you remember what it was like when you finally got *wheels* when you turned sixteen? Can you remember the difference it made when you got all that *mobility* and the possibilities it brought to your life? A whole new world emerged with just a small piece of paper with a set of numbers and the worst picture of you ever on it. Your adult self was born on the wheels of a driver's license.

Immediately, *you* were different. No longer were you dependent on your parents. You could be *separate*, grow up, and be your own person. There was freedom, independence, and choices to be discovered. You could also *belong* in a different way, maybe even to a new circle of friends. In that instant, your life changed forever.

Something even bigger happened to *you* when you were about eight months old. You got *mobility* for the first time. Just as when you were a teenager, it changed everything. It didn't merely change your notion of self; it gave you the *first* notion that you were a self. Unexpectedly, your brain realized that *you* were not your mother or father. Then your brain had to figure that out. With mobility came the realization that *I'm crawling but mom is not.* I'm over here, but dad is over there. Some part of you wondered, "What does this mean?" Then, it dawned on you. *You* realized that *they* were not *you*. This is the moment a baby has to begin to figure out what and who they are.

Consider that pure realization for a moment. Imagine what it must be like to realize that you're a separate *self* for the first time? There's nothing like abstract thought or language up and running at this time. All that's available is increased sensory intake, mobility, lots of emotional states, and the dawning comprehension that *I* am separate from the rest of the world. The first sense of a *self* is not an identity per se, but rather a sensory-motor *feeling* about separateness and belonging with others. At this age, your brain can only create a baseline *feeling* about *me-ness* and *We-ness*. That feeling travels with you in life, becoming part of your love style.

> The first sense of a self is a sensory-motor feeling
> about separateness and belonging with others.

Struggling with the *We*

From all outward appearances, they were the perfect example of the upwardly mobile, successful, and *conscious couple*. Jennifer and Todd were an Hispanic couple in their mid-forties who loved all things *transformational*. From Feng Shui, to fitness and Yoga, to yoni massage, they had studied with all of the masters of transformation.

Jennifer and Todd were perhaps the perfect example of how a *dueling* split *Right to Separate and Belong* could wreak utter havoc and chaos in a relationship. In our first meeting, Jennifer told me their plight, "We've lived in many places, from Buenos Aries to Boston, and trouble seems to follow us. There's always a distance between us. We keep opening up our core wounds with each other. From the time I was eleven years old, I've always felt *estranged* from love. No matter what I do or how much I change myself for Todd, I never feel like I'm enough. It just never feels like I'm loved for the incredible woman I am. There's always some way I should change to be enough. I feel *abandoned* and *disconnected* in this marriage." And that was merely the opening salvo.

Jennifer paused, staring straight into Todd's eyes as if to compose the big volley. With a voice that had more than just a bit of agitation, she made her meaning perfectly clear, "He doesn't *get* my true needs or who I am. If I hear him say I'm in my head one more time I'm going to scream. Most of all, Todd doesn't *see* me. When he doesn't *see* me, I pull away because I can't be vulnerable with him. Most of all, I never feel as if Todd is all *in*. Just when we start to feel close, he *pulls away*. It feels like the rug is always being pulled out from under my feet. It's frustrating, really. I mean, when do we get to be a *We?*" Jennifer loved Todd deeply, but didn't feel completely loved or part of a loving couple; that much was clear.

Not surprisingly, Todd wasn't exactly living in paradise either. "Well . . ." he said, drawing out his words as if he was choosing them very carefully. "I feel judged and not loved for who I am, too. She often does things without my input. I don't feel *respected* by Jennifer. I feel *controlled* a lot of the time. She gets upset when I want to get *away* into nature, or take a retreat *by myself*. I don't think she *gets* how important this is to *me*. When she gets upset, it seems like she's asking me to give up my identity. There's a connection between us—a deep one, even—but it feels like I'm being *intruded* on when she tries to get close like she does. We've worked on ourselves so our marriage could be better, and yet, it isn't." Such was the trouble in paradise for Jennifer and Todd.

Todd's last comment struck me. "*We worked on ourselves so our marriage could be better, and yet, it isn't.*" If working on your self was a straight line predictor of marital success, they should have passed with flying colors. When the *We* is not given its proper rights and focus, the couple is bound for trouble. If personal growth work is divorced from its role within your brain's attachment system, it misaligns and skews your love style in favor of the *me* over the *We*. This subverts your ability to create the bonds that love needs. A balance is needed between *me* and *We*.

Unhappy couples almost always have more *me* than *We*. If all or most of one's personal work is done as separate *Is*, the *We* is not invited to the transformation party. What's needed is what Dr. Daniel Siegel calls a *m/We*. There must be a strong *balance* between the *me* and the *We* for a couple to be healthy.

In this chapter, you'll experience the feeling of *Cherished and Protected*. That's the feeling love gives when you're sheltered within a cozy *couple cocoon*. You'll learn how a balanced *Right to Separate and Belong* is perhaps the most important thing for couples. This is your brain's foundational template for creating a *We*. One cannot underestimate its vital importance for creating a secure love style and a lasting bond with your beloved. Together, we'll learn how this right can be *split*. We'll also discover how to restore your right so you can create relationships that are neither distant nor smothering. You'll also understand how the *We* needs a *Right to Separate and Belong* as well. Lastly, you'll learn skills that can allow you to be a *me* within an empowering *We*.

So let's get acquainted with your *Right to Separate and Belong*!

The Goldilocks Zone for Love

Babies want to explore their world. Yet, they can't survive long without mom or dad nearby. Everything's so large, overwhelming, and maybe not so safe. In that moment of primal awareness, your brain must figure out two things: What does it mean to separate? What does it mean to belong? How your parents deal with your mobility and ability to separate from them will give you either a full *Right to Separate and Belong*, or some *split* version of that right. If you only get a permission slip to either separate *or* belong, that will play havoc with later, intimate relationships. On the other hand, if the parents deal with this new phase well, you'll feel *Cherished and Protected*. Let's explore this brave new world of the toddler.

If you only get a permission slip to separate or belong,
that will play havoc with later, intimate relationships.

This new phase of mobility and primal self-awareness will give you a lasting template for how you feel about being a self within a *We*. It will also inform what being a *We* means to being a *me*. This first template for navigating the self *and* a *We* is called the *Right to Separate and Belong*. It's the third *atom* in the molecule of secure love. This right is supremely essential for creating relationships.

The third right is different than the two preceding ones. First, the development of self-awareness changes everything. *The Right to Exist* and the *Right to Have Your Needs Met* are all about a baby's relationship to the *world*. The next two rights are about the relationship of the baby to *self*. Second, this right doesn't show up as missing. Instead, it gets *split* into *either* a right to separate *or* a right to belong. While there is a continuum here, the full right needs to balance the needs of the *me* and the *We*, i.e. the need of the self to separate and its need to belong. Achieving and maintaining that balance is a lifelong, learned art. Nobody is perfect here.

We all know the story of Goldilocks and the three bears, right? Walking through a forest, she scans a house and invites herself to dinner. Goldilocks sees three bowls of porridge. Eventually, she chose the bowl that was just right—not too hot and not too cold. The *Right to Separate and Belong* needs the same *Goldilocks Zone* to be fully empowering for the young child. Too much separation is not good. Too much belonging doesn't feel great either. The *We* is not suffocating and the *me* is not excluding. In that balanced place, a baby learns how being in a *We* contributes to the *me*—*and* how a *me* contributes to the *We* in positive ways.

A baby learns how being in a *We* contributes to the me
and how a me contributes to the *We* in positive ways.

Learning how the *We* contributes to the *me* sets the stage for later relationships. Have you ever seen a baby explore the room, and then bring back something interesting for mom or dad to look at? That's the child saying, "Hey, look what I found! I can contribute something interesting to you!" Then mom or dad says, "Wow, that's great honey. That's so exciting!" Perhaps the parent then shows the baby something about the toy or object they hadn't noticed. The baby learns how the *We* can help them learn and explore. The *We* is a give and take of mutual exploration between parent and child that *enriches* the child's sense of their self. Having this symbiotic sense of self is what allows people to create deep bonds later in life.

The feelings that a baby gets when they're allowed to separate and explore within the safety net of a caring *We* are the feelings of

Cherished and Protected. Do you remember *The Strange Situation* from Chapter Two? When mom left the room, once she returned, the secure children calmed down. What did they do next? They went out and explored the room and played with toys. While mom was there, they played with toys. When she returned, they played with toys. When mom was not there, without her watchful eyes looking over them, the exploration stopped. They got upset. Yet when mom came back, the secure children calmed down and went right back to exploration and play. That's what attachment theory calls a *secure base.* It's a feeling of safety that it's okay to explore our world, find out who we are, and then come home again to the loving, supportive arms of our parents or a committed partner.

The need for a secure We to anchor our common existential separateness isn't just for babies. We all require a secure base to feel emotionally grounded. Drs. Phillip Shaver and Mario Mikulincer created an adult version of *The Strange Situation* using airport departures between intimate partners. Predictably, the same three love styles show up. The anxious will hug with lots of intense emotions, barely letting go of each other. Those with an avoidant attachment will just drop you off at the skycap's booth to avoid pain. However, the secure will hug and calmly say, "I love you and I'll see you soon!" *How do you deal with airport departures?*

The Well Supported Self

When you have the liberty to explore, it's because you know you're safe and seen. The secure *Right to Separate and Belong* knows it can be properly *supported* to explore its world. There's a deeply embodied feeling of *freedom* without any sense that I must to go it alone. You know in your bones, without giving it another thought, that you deserve such support. Then you feel *emboldened* to explore the outermost edges of who you were meant to be. There's a deep knowing that independence is not an end unto itself. Both the securely attached infant and adult know they deserve more *back up* than that. Autonomy is experienced as a *positive interdependence* empowered by the watchful care of those who love you. There's no thought that you must sacrifice *me* to be a *We.*

When you have the full *Right to Separate and Belong*, you naturally seek out the proper mate who will support you. Our common existential mandate to separate and explore is meant to happen in community. Just like Columbus and Magellan, you have and deserve the support of Kings and Queens. It should never feel like you must go it alone. You feel *confident* that you can meet life head on. That's what a secure *Right to Separate and Belong* feels like.

With the right to belong and be your unique self, you get an all access pass to be a *fully* bonded *me*. There's no fear that a *We* will take away your freedom to explore or be yourself. Instead, it gives you the ability to bond with another in ways that support each of your dreams and interests. Within the *We* you always know you have the license to bring your full self. You feel *celebrated* because a secure *We* always revels in the *distinctiveness* you bring to it. Then you feel *inspired* to reach out for the stars of your own destiny.

Conversely, you know your contribution to the *We* is *important*. You also recognize how necessary a *We* is for helping you develop your own individuality. Do you remember the *stress relieving conversation* we talked about earlier that secure couples have at the end of the day? That's what I'm talking about and far more. Every securely attached person knows instinctively that it takes a *We* to *replenish* the *me*. That's the deep feeling of being *me* within a secure *We*—you feel *deeply held, sustained, and valuable.* This sense of unreserved care and protection comes in as the baseline reference feeling of *Cherished and Protected* for your relationships.

Few words in the English language have more romantic resonance and heartfelt power than the word *cherish*. Cherish comes from the Old French and Latin, originally meaning *dear, costly, and beloved*. When a woman is cherished, she feels a range of emotions. *Cherished* begins the moment she feels *highly regarded* and *admired* by her man. For some women, it means they are respected at a core level that's beyond surface issues like beauty or charm. Where there is cherishing, you're not taken for granted. Your man makes you feel like the most *special* woman on the planet. This feeling will not only be voiced by his words, but you will sense it in his actions, the look on his face, the sound of his voice, and in how he touches you. Your man is simply *enchanted* with you. Cherished is a fully embodied feeling in which a man communicates through body and soul how valuable you are to him.

Men want to feel cherished too, though to be honest, it's not the first word that comes to our mind. When we sense *appreciation* and *respect* from our women, we feel important and prized. We want to know that we're first in a woman's heart, above all others. This may come as a surprise, but when men know they're *prioritized* by their women, even above children and family, it allows men to feel cherished and *esteemed* by our women. In tough times, when our partner has our back, that's also when a man feels comfortable in his relationship. What allows us to feel truly cherished is for a woman to admire us for the man beneath the mantel of masculinity that we must wear just to be socially acceptable. If you allow us to be vulnerable and have our weaknesses, that's when we know that our woman values us above any roles we're playing as a *man*. Allowing us to be both masculine and human tells a man *I am devoted to you above all else*. We then feel cherished at our core.

When you're cherished, you will naturally feel *protected*. You'll hold each other with loving affection, no matter what happens in life. You're there for them in times of stress and joy and everything in between. To say that you cherish someone is a bold statement about how *sacred* they are to you. Deep in your heart, you simply *treasure* the absolute *blessing* of your beloved's spirit. Feeling blessed by the presence of your partner is a sure sign that you cherish them in a very deep way. It's this feeling of coupled *security* that allows adult partners to pursue and explore their dreams fully, knowing that the other is the net underneath the high wire act of their aspirations. It's the rare soul who desires to walk the tightrope of life without a safety net beneath them. Attachment science calls this *a secure base*.

> Coupled security allows partners to fully pursue and explore their dreams, knowing that the other is the net underneath the high wire act of their aspirations.

Once you understand the importance of a secure base for your developing brain, you'll never see the concept of *self-actualization* the same. Both as children and adults, we explore best when we know someone else is *watching over us*. Having a great *We* is the best way to give your brain the true freedom to explore your human potential completely. We were meant to have *back up* and proper support. For adults, this is what a secure base feels like. However, not everyone finds their *Goldilocks Zone*. When this happens, *trouble in paradise* is always awaiting them.

Jennifer Never Feels Seen

Let's look closer at what caused the long-term conflict between Jennifer and Todd. At first, it seemed on the surface as if they had the classic *pursuit/withdrawal* pattern going against them. She was quite anxious, while he was emotionally avoidant. However, if you peer beneath the common pattern, you'll notice they were having exactly the experience for which they had the rights for. There was nothing random about their conflict. To resolve a clash like this, you must get absolutely granular as to what's causing the big disconnect.

Jennifer and Todd's marital conflict was totally predictable given they *both* had a split *Right to Separate and Belong*. Jennifer had way too much *right to separate*, with very little *right to belong*. This gave her an anxious love style. Never having had the right to belong during her childhood, Jennifer opted to fight for that missing belonging and connection. She would sometimes go into flight mode to deal with her inner chaos too. This is called *situational avoidance*.

Todd was the opposite as he was given too much *right to belong* and not enough *right to separate*. His brain was fleeing from an intrusive mother who didn't give him a full right to separate and develop his full self. This gave him an avoidant love style. Too *little* right to belong drove Jennifer to pursue—too *much* right to belong caused Todd to withdraw—thus they became the other's worst nightmare. This is how *missing rights* become *relationship patterns*. With neither having a balanced *Goldilocks Zone*, building a *m/We* was impossible.

Jennifer's feelings of abandonment and disconnection were nothing new in her life. "In my family, it was every one for themselves. Mom and Dad simply *weren't there*." There was no secure base from which

Jennifer could explore her world safely. She was given a full right to be on her own, but not so much to belong. "As I try to remember my early childhood, there are no faces I can remember except in photos. I must not be important enough to be looked after. I feel so separate. I'm just not *seen*. I'm *invisible*. It all feels so scary . . . even playing! It's like I'm in *exile* with my toys. I'm so *invisible*." That's what a split *Right to Separate and Belong* feels like when you only get to separate. You don't feel seen and safe.

Talking about her later childhood, she continued, "I was a tomboy and would flip into *independent mode* like the boys did. *I was always on the lookout* for when I'd be on my own. But I was so lonely. I wanted somebody to love me so badly, but what I really wanted more than anything else was to make sure that they would *stay*."

Jennifer summed up her *cookie cutter* for love, "It's still the same today with Todd. Whenever I don't feel his love, or there's uncertainty, it creates *chaos* in my head. The only way I can restore any sense of clear-headedness is to create some certainty by myself. I can get very controlling. Or I try to comfort myself by not eating well or going shopping. Deep down, all I want is for Todd to create a *We* with me. I want to know I'm enough to be loved by him. I want to know he's all in and won't walk away. I'd like to experience the calmness, inner harmony, and peace that come from knowing you have a true partner who *sees* you." Not feeling seen is what it's like when you were given *too much of a right to separate but not to belong*. As for Todd, we'll get back to him shortly.

Cherished Wires Our Brain

The *Right to Separate and Belong* is initially wired into your brain between ages six months and a year. Most children learn to crawl between six and ten months, with walking beginning around the tenth month. The brain has developed quite a bit by this time. Around the eighth month, a child learns to differentiate themselves from their parents. A rudimentary *self* is born. Mobility and increased cognitive differentiation are tied together at this time.

The genes are spinning out the higher levels of the limbic system now. The emotional brain is more sophisticated. This results in better recognition and recall memory. Other limbic centers pertaining to emotional regulation have refined growth and function by now. The higher cortical brain is developing further. The brain is cognitively and emotionally exploding when the *Right to Separate and Belong* is being wired into a child's brain. The rights coming on-line now have much more to do with the development of the *self*.

What splits the right is how the parent reacts to this newfound mobility and selfhood. Again, all attachment is determined by contingent communication. If a child explores things that are possibly dangerous and the parent is *overly* protective, the child's ability to separate will be limited. Although done with the best of intentions, damage gets done. That's because mobility is the precursor to selfhood within the brain at this time. If we don't allow safe exploration, the child's ability to form a *self* will be limited.

We must remember the toddler *self* is actually a *sensory-motor experience* at this time. The toddler brain isn't creating anything like an abstract sense of selfhood or identity. It's more a fuzzy but dawning awareness that my body is separate from my parents. That sense of *embodied separation* is the initial state that will develop into selfhood in the years to come. In the meantime, it's the body-based experiences of exploration and separation that will color the feelings for all later experiences of self. *That embodied awareness around separation and belonging will become the template for later experiences around both selfhood and We-ness.*

Embodied awareness around separation and belonging
will become the template for later experiences of self.

A second way exploration can be limited is by having an intrusive parent who doesn't allow a child to play and explore on their own terms. Intrusion comes in a lot of forms. Say the parent plays with the child and determines the style of play. They may say things like, "Oh, let's not play with the fire truck. Let's play with the ball," or, "Be careful, you might fall on the jungle gym." If the child's natural expressions of exploration are blocked, controlled, or manipulated, that too will limit the experience of proper separation and therefore, selfhood. Here, a child learns *I can't be me.* The Neo-Reichians call those with this split version of this right, *the owned child.*

A child needs a certain amount of *freedom* while exploring to discover how *they* experience the world. If we impose our preferences, limits, experiences, fears, anxieties, agendas, scripts, or whatever onto their sensory-emotional uptake of life, we're keeping them from taking in the necessary raw experience to create their *own* sense of life's grand scheme. Those introductory exploratory journeys are the beginning of our selfhood.

However, the child also needs the *attuned input* of a secure parent to help them make sense of their world and inner experience. They need *supervision* as well as *separation.* That's where secure attachment comes into *play*, all puns intended. When a parent offers reflective responses back to the child, they feel important. It's perfectly okay to show a child something they may have missed about a toy or how to do something the first time, as long as too much input isn't offered. An attuned response may just be enjoying the child playing with a toy in a *wrong* way. The cherishing parent *joins them in their experience and rejoices with them in their explorations.* This helps a child feel esteemed in a big time way.

There will be times a secure parent will need to make a mad dash or limit something. However, if a child has been given the requisite freedom and encouragement to explore with attuned responses by a parent, they learn from these protective moments that the parent is carefully watching over them for any dangers. The child then realizes they are not only *cherished*, but *protected*. In that moment, they feel the secure base that enables them to feel safe in the world. When the fully embodied feeling of a secure base is added to the feelings of *Welcomed with Joy* and *Worthy and Nourished*, a child is well on their way to forming a secure love style.

On the other hand, say the parent has been overwhelmed by the needs of an infant child. When mobility first comes on-line, mom or dad may see that as a chance to have some separation for themselves. Here, they may say something like, "Oh, go over there, honey, and play with your toys." Or perhaps, "Daddy is working in the yard. Mommy has something better for you to do."

Here the right gets split in the opposite manner. The toddler receives a right to *separate* but very little freedom to *belong*. The secure feeling of a *We* gets a real hit. Their child gets the baseline feeling they need to do it all by themselves. Intertwining support will be replaced by staunch independence. In fact, a *We* may feel so rejecting that a child no longer feels comfortable being in a bonded relationship. Thus *We-ness* begins to feel dangerous to those who have a split *Right to Separate and Belong*. We may call this type the *disowned child*.

Intimacy and vulnerability will then become quarantined states. Some part of us will think, "Who needs that sort of rejection?" The feelings of *exiled* or *estranged* begin to replace the secure feelings of being safely enclosed within a *We*. When those sorts of emotions become the baseline state for a toddler's developing sense of self, it feels like they have no right for belonging or proper back up. They definitely won't feel seen.

If a child had a good enough experience with the *Right to Exist* and the *Right to Have Your Needs Met*, the *We* may take on a feeling of *Paradise Lost*. Here, a child gets freedom at the expense of feeling included. Often, as they grow older some part of them will then say, "Screw the *We!*" When that happens, *Paradise Lost* becomes *Paradise Rejected*. From here, there's no way to create a *We* when this becomes one's baseline feeling. A child's *excluded self* then becomes the *excluding self*. Eventually as an adult, they can only give an intimate partner their original feeling of *Paradise Lost*. I've seen many couples dealing with this issue in one form or another. Whatever we make about these early experiences become the backdrop feelings for our experience as a *self* and a *We*.

Often, as we grow older, some part of us will say, "Screw the *We*."
When that happens, *Paradise Lost* becomes *Paradise Rejected.*

Sometimes, the brain will use later childhood experiences to make a decision on whether or not it has a *Right to Separate and Belong*. Here, early imprints embedded in the amygdala team up with feelings from the higher, more cortical areas of the brain. As Dr. Catherine Pittman points out, there's a *cortex pathway* and an *amygdala pathway* for anxiety and fear. As a young child develops, those higher centers located in the cerebral cortex begin to play a part in how our rights develop. That means your brain eventually gets two *speakers* to play its emotional melodies; one coming from implicit memory, as I described earlier, and then eventually more cognitively based feelings. Seemingly, our brains are wired to feel in *stereo*. This is how later experiences influence our rights outside those first developmental windows.

When given inconsistent experiences, the brain can filibuster the vote on belonging, waiting until later. Early on I was hardly accepted by my mother. However, my grandmother did a lot to shore up my sense of belonging. It was hard to tell when I was four or five if I truly belonged or not. The tie breaker vote came when I was seven. Two things happened. First, my grandmother died of a heart attack. So there went my secure ties to belonging. At her funeral, I was numb. I couldn't allow myself to feel this loss.

Then, the tie breaker experience occurred. Six months later, I was at my cousin's wedding. A wild party was going on. I accidentally ran across four couples having sex in the barn. Two married couples had switched partners with each other, which shocked me. Who knew that could even happen? I ran back to the party frightened out of my mind with the chaos I was feeling. Here's the irony. Imagine for a moment what it might be like for a seven year old child running back to a crowd of drunks to find a *secure base*.

Eventually, I fled the crowd, sprinting as fast as my little legs could carry me all the way to the top of a hill that looked down on the party. Then my brain cast the vote. I said to myself, "I don't belong to this family. These people are embarrassing. I'm scared to be with them." The words hung in the summer air around me. From there, it was all separation with no sense of safe belonging. No part of *family* ever felt right after that. This decision came from both my amygdala and my higher, cortical brain. That's how you can fracture a *Right to Separate and Belong* at a later age.

Years later, I came to understand how my younger self equated *all* belonging with danger. No wonder I felt such anxiety in my two marriages at times. *We* meant weal and woe to some part of my brain. The real tragedy was that such a moment was hardly the entire story. Looking back, my family offered me many other times to belong. One uncle kept me for a month every summer on his farm. In the evenings, he and I would sit on his front porch overlooking the fields. We talked about atoms, stars, galaxies, dinosaurs, and more. Once he confided that I was like a son to him. That's belonging, but my brain deleted those memories.

Here's my point; no moment or its *meaning*, regardless of how tragic or traumatic it was, *should ever be allowed to determine the fate of an entire incarnation.* My young brain created a perceptual filter from that memory at seven that deleted a good many future instances of proper belonging, within my family and with others. While my mother was indeed scary, there were uncles, aunts, teachers, and friends who gave me many moments of secure belonging.

Just because your brain once split the *Right to Separate and Belong* doesn't mean that it was meant to be your entire, lifelong truth. I've worked with many clients to give them a fully balanced *Right to Separate and Belong*. One way to shift your rights is to remember the deletions and tell a more secure version of your story. Second, take a hard look at any global generalizations and beliefs you have about relationships. Third, adjust your official filter. You may be surprised how many hidden or deleted resources to belong you already have within you. It's a wonderful day when you realize that, just like Dorothy in *The Wizard of Oz*, you had the ruby red slippers of proper belonging and separation within you all the time.

Relationship Patterns

The first pattern to observe is *I always lose myself in relationships*. If a person had too much right to belong as a child, they will often create their identities based on the experience of others. Sometimes, they'll seek someone *bigger* than they are energetically to compensate for their deficient sense of self. One client wanted, "A man that is *larger than life* so we can be a power couple." As Dr. Robert Johnson observes, if a child has an anxious, overly protective parent, they'll learn to create a self from an *adopted standard*. Rather than creating a self from one's own experience, we learn a template for creating a self from others' experiences. Thus you may have learned to form your identity based on someone else's standards, expectations, values, and ideals. You often see this pattern in those with an anxious love style. With this patterning, they'll feel safest when they're holding onto someone. They can be clingy, overly dependent, and desperate to not distinguish themselves in a relationship.

Whenever you hear someone complaining, "I'm not me in this relationship," or, "I just get lost in my relationships," you may be dealing with someone who had too much of a right to belong. In order to find and create an authentic experience in love, they must learn to have their own experiences within a *We*. Running someone else's agenda doesn't work for creating a secure relationship. *Imitation* is never the basis of *intimacy* in any great relationship. Our unique, individual experiences are meant to empower our partner, rather than entrain their experiences within a false, adopted self. It's in the combining of two strong selves that the *We* is made even stronger.

Whenever you hear someone complaining that,
"I'm not me in this relationship," you may be dealing
with someone who had too much of a right to belong.

Those with this type of self template tend to *swallow their partners whole* in a relationship. If there's a sense of a *We* in their relationships, they'll complain that it's never on their terms. This, of course, is not a true *We*.

When someone can't separate, you may see them suddenly change religion or politics after beginning a new relationship. This may be a sign of not having a right to separate. The self-template under much of what has been called *co-dependency* is often a missing right to separate. Taking on another person's identity, values, interests, and needs eventually causes the relationship to fail. That's because few people want to marry themselves. On the other hand, these types have great abilities to create empathy. They can switch into a partner with the best of them.

Sometimes they'll talk about the other as if they're a *twin*. When I hear clients talking about finding their *twin flame*, I sometimes detect a missing right to separate. If someone is too much your *perfect mirror* it may be because you're copying them. Obviously, if the idea of a *soulmate* is seen through the eyes of a split *Right to Separate and Belong*, it can distort the entire concept and relationship. True soulmates never become overly identified with their relationship. Remember, the contract between soulmates is to bring out the *best self* of each other within the field of a mutually empowering *We*.

There are a few very popular identities for those who never got a right to separate. I'm sure you've heard someone say, "I'm nothing without you," or, "I can't be happy unless you are." These are the sorts of limiting identities that stop love in its tracks. Dr. John Gray advocates that partners are only responsible for about 10 percent of the happiness of their mate. Those in extraordinary relationships practice what he calls the *90-10 rule*. Each partner is responsible for 90 percent of their happiness by creating their own sense of fulfillment.

When we come to our relationships with the experience of a happy, secure love style it takes the burden off the relationship. However, if someone needs to borrow the experiences of their beloved, it weakens their bond. The *We* is drained because it takes two full *I*s to make a lasting *We*. This is one reason why it's so important to reclaim a balanced *Right to Separate and Belong*. When you're happy within yourselves, cherishing your partner becomes easier.

A second, opposite reaction may occur when there's too much right to separate. Sometimes a split right is handled with an avoidant strategy, called *the polarity partner syndrome*. This is the very opposite of the above pattern. Here you find folk whose mantra is, "I've just got to be me," even if their way of being is killing the *We*. They'll insist upon maintaining their uniqueness, because their early self was given too much separation. Interestingly, this reaction can also occur if someone was given too little right to separate. If a child was invaded, controlled, or subsumed into a parent's experience, you can get a similar reaction in the key of anxiousness.

In order to protect their self from intrusion, those with this patterning tend to have brittle boundaries. This is quite the opposite of those who lose themselves in relationships, who are *boundary-less*. It's as if the avoidant partner is saying, "Because I once didn't properly belong, I'll never let another person in too close." This erodes trust, intimacy, and any chance of vulnerability. Such walls invite suspicion, because those walls are seen as hiding something.

Brittle boundaries are often practiced by those with an avoidant love style, because at one time they had either too much right to belong, or only a right to separate. For instance, they may hold a tight schedule for any moments of togetherness. Many will keep too hard and fast rules regarding how they may be approached. They may insist that you adopt their rules for the relationship without much consideration for yours. This leads to conflict or disempowerment for their partner.

The secret to having great boundaries is to have a balanced *Right to Separate and Belong*. Those with a balanced right are neither boundary-less nor walled off. Instead, they tend to have *semi-permeable* boundaries. Every cell in your body is a living example of this. The cell survives by having a membrane that keeps the bad stuff out, yet allows the good stuff in. In relationships, semi-permeable boundaries allow for a proper flow of energy between two partners. A balanced right gives you a beautiful *Goldilocks Zone* for being neither too porous nor closed off. You're open enough to let them in. There's also appropriate distance. The secure self can flow between the states of a separate self and the protective bonds of a *We*.

When there's a balanced *Right to Separate and Belong*, we don't compromise our core identity. We will choose endearing communion over contrasting selves. The ultimate gift of a balanced *Right to Separate and Belong* is the deeply respectful intimacy it affords to both partners. This allows each self to be enriched by the spirit of the one we love, while preserving our deepest essence as a self. That's the true reward that comes from feeling *Cherished and Protected*. We become our best selves in a well-bonded way. However, there are other ways to create a self as we shall soon see.

In the ebb and flow of two selves sharing their essences
with semi-permeable boundaries, love flourishes.

Todd Feels Intruded

Now, let's step inside the mind of Todd, Jennifer's husband. His split *Right to Separate and Belong* matched hers like a glove. If Jennifer's worst fear was that someone would go away, Todd's worst fear was that someone would not let him get away. Therein was the very essence of their perpetual conflict.

Somewhere deep in his heart, Todd knew that something was off in a way he didn't quite understand. Todd explained, "Jennifer wants more of a *We*, but to be honest, I've never gotten what that means. As a result, I feel *empty* a lot of the time. I love her. I truly do. However, when she leans into me, I feel *uncomfortable* in some way. So I *lean out*. I'm *not as attached* as I'd like to feel with Jennifer. When I'm in nature or on a retreat working on myself, it feels like *I'm finally in control of my experience*. If I start getting too close, it feels like I'm being *intruded* on. That's when I *lose myself* so I pull back just to get a sense of *me* again. I want to *connect to myself*. While I love her, I don't feel as if I'm my better self within our relationship." If anything, Todd was one honest soul.

One can see their pattern clearly; his *freedom* triggered her *chaos* while *her chaos* triggered his need for *freedom*. His pull back instigated either an attack or pursuit by Jennifer. If he stayed close, all the alarm bells would go off in him. In Todd and Jennifer's relationship, the alarm bells were always going off in one of them. It all came together when Todd recounted, "My mother was always *intrusive*. I had to get away from her to have any sense of myself. Unfortunately, I could never get away. I spent most of my childhood feeling like I had *lost myself*."

That global feeling of *intrusion* wasn't just coming from Jennifer's need for closeness. It was the emotional echo of having a mother who didn't understand personal boundaries. By seeking too much closeness to her son, she gave Todd no right to separate. Since a young child needs physical separation to develop a healthy sense of inner self, his brain was desperate to escape the memory of his mother's intrusive face parked right in front of his nose. Flash forward about four decades. Now, the face of his wife replaces the face of his mother. It wasn't his marriage that was so much to blame as it was his memories. No wonder intimacy and a true *We* were so difficult for him to understand. This is what a split *Right to Separate and Belong* feels like when you can't properly separate.

Do you see how Jennifer's missing right to belong played right into Todd's missing right to separate? Jennifer was always on the lookout for when love would leave her on her own. Todd's need to separate gave her the only experience she had the rights for—the right to be on her own. Conversely, Todd's missing right to separate was always on the lookout for being invaded. Jennifer's anxious protests gave him the only experience he had the rights for—to be controlled or pursued. Curiously, when Jennifer had finally enough of things and withdrew, it triggered Todd's need to have someone fill in the gap of his experience. This caused him to be anxious and come back. Just so, their dueling rights would conflict until both restored a full *Right to Separate and Belong*. Only with a *balanced* right could a dynamic *We* be created between them.

Adult attachment research knows that a big challenge for those with an anxious love style is that they won't allow for a secure base. Drs. Mario Mukulincer and Phillip Shaver have observed in longitudinal studies of adult couples that the anxious tend to question their partner's supportiveness. They expect their loved ones not to be there. Moreover, they often don't acknowledge support, or won't seek it. Accordingly, the anxious often have quite a bit of difficulty experiencing any relationship as a secure base. Their system is wired to expect non-supportive behavior and to mistrust. Just so, in addition to not accepting any BS, Jennifer also had to learn to accept and let the good stuff in from Todd when he began to give it. Letting things in is also a part of feeling *Cherished and Protected*.

When Jennifer and Todd restored the natural balance of a proper *Right to Separate and Belong*, the doors to true intimacy were opened. For Jennifer, we added the feeling of *Cherished and Protected* to the little one inside her. She shared, "That's the feeling I wanted to feel my entire life; *exactly* what I wanted to feel. It's as if I've been waiting my entire life to feel this moment." It felt like a long overdue homecoming to her heart and soul.

For Todd, we added the feelings of safe and empowered to his little one. When their rights were balanced, both were able to create a powerful *We* that would empower the *me* in ways that neither could have imagined before. They discovered that the *m/We* is always more authentic and powerful than the *me* by itself. The most powerful *me* is a co-creation of two *me/s* within a deeply bonded *We*. This enables each partner to become their best self.

Rights of the *We*

Believe it or not, the *We* has a *Right to Separate and Belong* as well. When we begin to think of the rights of the *We*, there are two seminal issues we must explore; Does the *We* have a right to *separate* from the interests of each *me* and create an arbitrating third identity in your relationship? Also, does the *We* have a right to *belong* in each other's hearts? In every great couple, the *We* acts as system of checks and balances for the competing needs of the two partners. Yet the *We* in a secure relationship never sacrifices the interests, needs, growth, and potential of those partners. That's because *the We is the supremely cherishing soul of any relationship.*

The *We* is very much the emergent creation of the best of feminine and masculine energy. A secure *We* has a wonderful life-giving sense that protects the two *Is* as any mother would her children. It's always on the lookout for the deep needs of the couple, and how to nourish the highest purposes of everyone under its care. Some might call this feminine energy. In turn, the masculine must cherish and protect the *We* as we naturally do for all feminine energy. Every *me* on the planet is designed to be birthed within the loving bonds of a parental *We*. That need for a life-giving, self-supporting, and soul nourishing *We* remains with us as long as we have an attachment system.

The *We* is very much the emergent creation
of the best of feminine and masculine energy.

The *We* has a masculine side as well. It's a protective and guiding spirit who looks over us in the way all great fathers provide and look over their children. The *We* is constantly on the lookout for the bigger picture of support that both the couple and each *me* needs. In the middle of every extraordinary couple is a *We* that combines the best qualities of feminine and masculine polarity, energy, and qualities. This is how masculine and feminine *polarity* is supposed to work. *Polarity* between the sexes is meant to bring differences into a unified state of mutual belonging. For your attachment system, polarity was never meant to be merely about the differences.

Masculine and feminine arise within all people regardless of gender, identity, or sexuality. So here's my working, provisional definition of a secure *We*. The *We* is a reciprocal flow of cherishing energy and belonging that combines the finest resources and qualities of each partner into a unified field of intimate possibilities. This magnificent field of emergent energy surrounds the couple in a protective, beneficent, and empowering sheath we call love. Let's look at how this works out practically.

First, the *We* has a need to have its own identity in your relationship. While it's a combination of your two identities, resources, and internal programming that comes together, it also possesses a *more* quality. Too many couples attempt to make the *We* in their own image. Then the *We* becomes a war zone. This often happens when both members of a couple have done a lot of personal growth work. I've even seen it when two *I*s have attended my couples workshop. Both are sorting through the material looking for what matches their identities and needs the most. Then, they try to lay their concept of the *We* onto the partner. In turn, the other partner has filtered the workshop for what works for them. Each is defining the *We* according to the prisms of their own self-awareness, identity, needs, desires, wants, etc. That strategy will never work for a couple who wants to create a secure *We*.

One of the signs of a secure *We* is that the bond between partners allows them to have separate, unique experiences. Yet, there's also a *couple identity* that's different. This *couple identity* allows them to operate as a team, even when both have developed finely tuned personalities. If you have ever wanted to know how *big personalities* successfully couple up, it's because the *We* is at least as *big* and *finely tuned* as they are. Each created a *couple self* for their *big* selves.

Such signs of the *We* are not hard to find. You can spot a *couple self* in the very words a person uses in their day to day conversations. In a study at the University of Texas at Austin, Drs. James Pennebaker, Matthias Mehl, and Kate Niederhoffer discovered that just noticing the natural language used by people reveals the nature of their relationships. When someone is deeply connected to their partner, they use different pronouns. They're far more likely to use the words *we* and *us* rather than *I* or *me*.

In great couples, something else happens to the self-identity. Everyone navigates the *Ego Self* and the *Balanced Self* within them. A large part of the attachment process is knocking the *Ego Self* off its perch of self-importance. Most of us have gone through life thinking of our *self* in an *Ego Self* way. The *Ego Self* never creates a cherishing *We*. It takes humility to allow the *We* to become an independent identity within your relationship.

> The *Ego Self* rarely works well for creating a cherishing *We*. It takes humility to allow the *We* to have an independent identity within your relationship.

Ego Self often creates what I call *single identity*. You see it when singles have been solo for a long time, or when somebody has been divorced for a while. In the process of creating their lives, singles can get *stuck in their ways*. Single identity can be deadly to creating a new life with someone. It happens when two people own their own homes but want the other to give up their residence. Or one partner thinks that their furniture should be privileged over the other's prized belongings. Deciding where to live is often the first place the *Ego Self* gets revealed.

Many break-ups happen when someone cherishes their old lifestyle over designing a new life together. Or, as time goes by, they let things like career development, family needs, or the exigencies of an unexpected life crisis take precedence over the *We*. When a couple gets together, a true *We* will create a different lifestyle that combines the best of both worlds. There's some give and take involved here. If a couple cherishes each other they will *negotiate* rather than *negate* each other's lifestyles. In the process, a new lifestyle evolves from the *We* which emerges from their earnest attempts to attune to each other. From there, a new self emerges for the couple—the *We Self*—there's a merger at work here.

The second need of the *We* is that it be taken into your hearts and allowed to influence your identity. As children, the *Right to Separate and Belong* is about learning to feel safe as a *me* embedded in a *We*. However, as adults who have coupled, the game changes a bit. Now the game is about how a couple can embed the *We* in the *me*. The *We* needs to belong in our hearts the same way a child needs to belong in the protective circle of their parent's love. Moreover, that *We* must be allowed to influence our identities and all that flows from who we consider ourselves to be. Identity is precious for everyone on the planet. The trick for couples is to allow their identities to be influenced by each other and the *We Self*. That's what it means to cherish the *We* in a relationship.

When both partners allow the *We Self* to influence their identities, something magical happens in the relationship. The conflicts diminish. *Opposing* egos give way to *open* hearts. Compromise doesn't feel like compromise anymore. A field of cooperation and good will shapes the responses we give to our beloved.

SARK and Dr. John Waddell, in their book, *Succulent Wild Love*, offer couples a very creative way to handle their conflicts. Instead of offering *compromises* to each other, couples can suggest *joyful solutions*. Here you reach agreements by stepping into each other's shoes. You write down what it feels like in both sets of shoes and *explore* what's essential to both people. From there, you imagine something that works for both of you. It's a win-win for everyone.

However, before joyful solutions can be offered there needs to be an identity adjustment for both partners. When we offer any solution from the place of the *me* it inevitably feels like a *subtraction*; as if we're giving up something. Then we experience things like control, submission, or any other number of residual negative feelings. No wonder few people like the word *compromise*.

However, what if the *compromise* has been offered from a place where the *We* has been allowed to influence our *Ego Self*? Then we can offer a solution from a place I call the *We-dentity*. If you're coming from that place of selfhood, then the compromise will be felt like an *addition* to your *We-ness*. In that moment, the negotiation will no longer feel like a compromise, but will rather be experienced as a solution. *If you come to conflict with an identity that includes the We, you will experience very different feelings about compromises.*

When we come from a place of the *We*, solutions are joyful because some part of us is aligned with the greater purpose of the couple. If you want to end the conflicts and make compromises feel like joyful solutions, the answer may be allowing the *We* to have a place of belonging in your heart and sense of self. This is the deep magic that a *We* brings to a couple.

Two things naturally transpire when the *We* is allowed to belong in our hearts. First, where there's a strong *We*, both partners will *honor the experiences of the other*. A secure *We* respects the experiences of each partner. That doesn't mean we always enjoy our experiences or the experiences of our partner. (I'm not asking you to accept *any* abusive behavior, just to be clear.) Nobody's having a perfect experience in life, even the most self-actualized among us.

Where there is a strong *We*, both partners
will treasure the *We* in such a way that it
allows them to honor the experiences of the other.

Second, the cherishing couple will honor that experience and *find a way to navigate rather than negate their partner's experience*. Here you say, "Isn't it interesting they're having that experience of me? I wonder how I'm co-creating it with them." When you can step beyond your own hurt to honor the experience of your partner, you know the *We* is empowering you to cherish your partner's separate experience. You don't have to agree with it. Nor do you need to fight it. You simply honor it as their experience. Then both can stop making the other wrong and allow them to have their own experience. It's a better way to love. The *We* needs the entire gamut of experiences from both partners to create the closeness, intimacy, and vulnerability necessary to make your relationship a secure base.

The *We* needs the entire gamut of experiences from both
partners to create the closeness and vulnerability
that make your relationship a secure base.

The third need of the *We* is to *explore,* just as you do. Sometimes, couples get in ruts because some pattern has become routine, habitual, or comfortable. The *We* needs *attuned adaptability* to keep it fresh and viable. Sometimes, the bond between you will need something fresh to keep love alive. A great *We* can't be fed the same diet year in and year out. Our lives change. The *We* needs to explore too! Your *We* is about growth. Allow your union to explore the outer boundaries of intimacy with fresh experiences.

Cherished and Protected Skill Set

The key skill set behind maintaining a cherishing and protecting *We* is keeping the marital friendship strong. Maintaining a positive perspective not only allows the *We* to feel worthy but also cherished. The cherishing couple practices *fondness and admiration*. Secure love is a decision to magnify your partner's positive qualities while minimizing their negative qualities. They're each other's biggest fans. Sometime in the next week, take a few minutes and tell your partner what you cherish and adore about them. Share your fondness and admiration with them. Couples who cherish each other have a lot of fondness and admiration working in the background for each other. This enables them to remain the best of friends.

One good way to create fondness and appreciation in your relationship is to share *positive* traits you hold dear about your partner. Make sure you tell them about a *specific* instance or story regarding when they exhibited that wonderful characteristic too. You might start with saying things like, "You are so *loving*! Like the time you brought roses and Robitussin to my bedside when I was sick with the flu last winter." Or, "I so appreciate how *thoughtful* you are. I adore the way you plan our date nights so they are always interesting and fresh." If you do this regularly and often, it will change the tenor and feeling of your entire relationship.

Some great traits for appreciative partners to notice is how sensitive, reliable, sweet, truthful, fun, interesting, protecting, gentle, vulnerable, supportive, powerful, flexible, understanding, funny, decisive, committed, empathetic, or considerate they are. If you feel stumped, just Google "positive adjectives to describe people" and you will find a treasure of feelings to share with your beloved. A proven way to groove positivity into your relationship is to proclaim the *first week of every month* Fondness and Admiration Week. For six days share one positive trait and a specific instance of it with each other. On Sunday, do something really special to celebrate each other. Then watch your love soar.

A second skill is that secure partners help their partner make their *dreams* come true. As the Gottman research points out, whenever couples experience gridlock on specific problems, the *problem* often isn't *the problem*. The problem is the underlying dream of one or both partners that hasn't been recognized or supported. Extraordinary couples listen to each other's dreams and help each other make it happen. As song writers and poets have encouraged us, find lots of ways to make your beloved's dreams come true!

When you find many ways to make each other's dreams come true, you'll naturally cherish each other. Nothing makes us feel as cherished as when our beloved takes the time to learn our big dream, and then gets behind it. So, take some time every few months and check in on each other's dreams. Ask about their current dreams. Then find one hundred ways to make dreams come true for each other. Now that's a cherishing *We*!

My Right to Feel Cherished

By now you know the drill here. Find someone who knows you well. Then just say to them, "I have a balanced *Right to Separate and Belong*." Then continue as before.

If you have a split *Right to Separate and Belong*, you'll want to find somebody who can help you reset that split. In the meantime, you may want to create a new perceptual filter for yourself. On a 4 by 6 index card, write the following:

Ways I Can Feel OK to Be "Me" in a Supportive "We"

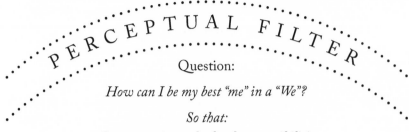

PERCEPTUAL FILTER

Question:

How can I be my best "me" in a "We"?

So that:

• *I can experience the freedom, possibilities,*
growth and protection of a "We"

For the next few weeks, read this card two to four times a day. Read it in the morning and just before you lay your head on the pillow at night. Notice any ways that you're being cherished and protected in life. Look into the mirror and say to yourself, "I can be a *me* and a *We*." *Both* are your birthright in life.

If you would like to begin restoring a balanced *Right to Separate and Belong*, go to *www.garysalyer.com/lovemanual*. Again, you'll find more customized filters designed to help you create a personalized experience with this right. Isn't it time you start reclaiming your right to have a *me* and a *We* in a loving relationship so you *experience* what it's like to be well supported, seen, and securely bonded?

Seven

Empowered with Choice

Choices—everybody loves them—freedom to choose lies at the heart of the human experience. The whole point of being human is to choose, learn, and grow from our experiences. Some cosmologists have argued that the universe was rigged at the quantum level to eventually spawn not only life, but conscious life that's self-determining and aware of that fact. Humans are a sentient species. We not only make choices but are conscious of our decisions.

One of the most beautiful examples of selfhood and choice in its pristine childhood innocence can be seen in an online video, *A Cashier Asked a Girl Why She Wanted a Black Doll.* The video begins by showing a cute, blonde two year old Caucasian girl, Sophia. She's playing joyfully and intently with an African American doll. Sophia thinks she and the doll look alike because, "we are both pretty girls." As her mother tells the story, little Sophia spent twenty minutes looking at all of the dolls in the toy store. She kept coming back to one African American *doctor doll.* When they got to the checkout, the cashier asked, "Are you certain this is the doll you really want, honey? This doll doesn't look like you. But we have lots of other dolls that look just like you, dear!"

The viewer is next privileged to witness one of the most dazzling acts of pure, undiluted childhood choice. Undeterred by the cashier's comments, little Sophia stands firm by declaring, "She *does* look like me! *She's* a doctor and *I'm* a doctor. *She's* a pretty girl and *I'm* a pretty girl!" We next see Sophia as she plays with the doll saying, "I'm a doctor." You got to love this girl's spunk.

The story is truly heartwarming. Yet something much more significant is going on at a deeper level. For little Sophia, something more basic was being confirmed and wired into her young brain by a very wise and loving mother. Sophia was allowed to choose what *she* really wanted. She was exercising a full *Right to Create Your Own Experience*. When little Sophia boldly stood up for her choice by telling the clerk that her idea of a cute doll wasn't the experience she wanted, Sophia exercised her *Right to Assert*. If you can grasp the sort of secure, loving experience it takes to empower a child to stand up to an adult under such circumstances, then you intuitively understand the rights I'll be explaining in this chapter. Sophia obviously felt *Empowered with Choice*.

A Ghostwriter Wrote My Life

As Emily walked through the door of my office, I couldn't help but notice how vivacious she was. Bright, warm, and friendly, Emily possessed a wicked sense of humor and worked hard in the real estate and financial sector. She had been divorced for about five years, after immigrating to the United States from South America with her husband many years ago.

Typically, rights are formed in the first three years, or at least before age seven. Interestingly, this was not the case for Emily. She shared in utter exasperation, "When I was fifteen, I was given to a man in an arranged marriage. Eduardo was *twenty four years* older than me. It felt like I had just been *auctioned off* to an old man. Unbelievably, I got pregnant on the first night. I had three children before I was twenty. At first, the marriage was *tolerable*. Eventually, I just couldn't hide my lack of sexual attraction. That's when the physical abuse started. I learned to put on a mask and hide my true self in the marriage. Everything about *me* went numb. The joy went out of my life. It's like Dr. Brené Brown says; *if we numb our pain, we numb our joy too.*" Later I discover that one in five girls in South America is given away in child marriages. In Brazil, nearly a third of young girls will be married off before they're eighteen.

Emily was very clear about what she wanted from love going forward. "Next time I'm in love," she stated directly, "I want *more* of *me* in my relationship. More than anything else, I want a partner to see *me* as *I am*. I want a relationship that I don't have to play a *role* or hide behind a *mask* to be in. I want to be *me* and to be my *true self*. I want to fall in love deeply, totally, passionately, and completely. I was *never allowed* to fall in love the first time. This time, I want to fall in love the way real lovers do."

Emily had a missing *Right to Create Your Own Experience,* and also a missing *Right to Assert* due to the physical abuse. Given how rights are usually disabled, I assumed we could find the originating cause well before she was *auctioned off to marriage*. That turned out to not to be the case. Until that dreadful day, Emily had experienced a very secure childhood with her parents. While they thought they were making sure she would be provided for, her parents' well-meaning intentions undid Emily's secure love style.

This decision robbed Emily of the *Right to Create Your Own Experience*. As she lamented, "Looking back, I've had two lives. I had a truly happy childhood until the day they auctioned me off to Eduardo. I didn't get to *choose* what happened to me. My parents wrote a terrible script for my life. *It feels like a ghostwriter wrote my life.* I've lived a story I didn't compose. I haven't gotten to live *my* life since I was fifteen. Going forward, *I want to write my own story*. I long to write a story where I can fall in love and there isn't a shred of *obligation*." Have you ever felt that way?

In this chapter, you'll experience how the feeling of *Empowered with Choice* creates secure love. We'll go deep into the *Right to Create Your Own Experience* and the *Right to Assert*. You'll learn how these twin rights can be limited or lost. Of course, I'll show you how to recover them as well. You'll also learn to recognize the relationship patterns that come from these missing rights. Feeling empowered is so necessary for sustaining love. Couples will learn how to move beyond their stalemates to become soulmates. I'll also show you how to turn your *dueling rights* into a duet of dynamic partnership. The *We* needs to be empowered, too, so I'll show you how to do that as well. Lastly, you'll learn specific skills that all secure partners use to navigate the inevitable power issues that arise in any relationship. Then you can both feel at choice with each other. Love needs to express itself.

It's time to meet the *Right to Create Your Own Experience* and the *Right to Assert*!

The Rights to Feel Empowered

The fourth feeling of those who are securely loved is *Empowered with Choice*. This is the *West Pole* of your inner GPS for love. Underneath the fourth feeling of a secure love style are the *Right to Create Your Own Experience* and the *Right to Assert*.

In the story about Sophia, we see these two rights clearly in play. First, Sophia exercised her right to create an *internal* experience of her *self*. Second, she engaged in the *external* act of declaring a choice for a certain doll. Internally, Sophia considered herself to be a *doctor* and a *pretty girl*. She then made an *external choice that echoed her internal experience* when she told the cashier her choice was firm. That was her taking control of *external* experience by asserting her voice and choice.

With little Sophia one sees choice in its dual-natured simplicity. We need to have *both* internal and external experience to fully implement a choice in our lives. It takes two rights to create an effective human being who can be fully *at choice*. These two rights come in at the same time since you need to affect both internal as well as external reality in order to exercise a truly empowered sense of self and choice. The ability to create *internal* experience I call the *Right to Create Your Own Experience*. Conversely, the ability to affect, implement, and declare to one's *external* environment what our inner self desires is described as the *Right to Assert*. Together, these two rights give us the ability to choose, which is to say, the power to create both our internal and external realities.

Our lives reflect what has *already* occurred in our minds. Your *self* is naturally powerful. The only real question is whether you have the power and permission to create what you truly want. Our pre-frontal cortex allows us to look backwards and forward in time so we can plot the effects of our decisions. This allows us to learn the consequences of our choices. Thus we discover that life and love aren't happening to us, but are something we've *created*.

Your *self* is naturally powerful. The only real question is
whether you have the permission to create what you truly want.

A big part of being at choice is learning the lessons from our inner and external experiences. Self-reflection allows us to decide if the experience we've chosen is what we wanted, or whether there's something even better we would like. We can learn, grow, and evolve through every decision we make. Choice plays quite a large part in creating the love you deserve. Being *at choice* in your relationships is the issue underneath the two rights I'll be addressing in this chapter. These rights are powerful templates you'll need to create the love you want. Are you ready to feel at choice with love and have a *say* in your relationships?

The Expressive Self

Power shows up in many ways. In the transformational world you can find it everywhere, with marketing geared towards things like *personal power*, *feminine power*, etc. There are good reasons for this. Depression is rampant in our society. As I write this, more than 15 million American adults, or about 6.7 percent of the population over age 18, have some form of persistent depression. Worldwide, it's estimated that more than 300 million suffer from debilitating hopelessness and despair. That's a lot of global disempowerment. The results of not having the right to feel *Empowered with Choice* are very debilitating. We need a strong sense of personal empowerment to be able to thrive in life and love.

What does *power* look like within a secure love style? The philosopher Friedrich Nietzsche argued that the desire to attain power was *the* driving force in humans. By *power* he meant the inner push and search for achievement, ambition, and striving to attain the highest possible status in life. While Nietzsche tried to distinguish carefully between power as raw force and power understood as *self-overcoming*, his views have been wrongly understood by many. Our primate brain is constantly searching for power and raw dominance. It will strive for power even when survival is at stake. In terms of secure bonds, that kind of power is a dead end strategy. There's no love in pure power. Here, we trade intimacy for supremacy and then wonder why we're so lonely in our relationships.

Psychologist Dr. Rollo May points out that thriving people need both *love and will*. Dr. May worked with patients who had severe anxiety. Never shying away from controversy, he once argued, "Anxiety is good for you as long as it is not out of proportion to the situation." That's interesting for those with an anxious love style, isn't it? However, underneath states like anxiety and depression, he clearly perceived the role that disempowerment plays in people's unfolding lives. Dr. May astutely observed in his classic book, *Love and Will*, that, "Depression is the inability to construct a future." In many of these cases, there's often a missing *Right to Create Your Own Experience* and/or a missing *Right to Assert* for the nearly 300 million people who suffer from depression.

Depression is the inability to construct a future.
This may be due to not feeling Empowered with Choice.

Dr. May's style of therapy was to increase someone's sense of *freedom* by helping them see the possibilities which they could not see. When they no longer felt trapped, the depression lifted. This resulted in them taking their lives into their own hands. In NLP circles we call this, *adding resources to the map*. Dr. May was constantly advocating for everyone to determine new values for themselves. The goal was to grasp our capacity to *mold ourselves*. This ability to take personal development into your own hands thoroughly depends on having a full *Right to Create Your Own Experience*.

Nothing could be more important for creating the relationship you want than a strong *Right to Create Your Own Experience*. Love is a co-created experience between two people. If the template or permission slip for creating new experiences is missing, love can only be fashioned on a platform of limited options and resources. Such a relationship will not fit either person. For partners to respond in an attuned manner, both must be able to generate new experiences with each other. Empathy needs a permission slip to actively generate new possibilities of aligned, contingent responses. Nothing is worse than when our beloved shows up like an autobot for love. A lasting relationship needs both partners to have a sturdy sense of *personal* power to create the sense of empowered *We-ness*.

So what does it feel like when you have a full *Right to Create Your Own Experience*? *Power* comes from the Anglo-French word meaning *to be able*. *Potent* and *potential* also come from this ancient root. When you're *Empowered with Choice*, anxiety and fear melt into calm inner assurance. For women especially, there's no sense of *submission* to your partner's agenda. Instead there's a sense of *unbridled confidence* that you can craft what you want to happen. One woman said when she's empowered by her partner, her *self-esteem soars*. Then she can come from a place of *enhancement* versus *timidity* in her relationship. You're able to explore the possibilities in life and create an inner reality together. *Choice* becomes the operative word in your life.

From this place, your inner potentialities are *endless*. Remember, this right is all about actively choosing your *inner* experience. There's a freedom to be your best self and explore your *capabilities*. Your choices are *unshackled* from the usual insecurities. You're at liberty to imagine wildly and dream big. *Change* is now your friend. Failure is experienced as feedback rather than bone crushing defeat. Taking the next step feels natural, comfortable and good. You can take *appropriate risks* because you instinctively discern that you're only a choice away from the necessary course correction to make it all good again, or maybe even great! You can be *decisive* and make *bold* executive moves. Your experience fits you like a glove.

Those with a *Right to Create Your Own Experience* instinctively feel like a mover and a shaker in their lives. This right enables the *imaginative impulse* in all of us. The *dreamer* makes its abode here. When someone has this right, they rarely get stuck in a rut. But if they *do* get stuck, they'll seek out someone who can restore their natural state of originality and creative resourcefulness.

Those with a Right to Create Your Own Experience feel like a mover and shaker in life. The dreamer lives here.

The *Right to Assert* feels similar, but has a few different emotional hues. This right is about affecting your *external* world. When you have a full *Right to Assert*, giving voice to your thoughts feels natural and good. You can make requests, not just because you're worthy to do so, but because anything less would be *inauthentic* for your empowered, expressive self. If there's a disagreement on something, you tactfully and skillfully speak up without hesitation. When you have a *Right to Assert*, you know that sometimes you must rock the boat to serve the *We*. Nevertheless, in a secure relationship assertion is paired with attunement, so the receiver of the message may be empowered to listen and give what is needed.

Many women feel most *Empowered with Choice* when their man is open to the conversation that's needed between them. Even if the conversation is uncomfortable, saying *Yes* to the dialogue feels very empowering for most women. When a man opens himself to his woman's influence and stops the stonewalling, she can voice her truth. For men, this open space is where you'll find the peace and respect you crave from your partner.

As a couple, you're able to give voice and choice to the wonders of mutually designed experiences in your common life together. Here's some advice for my men readers. Women feel most empowered to assert when their opinions are valued, respected, accepted, and honored by their partner. Where there's a secure *Right to Assert*, accepting that you have a difference of opinion replaces second guessing your spouse. When each partner's voice feels respected, conflict turns into collaboration. One man put it best, "Truth telling is the key thing in terms of how we empower each other and keep our union tight." That's a smart man who understands why men and women need a secure *Right to Assert*.

When you have a *Right to Assert*, you're fully allowed to have your wins and victories in life. Sabotage ceases while success increases. You no longer feel timid or pull back from your full expression. Life ceases to be hard. You can choose the high end option rather than the *blue light special* version of what you want. *Affirming your dreams* becomes your norm. Indeed, you can *be the author* of your reality. You may express your inner reality fully in your daily life. Every inch of you knows that you can impress upon reality the stamp of your most authentic self. This makes you a *living poet* who expresses your essence in the rhythmic nuances of a well-created life. The motto for creating the fabric of your life becomes, *"Why be the garment when you can be the tailor?"*

The motto for creating the fabric of your life becomes,
"Why be the garment when you can be the tailor?"

Adult Experience Counts

Attachment research has tracked people like Emily for thirty and forty years in various longitudinal studies. This field is called *Adult Attachment*. We know that secure love styles can be lost later in life too. Sometimes, if the experience is deep enough, teenage and adult experiences can rewire our brains. Dr. Glenn Roisman at the University of Minnesota tracked the attachment styles of babies to ascertain how a child's love style would develop into adulthood. Dr. Roisman discovered that only 11 percent of babies who were classified as either avoidant or anxious had gained a secure love style by age nineteen. In another study based on the same population sample, it was further revealed that nearly 39 percent of the secure babies had *lost* their secure love style by age nineteen. Emily would have fit right in there with them.

Adult experience taught Emily's brain that choices were off the menu for love. Accessing her true self would have been too painful to bear given that she was trapped inside a loveless, choice-less marriage. We notice that culture played a big part in this lost secure love style too. The larger point in Emily's story is that *all experience affects your attachment system*. While childhood is the big predictor, adult experience also factors into your love style. The corollary is, *If it changed as an adult, then it can change again*. I pointed that out to Emily after a few sessions. She needed to know that if her brain was once secure, then it already knew its way *home*. Her brain did just that. Emily found her way home to a secure love style and is now happily married, writing her new own story with a loving man.

Empowered Wires Our Brain

Between 12 to 24 months of age, the brain gets wired for the *Right to Create Your Own Experience* and the *Right to Assert*. These two rights run in tandem. A child's brain undergoes tremendous development, especially in the language area at this time. They now have more neurological support for body movement and balance. New synapses are connected together. This results in the onset of language capabilities. Studies show that a child's vocabulary will quadruple as their brain explodes with new neural connections. The cortex and the limbic areas continue to develop, creating more self-awareness. This enables their concept of a *self* to go way beyond what they experienced in the *Right to Separate and Belong.*

With all of these physical and mental abilities coming online, they must now integrate these new *magical powers* into their sense of *self* along with the vulnerabilities that come from still being a little one. It's the toddler version of *Mission Impossible.* It's as if they got a message from the universe; "Good morning, little one. Your brain just got a lot more sophisticated. You now have many physical and mental powers that you never knew you had. Word has it, however, that you're still very much defenseless and there's much you need to learn. You still need protection and guidance. Your mission, should you choose to accept it, is to explore your new powers while integrating your full humanity. This tape will continue with new orders as you grow older." Imagine waking up one morning and getting that *mission impossible.*

A child is now a fully thinking, feeling self that's dedicated to exploring their potential. At this point, a child's brain must figure out what that means. When the child's attention turns toward the *inner* experience of selfhood, it must deal with the self's agency in terms of it being *both* strong and weak, good and bad, vulnerable and magnificent, big and little, as well as all the other polarities in life, like love and hate, mean and nice, etc. That's where the *Right to Create Your Own Experience* comes into play. An integrated right allows the child to accept and express the full range of experiences that come with being human. They need a complete permission slip to articulate their full humanity *and* to feel their personal power.

The child's attention must also turn toward the *external* experience of their selfhood in order to understand what all of these new powers mean. Here, the self's agency is tracked in terms of its *effectiveness* in their relationships. A child's brain is learning what it means to assert with voice and choice. The issue is whether they're controlled by themselves or others, i.e., do they get *free will.*

They're also exploring their new powers of language and what kinds of communication are permissible and effective. A toddler's brain is seeking to comprehend what kind of power comes from having words. When a child is permitted to express both *Yes* and *No* (within reason, of course), they're given a permission slip to have their wins and successes in life. A sense of agency and personal power is then created. Their reward is a full *Right to Assert*. The *Right to Assert* is what's behind *the terrible twos*. Although this can be challenging, it's necessary to navigate this time well with your child. Where there's a will, there's a well child.

Losing Your Fully Human Self

A Right to Create Your Own Experience can be lost in many ways. Some have a low grade version because at some point, they were overly controlled. As a result, they lost their ability to choose who they want to be when they're in a relationship. Those with a low grade lost right tend to complain that they *lose themselves in relationships,* the same way those with a split *Right to Separate and Belong* do. The difference is that they lost the right, not because of parental intrusiveness, but rather due to a sense of losing control and choice. It's a tricky distinction that can be difficult to see.

There's also a middle grade version for this right. If the amount of parental control increases, for instance, in a very religious or ultra-conservative household, then the missing sense of empowerment increases. Emily falls into this camp. Here, the sense of lost choice and personal empowerment is much more pronounced.

Then there's the high grade version of this lost right. Here, you often find the presence of a genuinely narcissistic parent behind the scenes. This severely impacts the child's developing sense of selfhood well beyond what we saw in Emily's case. Imagine a narcissistic parent who needs a child to reflect positively upon *them* (picture the proverbial *stage mom* or overbearing *sports dad*). The Neo-Reichians call these children the *used child.*

Here a child exists to mirror the parent, rather than the parent mirroring the child. The child learns they exist only to reflect well on either mom or dad. If they have a moment of weakness, the parent will reject that feeling or state in the child because it doesn't make them *look good.* As a result, children will learn to suppress the vulnerable half of human experiences in order to gain approval. Going forward, it will be difficult for them to express any authentic sense of *me* in a significant relationship.

A child's brain then splits their *self-image* into two inauthentic parts—the *good me* and the *bad me.* They learn to develop a *false self* that may only experience their good traits and states. Moreover, these inner states must *enhance the experience of significant others rather than their own.* Only positive, grandiose states will be allowed on the list of approved experiences. Conversely, anything that feels remotely weak or vulnerable will be highly defended against, as if it were a toxic reality. These children will grow up unable to handle their basic humanity. Repairing the connection between these two internal images of the self is what it means to make a bond with your brain if you have this wound.

A child receiving such poor, self-interested reflection inevitably develops a *grandiose false self.* This is the high grade version of the lost right. That grandiose self is described as the *narcissistic wound* by the Neo-Reichians. When the most common human traits are classified as toxic, it becomes difficult to create your own experience. Such parents don't realize that strength comes from weakness, integrity from vulnerability, and a host of other human paradoxes that act as catalyst for our self's true potential. These children will be condemned to creating half of a human experience.

The basic message a child receives is that they can't be who they are. Instead the parent communicates, *"Be who I need you to be."* The child is barraged with messages on a daily basis which communicate they are too much or too little, too lively or too quiet, too exciting or too dull, too smart or too dumb, too pretty or too ugly, too fat or too thin, too independent or too dependent, too active or too passive, or just plain, "You're wrong for not making me look good." In short, they cannot be authentically themselves.

Sometimes a parent blames a child for their fate in life. Or, the parent is jealous of the child's intelligence, looks, likeability, etc. They criticize them either implicitly or explicitly. Here, a child is given too much permission to look at their weaknesses and aren't allowed to embrace their strong sides. Laying guilt trips on a child can also disable the *Right to Create Your Own Experience.*

Here, the right goes in the opposite direction of grandiosity and arrogance. You get the right to be modest, unassuming, or humble to an extreme. Such people are constantly looking at their self-perceived faults and what they *still need to work on.* On a first date, they'll *front their faults* as a way of creating intimacy. This, however, is not real humility. It's personal empowerment in a state of disablement.

Neither grandiosity nor obsequiousness can express this right well. There's a *Goldilocks Zone* in which you can find your true power. Knowing your abilities is never arrogance. Once, Reggie Jackson, the great baseball slugger, when chided by a reporter that he was arrogant, quipped, "It ain't arrogance if you can do it." Every talent has limits. But it's also okay to feel your fabulousness. *You have a full right to be flawed and fabulous all at the same time.*

It's okay to be flawed and fabulous all at the same time.

Lost Voice and Choice

The *Right to Assert* is lost in a different way. This right is not so much lost as it is conquered and defeated. When a parent is over-controlling, punishing, and stifling of a child's voice, it crushes their will. From the first utterance of the word *No* during the terrible twos, until the last act of rebellion as a teenager, the parent counters the child's efforts to choose with controlling or dominating responses. This ranges from the know it all authoritarian parent to the physically abusive mother and/or father.

Whenever a person has endured physical abuse, this is the missing right that's often driving their painful experience. The Neo-Reichians call this the *defeated child.* Later in life a missing *Right to Assert* shows up as a clear and persistent pattern of *self-defeat and sabotage.* These are the people who typically *grab defeat from the jaws of victory.* You may think of the career self-saboteur here.

This has tragic results for any human being. As Nietzsche pointed out, an important part of our nature is to exercise a *will to power.* In the face of such overwhelming domination, a child who can't freely choose their successes will reach for defeat as a substitute form of *will power*. It's as if they're saying, "If I can't have what I want, then I'll choose what I *don't* want on purpose."

What you'll never see is them saying, "This doesn't work for me." Instead, they'll grin and bear the pain. For this reason, the Neo-Reichians call this missing right the *masochistic wound*. They constantly hurt themselves by choosing abuse or frustrating patterns where they simply must lose. Like a Timex watch they *take a licking and keep on ticking*. If you take away their sense of defeat, it will feel like you're taking away their identity. Choosing the Rolex experience they really want from love is totally off their map.

Dr. Robert Johnson describes this as, *"The hopeless sense of being trapped in an endless circle of maximum effort leading to defeat."* They'll constantly complain about working their tails off but not getting anywhere, or getting the same results with their partners. Some will stay in a relationship forever, working hard on a love that will never pan out or deliver the goods. When the reference feeling for love becomes *working hard*, creating a sense of peace and ease will be most difficult. *Struggling* love replaces secure love for those with a missing *Right to Assert*. Secure love isn't hard like that.

> Maximum effort leading to defeat is
> what a missing Right to Assert most feels like.

When they can't have what they want, hope defines their choices. If there's been abuse, the brain will *split* the image of the *parent* into his or her good and bad parts (just as it did the image of their own *self* in the previous right.) A child's brain creates both a good and bad image of the parent. This allows the child to gain some measure of control over the internal experience of their "caretaker."

So where does the good image of the parent go? It takes residence in their hopes to have a loving parent someday. Thus a child who's not securely loved develops two images for an abusive parent. One image will be the internalized bad *devil* parent who lives in the present. The other image will be the good *angel* parent who dwells in the future, along with their other hopes. The good parent then becomes increasingly idealized as time goes on.

When this happens, the child begins to run a *hope structure* in their minds for love. Due to a split image of the parent, those who lived with abuse *must always have both abuse and hope present in their later relationships.* *Love* must therefore have an abusive quality in some way to be *survivable.* Moreover, secure love can only live in their future hopes, yet never be present now. That's a real bind.

Abusive Hopes

This has huge implications for the dating world. Consciously, a single may think they're looking for a wonderfully loving partner when they go online or attend a Meetup group. However, they'll almost always be attracted to somebody who will be abusive in some way. Then, they'll work their tails off to try and spin their partner into the idealized parent who they always hoped would show up. In this way, they'll turn love into something for which they must hope for indefinitely, while never actually having the secure love for which they so long. This is why many women and men stay in abusive relationships well past the time they should have packed their bags. If your friends have said that you're *addicted* to bad love, they may be right. However, there's a deeper reason you may need to explore if you see yourself in this missing right.

The nature of hope becomes the more profound problem if there's a missing *Right to Assert.* When a child's brain splits the parent in this way, it primes them to only *hope* for love. The brain learns that they cannot actually *have* love in the present now. As such, *there is only a right to hope* for real, secure love to come knocking on their door *in the future.* This is the peril of running a *hope structure.* People with this missing right can't actually have a good experience in love. They may only hope for one. In turn, that has several results.

When you are running a *hope structure*, you
only have the right to hope for love, but never to have love.

First, they'll *idealize their partner* in ways that aren't reasonable. That sets them up for continual disappointment. If they do find a good match, they'll never be able to completely love them; no real person will ever match up to this highly idealized image of love. Some will be prone to do the *fear of missing out* thing with their dates because of a runaway hope structure.

Second, they'll usually be living in *the future*, but rarely in *the present*. Instead of seeing the abuse in the present, they'll hope their date or spouse will change into who they want them to be in some *tomorrow*. In this way, they actually can't see their dates or partners for who they are. Moreover, they'll deselect the good ones and select the bad ones, all in an effort to keep *hope* alive.

Third, their relationships will be built around trying *to change an abusive relationship into a good one*. As a result, they're always working very hard on a relationship that's impossible to navigate. This is the *signature state* of those with a missing *Right to Assert—they work their tails off in dead-end relationships*. All of this is due to an out of control hope structure running ubiquitously in the background. Hope tells them to *hang in there* until it either becomes strictly intolerable or dangerous, or they're so exhausted that they can't possibly stay. Only then will they exit the relationship.

The inevitable end for all such hope structures is that they set the person up for real hopelessness. Until you reclaim your *Right to Assert*, you can't actually *have* the loving, secure relationship you deserve. In truth, you deserve *so* much more, and you deserve it *now*!

The inevitable end for all hope structures
is they set you up for real hopelessness.

A Bad Case of the *Bends*

I understand this right from the inside out. When I was two, I remember telling my mother, "No!" while I was jumping up and down on the bed. She told me to stop several times. But I did what many toddlers do—I asserted my right to say, "No!" My mother's response was swift. She hit me with a backhanded fist that sent me careening off a bed post. The effect was swift and lasting. I never, ever said the word *No* to my mother again. My family praised me for being such a *good little boy*. Little did they know why!

That was the first incident I remember, but it wasn't the last as she often used physical force as a form of discipline. In elementary school she raged against me again. Beating me with a kitchen chair, I remember being crouched in the turtle position, scared to death. It seemed like I might be killed. Suddenly, anger rose up in my heart and soul. I thought to myself, "This is so unfair." In utter defiance, my brain came up with a solution, "I will never bow to this! *You can bend me, but you can never break me.*" It sounded good at the time. This *solution* seemed like a way to reclaim my authority with an impossibly oppressive mother. That was the positive intent of my young brain. However, it was also the moment I lost much of my *Right to Assert* for years to come, though I didn't see it.

Later in life, my best friend once shared with me, "I don't understand you, Gary. You're one of the most assertive intellectuals I have ever seen. Yet when you're with a woman, you turn into a wimp. What's going on?" That's because the template I learned was about *not asserting with women.* And did that ever cost me dearly in my later relationships! The missing right didn't cover every aspect of life. My brain learned to limit assertion only *in an intimate relationship with a woman.* So, just because you lost this right for love, doesn't necessarily mean you lost it in every area.

Growing up, an entire identity was built around this decision. I thought this was my *finest* moment, when I *reclaimed* my *inner power.* Years later, I told this story to another therapist trained in NLP. As I came to the end of the story, I said glowingly, "That was the day *I* was born. All of the determination that made me a Ph.D. came that day." Carl listened, and then asked, "So, Gary, what's it like going through life bent over backwards?" What a humbling reframe.

If you're always bending over backwards in your relationship, you may have a missing Right to Assert.

When Carl said those words, a thunderclap of clarity went through my soul. I realized what a Faustian bargain I'd made with my *Right to Assert* by sanctioning *bending over backwards* as my way to assert. I had gone through the rest of my life as the man who was always bent over backwards in his relationships. To my old identity, my best moment was the day I gave up my *Right to Assert*.

Whatever that day was for you, I have a new truth to tell you; *deep down, we never lose our rights completely.* They just go underground, waiting for us to set them free again. The brain stores them away, safely pulling them offline, until the day we can train our brains that it's *Safe to Love Again*. When I work with clients, my job is to provide an alternative, *attuned parental experience* for early memories, so their brain can go back and learn the art of secure selfhood. NLP calls this *re-imprinting*. It's a powerful technique that allows the brain to relearn early memories in a secure way. Then the rights can come out of hiding. Love returns in the way it's supposed to be. This is the actual deep work I do with clients.

These days I have a full *Right to Assert*. It makes all the difference in my life. So can you, even if you suffered abuse in childhood. I'm here to tell you my *secure* story of abuse so that you can reclaim yours. My personal stories are told to empower you with the choice that is your birthright! If I can do it, so can you.

Relationship Patterns

For those with a missing *Right to Create Your Own Experience*, creating true intimacy will be a challenge. Sometimes it feels as if a ghostwriter is writing their relationship script. Moreover, when a person can't create their own experience, then creating any *We* experience will be difficult. If they have a low grade version of the missing right, they won't be able to individuate effectively; they will feel lost in the relationship. In turn, the other partner will feel like they don't have a partner, but rather a *twin*. They've lost the *right to be their own standard for experience*.

If they have the high grade, narcissistic version of the missing right, then the big complaint by a partner will concern their *grandiosity*. The entire relationship will feel like a *front* due to the false self of the grandiose partner. When you're with someone who can't be real about their vulnerabilities, it feels lonely. The grandiose partner will resist any attempts at true intimacy, since being in close quarters makes it very difficult to maintain their false, grandiose sense of self. Within an intimate relationship, we learn about each other's vulnerabilities and weaknesses as a matter of course. As a result, they'll hide behind a mask of magnificence. Grandiosity makes the entire relationship feel like a fake.

Partners in this kind of relationship will only feel valued for promoting their partner's sense of self. Those with the narcissistic version tend to turn their mates into a *trophy mate*. If the trophy mate loses money in the stock market or gains a few pounds, they often go on to the next trophy mate. There's a profound underlying sense of being used or manipulated. If you habitually feel *used*, you may be with someone who has the narcissistic wound.

Those with a missing *Right to Assert* will first and foremost become masters of choosing a losing strategy for love. Dr. Robert Johnson calls them a *one trick pony*. I'll paraphrase five of his losing strategies for love. First, their pattern may be to choose subservience, and then play the martyr card for the sense of righteousness it provides. A second strategy is to delay any real attempts at change. This is where you complain endlessly about the relationship or your partner but brush off implementing any winning strategies. Some adore laying the victim card on their partner.

The third way to choose defeat is to flood yourself with so many problems that you can't effectively fix any of them. The fourth way is one I often see in couples; the *Oh, did I do something wrong?* pattern. Here, the spouse knows right where their partner's pet peeve is parked. They'll do something to provoke their mate, and then act innocent when called on it. Fifth, some just won't allow themselves to enjoy a great relationship. These are the habitual *minimizers* who are the killjoys of any great relationship. No matter what the partner does, it's never, ever good enough. This is how a broken will shows up in love.

Those with a missing *Right to Assert* often have a *savior complex*. Buried within a hope structure is the belief that if the *bad parent* is given enough help, they'll change. The child begins to think *they* can change them. When they grow up, they'll pick people who will reprise the role of the parent, so they can save them from their personal maladies. For instance, a man will attempt to save a woman financially, or a woman may try to save a man emotionally.

However, being a savior will absolutely destroy any chance to create secure love. First, nobody wants a savior. Second, it destroys any sense of equality, and therefore intimacy, between romantic partners. The partner being saved will resist the *salvation*, which utterly frustrates the savior partner. If the savior persists (which anyone running such a hope structure will inevitably do), their partner often resents them. Being a savior never creates secure love.

Trouble Creating a Future Together

Judy was a frustrated and despondent single woman wanting to find love after her second divorce. Then she met Chris at a college reunion. Love was soon in the air. Judy's core missing rights revolved around having a split *Right to Separate and Belong* with almost no right to belong. She also had a wounded *Right to Assert*.

Chris, on the other hand, had almost no *Right to Create Your Own Experience*. His *Right to Assert* was profoundly disabled, more so than hers. This created a very painful pattern of *dueling rights* between Judy and Chris. Their missing rights collided within a few short months. Her missing right to belong ran straight into his missing right to create loving experiences, including with *her*.

Judy confided in an early session, "All I remember is spending my entire childhood wishing I could have a loving connection with mom and dad. Mom was angry at life while dad was a drunk. I kept thinking, *if I only worked harder, it would all change*. When I look back at my relationships, I've been in two physically abusive marriages. Most of the men I've dated since my last divorce have not been emotionally present. I keep *hoping*, '*If I stay, it will change.*' But it never does." Judy had a classic split *Right to Separate and Belong* along with a damaged *Right to Assert*.

Enter Chris. He was recently divorced after twenty plus years of marriage. Chris was the ever so nice man Judy had longed to be with over the years. Judy was the kind, powerful woman that Chris had dreamed of so long ago, before he married his now ex-wife. It was a *match made in heaven*—or so they thought. Then the holidays arrived. Judy was busy making plans to be together with each other's families in her fantasy version of Christmas.

However, Chris' missing *Right to Assert* was about to raise its hoary head. His sons were not ready for another woman *so soon*. Never mind that Chris and his wife had separated three years ago. His sons were not going to have anything to do with Judy. It was how Chris handled the situation, or rather, *didn't* handle it that caused the hurt in Judy.

About a week before Christmas, Judy bolted into my office. Her eyes were swollen and red. I could tell she had been in tears on the drive over. "It's obvious I'm not the priority to Chris that I want to be. I'm beginning to see why his marriage failed. He has no spine! I need him to stand up for me! I should be included!" Judy then began to tell me the story she was telling herself, "Chris was controlled and dominated by his ex-wife Leena for his entire marriage. I figured with a better woman, Chris would get his *male mojo* back. That's not happening. He's a wimp." In her story about Chris, we notice something else. Couples always know the deal with their partners. Some part of us always knows. The trick for most people is to not only recognize it, but to acknowledge it.

Fortunately, they both agreed to work with me. Before our first session together Judy blew up at Chris. Judy too had a missing *Right to Assert*, though not quite to the same level as Chris. Judy could assert *only* when she was extremely upset. I call this pattern *Vesuvius Assertion*. Here, you keep everything inside until you finally blow up like a volcano. As with all forms of uncensored expression, this is a very deadly form of assertion that almost always leads to criticism and contempt being laid on the other.

Vesuvius Assertion is when you keep everything inside until you finally blow up. This is not the secure Right to Assert.

When Chris came in, I saw a man who was now doubly disempowered. He entered the door with slouched shoulders and a downcast countenance on his face. I took the opportunity to ask him how he felt about what just happened. Chris looked down at the carpet with an utterly crestfallen look, "I can't seem to make anybody happy. *It feels like I can't win for losing.* I feel so *defeated* sometimes. Take what just happened with Judy. I didn't want to rock the boat too early with my boys, but then I pissed off Judy. There was no way I could make everybody happy." I noticed right off the bat that nowhere did Chris ever consider what might make *him* happy. He never asked himself, "*What is the experience I want to create with my sons and Judy?*" It was all focused on others' experience.

We learned more about his missing template for choice and voice going forward. The big rule for belonging in his family was *make sure everybody is happy, especially mom.* When I asked Chris about this, he said, "I learned early to never thwart or dishonor my mother. When I disobeyed any of her rules, she had a look that made me feel ashamed. I followed the rules—*all of them*—so I didn't make her feel bad." His brain was trained to look out for mom's experience rather than his own. When he married, that role would be reprised by his wife to match the early template he learned from mom.

When Chris was six, an incident convinced his young brain that speaking up wasn't tolerable. "My father never allowed us to talk back to him," he shared. "I remember starting school. Mom asked dad if he would walk me to the bus stop. When the bus came by, he put me on the wrong bus. I tried to say something but he cut me off, saying, "I'm the authority here, son. I'll say what's best for you. Just do as I say. Get on the bus." With that, I got on the wrong bus, went to the wrong school, and I knew it. I didn't speak up. I learned from dad that my opinion was not important. From then on, I didn't feel comfortable speaking my mind." When I pointed out that his emasculating father-in-law had reprised the role of his father, while his wife had reprised the role of his mother, the lights began to come on in Chris. He was reliving an old template for love.

When his sons and ex-wife wanted to exclude Judy for the holidays, Chris' brain had no defense. He had no rights to do otherwise. His inability to create his own experience and to assert gave Judy her worst nightmare. She got no right to belong. When she blew up at Chris, he felt emasculated with no *Right to Create Your Own Experience* or *Right to Assert.* Chris was living his worst nightmare. This was their pattern of dueling rights.

It took some time to restore their rights, but we finally got there. Chris began to set limits with his sons and ex-wife. One day he stood up, saying to them (in so many words), "This is the woman I love. From here on out, we'll be doing things with her included. Judy and I are creating a life together. You're welcome to celebrate our love with us." When Judy finally belonged, she naturally empowered Chris. Love began to blossom.

About a year later, Judy and Chris tied the knot. They're now creating a charity for unemployed women. Neither could be happier. Judy and Chris are co-creating a dream that both feel great about. Earlier, both shared how they wanted to *do something big* with their lives. When you have the right to make each other feel *Empowered with Choice*, creating a bright future together is easy. You naturally help make each other's dreams come true.

Rights of the *We*

For a couple to create a grand, lasting future, the *We* must have the *Right to Create Your Own Experience*. It must also possess a *Right to Assert.* A couple's third partner is the deeply imaginative, highly creative, inspiring place of bonding that desires to create the very best version of your futures together. Mediocrity has absolutely no place in a fully empowered *We*. Your attachment system is geared to create a *We* because it's the child of the grand, cosmic evolutionary impulse that's been creating *something more* ever since the Big Bang. Never forget that deep truth about the We.

Within the purposes of an attachment system, your brain seeks something I call *secure empowerment*. This is the ability to fashion your experience without recourse to domination, control, one-upmanship, manipulation, or any other form of head games. Secure empowerment is a reciprocating feeling of equality between two attuned partners. Your brain seeks secure empowerment because love changes the nature of power.

Your brain seeks secure empowerment
because love changes the nature of power.

Great couples experience the power of a bond where each adds to the capacities and potential of the other. In a secure relationship, partners gain power from the other in a way that doesn't drain them or the *We*. In a secure *We* you'll only find a place that reenergizes your life in empowering ways.

When a *We* is granted a right to create securely loving experiences, it's also allowed to craft options. Consciously loving couples are aware that love sometimes needs a different set of choices to stay strong. Sometimes, a *We* needs to choose a better strategy so the needs and dreams of both partners are honored and empowered. If a couple allows the *We* space to dream and choose new options, the sky is the limit for their potential as individuals and as a couple. A secure *We* is not only given a right to *explore* but to actually *create* new experiences based upon that exploration.

What allows a couple to design their experience together? The actor Matthew McConaughey has a brilliant strategy. Writing in a blog, he shares, "I ask myself before making a choice, '*What experience am I going to have in this?*' I give less of a damn about the result." He goes on to share about the time he traded in a much loved truck for a sports car. Matthew figured a 300 ZX would make him more popular with the ladies. (If you're a woman, feel free to substitute Jimmy Choo heels or Valentino shoes here.)

The inner experience was different than what he expected, however. Matthew became more conscious of things like his own appearance, or whether there were fingerprints on the car. With so much emphasis on him, women were less interested. Then he figured it out; the ladies were more interested in their own experience with him. When Matthew realized his new car wasn't giving him the desired experience, he scrapped it. Matthew returned to creating an internal experience that was more authentic; he went back to driving a truck. The results took care of themselves.

There's a lesson here for couples. It's the internal and shared experience of the *We* that dictates the results of their union. When the experience is right between a couple, positive results usually follow. So, what if buying a new home doesn't give your *We* a better experience? You may want to let your *We* have some options so it can give you a more authentic experience in love. Or, if creating that new business is stressing you both out, you may need to re-visit the experience you're choosing together.

Whatever you've chosen as a couple, notice the *experience* it generates. Observe it just as you would the experience that's inside you. Strong couples choose, observe, evaluate, and then choose again if necessary. They don't allow the *We* to get stuck in a rut or a preconceived plan. You may also need to notice the experience that you're *not* having. That's important too. Sometimes, it's the absence of an experience that the *We* is trying to communicate.

Partners give the We a right to create experience when they notice and observe the experience that's between them. Simply noticing the *We* is a great way to create secure experience. The beauty is that inner experience always leads to a result—either for good or bad. So, *notice the experience between you.* Dare to ask the *We* what experience it wants to create. Then allow it some options so the *We* can choose a better, more authentic and empowering experience for both of you.

Partners give the *We* a right to create experience when they notice and observe the experience between them.

The *We* must also be allowed to be fully human. Every *We* has its good and bad sides as well as its weaknesses and strengths. The *We* is still human, right? Couples must not over idealize the *We*. Few couples are walking Hallmark cards. We rise and fall as a couple. We also get back up and continue walking the path of secure love. That's the authentic experience of secure love. It's precisely by embracing the full range of love's foibles that couples empower the *We* to become more than they dreamed. There's power in honesty.

Debbie Ford reminds us that when you own up to both your shadow and light sides as a couple, you'll discover the freedom to create the love you want. She suggests in her book, *The Dark Side of the Light Chasers* that couples make a list of each other's dark and light sides or *sub-personalities* and name them. You may find dark sub-personalities like Rick Rebel, Do It My Way Donna, Controlling Carl, Contemptuous Carrie, and more. You may also find some light ones like Lover Boy Larry, Sensual Sally, or Perceptive Priscilla.

When a sub-personality enters the energetic space of the *We*, you can both notice it! Instead of saying something like, "You're so contemptuous toward me right now," you might say, "Can you go talk to Contemptuous Carrie?" If *you're* being Carrie, you might observe your words and say, "I'm sorry, I think Contemptuous Carrie has entered the *We*. Let me see what I can do about her. I'll be back soon." Then think of a more secure, positive persona to bring back to your beloved. When you own up to the dark and light sides of your relationship, it opens up your true power as a couple to transcend these states. From here, you gain the freedom to choose your experience as a couple in any given moment.

The *We* must be given a full *Right to Assert* as well. Carol Gilligan once observed that, *"There can be no relationship without voice, and there can be no voice without relationship."* Every *We* needs a voice to even be considered a *relationship*. Suppose for a moment that your *We* has a full right to feel worthy. What good would it do you to feel worthy if you can't assert that worthiness? All of the rights work in conjunction with each other. The *Right to Assert* empowers all of the other rights to express themselves. Only when the *We* has a voice can it express itself.

"There can be no relationship without voice, and
there can be no voice without relationship."

What are the benefits of empowering the *We*? First, giving the *We* a *Right to Assert* enables a *positive feedback loop*. Feedback is a key component to creating any experience you wish to have. When one or both partners fail to assert their truths in a timely manner, it creates a *negative feedback loop* between them. The longer we delay telling our truths to each other, the more likely the eventual communication will be overly negative. A strong *We* is never based on a *take it, take it, get fed up, explode* strategy for asserting. That's a losing strategy which creates negative, debilitating feedback loops between partners.

When partners tell their truths *in a timely manner*, this allows for positive feedback loops. *Instead of "taking it" until we're fed up, we talk about it until we're fond of each other again.* Rather than building up more and more negative emotions toward our partner by staying quiet, asserting generates positive feelings.

Second, a space for empowered *vulnerability* and *deep intimacy* is created. When the *We* is given a full *Right to Assert*, it opens up a space in which both partners may talk more immediately. The *We* is allowed to make micro course corrections instead of there being major detours into resentment or conflict. This completes the positive feedback loop between the partners. Remember those bids for attention and support we talked about? Well, they're all dependent on a *Right to Assert!*

Empowered with Choice Skill Set

Couples research verifies the importance of a full *Right to Create Your Own Experience*. Dr. John Gottman discovered that people with the highest expectations most often end up with the highest quality marriages. As Dr. Gottman admonishes, this works so much better than, "looking the other way and letting things slide." In addition, his research on newly married couples confirmed that those newlyweds who tolerated high levels of negativity like criticism, defensiveness, contempt, and emotional distance wound up with less satisfying or even dissatisfying marriages down the road. Dr. Gottman calls these the *four horsemen*. You must avoid them.

What's more, couples who refused to put up with negativity were far happier later on down the path of love. Those who insisted on exercising their *Right to Assert* by kindly objecting to harsh tactics, contemptuousness, defensiveness, and the like, were happier in their marriages. A critical goal for any relationship is to create an ambiance that actively empowers each partner to speak up honestly about their experiences, values, convictions, needs, desires, and whatever else they want to address.

Couples must be willing to rock the boat sometimes. But you *must* rock the boat of love in a secure way. Having great conflict skills lies at the heart of a secure love style. One effective tool I'd like to share is the *Feedback Wheel* from Terry Real. It's actually quite elegant and simple. Before you begin, remind yourself that you love this person. Approach it from a caring perspective rather than a critical one. Always remember why you're giving feedback. The point is not to hurt them or to prove your point. Rather, the point is to create a more secure connection so that you both feel loved going forth. Assertion works best when you remember you love them. There are five steps for giving feedback to your partner.

All great couples must be willing to rock the boat
sometimes. But you must rock the boat in a secure way.

First, tell your partner what you saw and heard from that particular incident. This must be totally objective, like a fly on the wall would say it. Judgments, name calling, and inflammatory or subjective language are strictly off limits. It sounds like this, "Today, I noticed the toilet seat was up again. I didn't see it and nearly fell in." Or, "You were late for dinner and didn't let me know ahead of time." Notice, it's not a long and protracted oration. You keep it simple and behavioral. It should be no more than a few simple sentences.

Second, tell them the story you made up about the incident that's running in your head. Here you own the fact that your brain made up an experience about it. Some part of you exercised its *Right to Create Your Own Experience,* and now, you take responsibility for it. You also practice vulnerability and intimacy by asserting it.

You might say, "When you were late for dinner and didn't let me know, the story I told myself was that you didn't care about me." Remember that you aren't a mind reader and this truly is *your* experience. Practice the *humility* that your truth is your truth, but it may not be *the* truth. Own up to the fact that your brain has generated an experience that may or may not be accurate. *Remember, your partner is always an experience in your brain.* Keep that in mind at all times!

Third, tell your partner how you felt about the experience. You can share how angry it made you feel or how hurt you were. However, tell them in a way that takes personal responsibility for those hurt feelings. Tell your partner how the story *you made up* in your mind made you feel. Don't say, "*YOU* made me feel *X*, *Y* and *Z*." Instead say, "When I thought you didn't care about me, it made me feel angry." In this way, you can move past accusations that build up resistance in your partner. Notice these are simple declarations. If any of these steps is more than three sentences, it diffuses the effectiveness of the sharing. It feels like *piling on* which only creates resistance in our partner.

If you're discussing a previous fight or *regrettable incident*, you might want to share what the *trigger* was that caused your regrettable action. If you're listening, you may want to get more info by saying, "I'm curious; is there a story behind your reaction?" You might consider asking what's behind that regrettable incident.

If you're the speaker, talk about any childhood wounds or old relationship hurts that got stirred up or triggered. You might say, "I'm really sensitive when somebody doesn't listen to me, because my father never took interest in me. I always feel so unloved when I think someone isn't listening to me. Then I get angrier than I should." Share whatever's behind the trigger. If you're the speaker, you must share your back story without criticism or contempt for your partner. If you're the listener, you should be accepting. Invite them into an understanding and safe place. You may add this piece if you're processing a regrettable or unfortunate incident, like a fight. Understanding each other's enduring vulnerabilities goes a long way towards heading off the next quarrel.

Fourth, tell them what you would prefer, or what you would like to see happen in the future. Telling a partner what they did wrong doesn't allow you to get what you want. This is the real problem with criticism; it doesn't ask for what you want in the future. To be honest, criticism is for wimps. Instead, give them a recipe for success. The actual *Right to Assert* will say what it wants and not just what it didn't want. Here you say, "In the future, I would love it if you were on time for dinner, or text me if you're running late." Or, "I didn't understand your comment. If you were being critical of me, can you explain what you meant? If not, tell me how I could have heard it differently?"

You can also practice the NLP Feedback Loop by saying what you appreciated, and then what you would like more of. As an example, "*I appreciate* that you showed up for dinner. *What I would love to see more* of in the future is showing up on time or texting me to let me know if you'll be late." This adds appreciation to the conversation. Appreciation is almost always appropriate when delivering feedback. When you securely make your requests, it empowers your partner to give you what you want. This is the ultimate way to empower each other with choice when a conflict is looming between you. Feedback must empower the other too.

Later, you can take a few moments to reflect on your interaction and the process you had with your partner. Here, you may ask yourself these golden questions: Did that story I told myself empower me? Did that story or filter help me to have a better experience with them? Was the story I told myself appropriate given their feedback? Did that interpretation empower the *We*?

If the answer is *No* to any of these, you may want to notice *how* your brain made up that experience. You may also want to revise how you make up stories about your partner, and look at any negative filters you have that aren't fair to them. Try to tell more empowering stories about each other. Giving your partner the benefit of the doubt can do marvels for creating a secure relationship.

On the other hand, sometimes you may need to accept that something is the truth for you, and then decide to let it go or find another way to deal with it. *The fifth step is letting it go.* How they respond is up to them. If you're on the receiving end of one of these conversations, truly listen. Listen *deeply* and realize this is your beloved sharing *their* experience. Don't make it too personal. It's actually not always about you. But then again, it may be. Allow them to influence you so that you both feel *Empowered with Choice*. Remember, nothing empowers your partner with choice more than when you accept influence. As couple science knows so well, it's one of the big predictors for relationship success.

Empowering Your Triggered Self

Every couple gets triggered beyond their ability to use these conflict management tools from time to time. When that happens, the most empowering thing you can do for yourself and your partner is to take a *time out*. Habitual, volatile, triggered states called *flooding* forecast the demise of a relationship with over 90% predictability. The clues that you're flooded include harsh startups and abundant use of what Dr. John Gottman calls the four horsemen—criticism, defensiveness, contempt, and stonewalling. Or, you keep arguing the same point over and over, expecting that on the 30ᵗʰ time they'll magically understand or agree. The goal in almost all of these triggered conversations is to be *right*—even at the expense of the relationship. Whichever way, out of control *chaos* or *rigidity* rules the moment.

Physiologically, you're under distress. Cortisol is raging in your body. You'll have a rapid heartbeat (usually above 100 beats per minute), higher blood pressure, and sweating of the palms. Worst of all, secretly, your reptile brain has turned down the blood flow to your pre-frontal cortex—the human part of your brain. Flooded partners no longer have access to empathy, understanding, compromise, or any sense of attuned logic. In fact, it's not *you* that's talking at all—what's actually talking is your *reptile brain*—and nothing good comes from two reptiles arguing over their hurts. I call this *reptile repartee*. One thing is for sure—*you* are definitely not empowered with choice when you're flooded—rather, you're in a *reactive state*. The ability to respond in a secure, choice-full way has been taken off the table.

The only remedy is to *stop talking immediately* and to take a time out. This should be done at the first sign of flooding. Don't wait. And don't say, "Oh, I'm not *that* upset. I can handle this." Be honest with yourself. Trust me, you *won't* handle it well. I can't admonish you enough to stop the conversation for at least 20–30 minutes until your human brain comes back online. Some people may need a little longer. The seeds of most divorces or breakups happen during these times. It's important for every couple to have a *previously agreed upon* signal that a time out is needed. We call this a *dead stop contract*. You both stop talking *immediately*—not another word is said. There's no making your last point or getting the final word in.

The initiating partner may say, "I need to take a break. I promise I'll return in 30 minutes so I can be a more loving partner. I can't understand you now and I want to protect you and our relationship. Please let me have a time out." If you discover that you need more time, let them know. But give them a revised time for when you'll come back, too.

It's important to promise that you'll return to the conversation and when because nobody wants to feel abandoned or stonewalled. Not doing so just fires up the other person even more. It's also imperative to let them walk away, especially if you're the anxious type that wants to pursue them into the next room. Pursuing is a sure fire way to put gas on the fire. Sometimes, if it's a very heated conversation, you may need to wait for 24–48 hours (but not much longer).

While taking a break, practice *self soothing*. Don't ruminate on the conflict—let it go for a while. If you go away and continue the fight in your head, taking a time out won't help. Find something to do that relaxes you. Enjoy some deep breathing, take a walk, listen to soothing music, or do something fun. Above all, remind yourself that you love this person when the time out is over.

When you return to the conversation, it will be as if two different people are now having that same discussion (unless you go back with a harsh startup, criticism, or other losing strategies for love). This is how secure couples empower each other when they're triggered. They take time outs so they can return to the conversation from a *treasuring* place, rather than a *triggered* place. Cultivating a more loving *second consciousness*, as Terry Real calls it, is the key here. That triggered *first consciousness* is deadly for love. What's needed is to come from a place of compassion, understanding, empathy, compromise, and our highest, most loving self. To do so, you may need to process the regrettable incident as outlined above.

Dr. Sue Johnson calls these conversations *demon dialogues*. The destructive, disempowering effects of such conflicts cannot be underestimated. The most empowering thing you can do when you're flooded or triggered is to allow your human brain to reset from *reptile mode*. One client called this, "resetting my dragon brain." Resetting your brain allows kindness and thoughtfulness to re-enter the conversation.

Time out skills are a must for every couple. Above all, remember that you're not wrong for these moments; you're just human. Therefore, make sure you have a plan in place before conflicts happen. That's how all secure couples empower themselves so love can rule the day, rather than the reptile brain! Taking a time out is a great way to cherish and protect *The Four Feelings* from any un-cherishing and disempowering feelings created by these skirmishes. If you're single and starting a relationship, have this conversation early; it just might save your relationship later.

My Right to Feel Empowered

By now you know the drill. Find someone who knows you well. Say to them, "I have a full *Right to Create My Own Experience.*" Follow with, "I have a *Right to Assert.*" Continue as before.

If you don't have a full *Right to Create Your Own Experience* or *Right to Assert,* you'll want to find somebody who can help you reset those missing rights. In the meantime, you may want to create a new perceptual filter for yourself. On a 4 by 6 index card write:

Ways I Can Feel OK to Speak Up and Express My Full Self

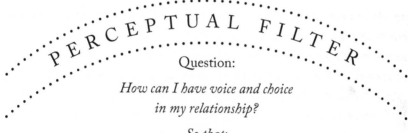

PERCEPTUAL FILTER

Question:
*How can I have voice and choice
in my relationship?*

So that:
• *I can choose to assert, create my experience,
and empower our We to be stronger and better.*

For the next few weeks, read this card two to four times a day. Read it in the morning and just before you fall asleep at night. Notice any ways that you are *Empowered with Choice* in life. You might notice you have more empowering moments than you remember. Look in the mirror and say aloud, "I can have both choice and voice."

If you would like to begin reclaiming your *Right to Create Your Own Experience* and/or *Right to Assert,* go to *www.garysalyer.com/lovemanual* where you can access additional, customized filters. Here you can choose your very own, personalized experience with this right. What better way is there to begin practicing the *Right to Create Your Own Experience* than to select your very own filter from the digital workbook?

Eight

To Love and Be Loved

When my son was three and four, Kenny loved his evening bedtime stories. Sometimes, I would change parts of the plot or how the story ended. Immediately, Kenny would cry foul and say, "HEY! That's not how it goes, Dad!" I'd continue with the *rearranged* story until he would say, "*Daaaadddd*! You *know* that's not how the story goes!" I would always reply, "Well, that's how it goes tonight, my son!" Sometimes he would be waiting for the ending to change. Kenny would say, "I want to change it tonight, Dad! It's my turn!" Mom would shake her head at what was going on in his bedroom. Unwittingly, I was teaching my son that our stories *can* change. We don't have to keep reading or writing the same story about love.

Kenny's room was a walk-in closet that I had remodeled into a miniature bedroom just for him. We lived in student housing and had to make some adjustments to make our budget work. Outside the room, we hung a picture of a deer that I had drawn some years before. During that time, Kenny had been plagued by fears of the boogieman. While reading to him one evening, he stopped me and pointed to my drawing. With some consternation, Kenny exclaimed, "Dad, I don't like that deer. It's looking at me funny." Now the boogieman was in the picture! Exasperated, I wondered how to calm his fears.

The picture showed a deer with huge black eyes that seemed to be looking at you. I pondered if I needed to take it down. Then, a stroke of genius hit me, "*What if his story about the deer changed?*" After pausing a moment, I said, "Kenny, that's Rusty the deer. I created him in love to watch over you. Every night, Rusty stays awake looking over you, making sure that no boogieman ever comes in your room." Kenny took that in before exclaiming, "Dad, I *like* that deer! I *like* Rusty! He's a *good* deer!" My son never feared the boogieman again. When we know we're loved, there's no boogieman able to stop us in life. We feel a sense of safety that allows us to love and be loved. Love can change your story, too.

When we know we're loved, there's no boogieman able to stop us in life or love.

Sabrina's Double Life

The needle on Sabrina's GPS for love was pointing toward big time marital trouble, heartache, and loss. When Sabrina walked into the office, she sat on the couch where couples usually sit. Placing her handbag beside her, the couch caught her eyes again. With a deep sigh, she began to confess. "My husband should be here but he can't know about this," she began. "John and I have been married for fifteen years. We have a wonderful marriage and three beautiful children. There's no other man I would rather be with, yet I've been having an affair every six months since the beginning." Sabrina hesitated as if the weight of the world were on her shoulders.

Looking down at the carpet, she continued, "We kind of *hook up* four or five times, and then I get back to being a wife again. It's not what you might think, though. I love my husband dearly. He's my best friend, the absolute most loving husband, and the best father I could ever ask for. It's just the sex . . ." she said hesitantly. I asked her to explain. She answered, "I don't really *enjoy* sex with my husband. I just can't seem to have hot, passionate sex with him. The only time I can be an out of control woman is when I'm having an affair. Don't get me wrong, a lot of women would be perfectly happy with him in bed. *I just can't let loose with him.* This isn't John's fault. What I want more than anything is to make love to my husband and lose my mind like I do with the men that don't mean a thing to me. I can't live this double life any longer." With that, Sabrina broke down in tears.

It was clear to me that Sabrina had a split *Right to Love and Be Loved* sexually. For the record, her behavior had little to do with any missing code of *morality*. Her affairs were the result of a split right to have hot sex *and* love in the same relationship. Sabrina had no right for passion and partnership packaged together.

When you can't have passion and partnership together,
it's a sign of a split Right to Love and Be Loved.

In this chapter, you'll experience what it means to feel fully lovable and loving. We'll explore the intimate depths of a full *Right to Love and Be Loved.* You'll learn how this right can be split and the ways it may be reclaimed as the crown jewel of your love style. Of course, I'll show you the typical relationship patterns that accompany a split *Right to Love and Be Loved.* Going beyond that, couples will discover how to create deep intimacy, including the erotic delights of love. Singles will learn how to set the table for a fully intimate relationship. The *We* also needs a *Right to Love and Be Loved,* so I'll show you how that shows up too. Finally, I'll teach you skills to add increased depth and passion into your relationship.

Let's meet the final right, your *Right to Love and Be Loved*!

The Right to Feel Lovable and Loving

By the time a child reaches their third birthday, they know if they're well-loved or not. The third year of life is when your brain adds up the *math* from the first five rights, so to speak. The upper levels of the cortical brain are coming on-line for the first time. They begin to notice what's happened in the lower levels of the sub-cortical brain, especially all those feelings housed in implicit memory. Soon, the upper brain begins to add things up, emotionally. It creates an inventory of what's already happened attachment-wise. When your upper brain adds up the lower brain attachment *math*, it creates the *Right to Love and Be Loved* in order to integrate your entire attachment style.

From ages 24 to 36 months, your brain figures out if you're securely loved or not. Following that, it decides if you are *lovable*. At the same time your brain is doing the emotional math, it's also turning on a child's latent sexuality. A child's brain will add up *The Four Feelings* we've talked about: *Welcomed, Worthy, Cherished*, and *Empowered*. If the math adds up to *four* positive feelings, they'll have a secure love style. However, if all four of those feelings are not present, the brain will deduce that they aren't securely loved. Your brain usually opts for either an anxious or avoidant love style at that point. Our native sense of sexuality is coming online too, so this right has some nuances that previous rights didn't include.

With the *Right to Love and Be Loved*, your brain completes the starter set of templates it uses to navigate every relationship. This right can subtly affect many areas of your life. I don't know how many times I've seen someone speak on stage, and then quickly exit before the applause stops. It's sometimes a sign when a person can't receive adulation, appreciation, and love from an audience or boss that something deeper is going on. When those people sign up to work with me on their relationships, many have a problem with the *Right to Love and Be Loved*. If you can't accept a raving fan club, praise from a superior at work, or anyone else in your life, a split *Right to Love and Be Loved* may be in play.

Likewise, some people will tell me they don't feel appreciated by their loved one. When you check in with the other partner, you may hear them complain in utter frustration that their spouse won't *take in* their love. For these partners, nothing they do seems to register or settle in. Loving such a spouse feels futile and wearisome. *When you can't be loved, you can't truly love well either.* If this right becomes split, it can undo the best of relationships.

If you've told yourself any story that makes you feel less than lovable, maybe it's time to swap out that old tale for a better one. It's time to change your story with love and drive that boogieman out of your life. You have the right to feel fully loved, lovable, and loving. Let's start by understanding how loving is *supposed* to feel.

The Fully Loving Self

By the time you were ten to eighteen months old, your brain had already created your *love style*. That's the lesson we learned from attachment theory and *The Strange Situation*. During the first two years of life, your brain was given four reference feelings for feeling securely loved or not: *Welcomed with Joy, Worthy and Nourished, Cherished and Protected*, and *Empowered with Choice*. Underneath those four reference feelings lie five *rights*: the *Right to Exist, Right to Have Your Needs Met, Right to Separate and Belong, Right to Create Your Own Experience*, and *Right to Assert*.

During the third year of life your brain began to add these experiences up. Because the *Right to Love and Be Loved* falls outside the period of *The Strange Situation*, it's best to think of it as a *summary right* and generalized feeling about love. This right needs all of the previous experiences to complete your love style. It doesn't *determine* your love style so much as *it is determined by* your love style and the first four reference feelings. So, technically speaking, feeling loved and lovable (or not) is how your brain feels about the first four feelings it received from parents and caretakers. While that last statement is not totally accurate, it's still very much the case. This right puts the *polish* on your love style. Yet, it also possesses its own independent and unique expressions.

As a summary right, the *Right to Love and Be Loved* is also part of your brain's GPS for love. If the *Four Feelings of Secure Love* are the North, South, East, and West Poles that your brain uses to determine if it's loved, this right and its reference feeling of *Lovable* is the needle on your brain's internal love compass. It's therefore the feeling we often notice first. Together, the *needle*, i.e. the *Right to Love and Be Loved* plus *The Four Feelings*, become your brain's complete GPS for love. This right, along with its reference feeling of *Lovable*, works in tandem with the other feelings of *Welcomed, Worthy, Cherished*, and *Empowered* to steer your experiences with love. That's how your love compass works.

The Right to Love and Be Loved and the feeling
of being Lovable is the needle on your brain's GPS for love.

When your brain adds up *The Four Feelings*, the sum is actually greater than its parts. Having a pre-frontal cortex that can step into another person's mind makes our attachment system different than other mammals. Our brain needs something *more* to match the *more* that our brains bring to the game of love. For humans, that something *more* is a feeling of *intimacy*. Everyone has the need for a caring partner to step inside our minds and know us deeply.

Due to our ability to step inside another human being's mind, what attachment calls *theory of mind*, the *Right to Love and Be Loved* goes beyond mammalian and primate bonding. This is *the right to intimacy* for humans. Humans long for something more than safe bonds. That something more we call intimacy. Intimacy is a feeling of being known, along with a sense of close or warm friendship. Eventually, the compassionate friendship *catches fire*, creating a sexual passion that burns brightly within a couple's sense of deeply fulfilling closeness. These two experiences—emotional and sexual familiarity—combine into one unifying experience for couples.

This right gives you *a permission slip to feel both emotionally intimate and sexually passionate*. While it's only a first *primer* for emotional and bodily closeness as a child, the basic energetic contours for later adult relationships are all present in its earliest form. From the beginning, the securely loved child is given lots of healthy touch. A natural, grounded sensuality (in the general, bodily sense) occurs when we hold babies close to our body. Babies feel loved when we stroke their faces and gently caress their cheeks.

Having a full right to intimacy means we feel most loved when we're deeply connected to someone. Nothing less will do when there's a full *Right to Love and Be Loved*. Once you have this right, there's a warm feeling that you deserve a place in someone's heart. Further, they deserve a place in your heart, too. You know in every cell of your body that nothing less than feeling profoundly connected, adored, and prized is your birthright in any relationship. In a word, you feel *lovable and fully loving*.

Lovable is a warm feeling that you deserve a place
in someone's heart and they deserve a place in yours.

One woman described her *Right to Love and Be Loved* as a feeling of *radiance* from her toes to her head. There's *lightness* in your being that stems from knowing that you're made of the very stuff from which love comes. In your relationship, there's an indescribable feeling of *oneness* with your partner. It feels safe and good to open yourself up completely to this person. You're able to be *vulnerable* about your highest truths and your deepest wounds. It's not an accident this right follows upon the right which allows you to own up to your entire humanity, including your strong and weak sides.

When you feel this lovable, you naturally pick partners who will genuinely listen to your wounds without judging you. You therefore feel *received* by your partner. When you have this right, nothing less will ever be tolerated as a substitute for real love. If such is not the case, a full *Right to Love and Be Loved* allows you to either seek an attuned correction, or to move on to someone who reflects back the inestimable lovability you know is true about you—warts and all!

The right to feel deep intimacy and oneness naturally includes sexual pleasure as well. There's full permission to express love in all of the *pleasurable* ways that your bodies were designed. You're open to the full range of pleasures that your body and your partner's body offers. Even more, you know that sexual pleasures are a means to experience each other's *full presence* in ways that go beyond words. Such a sexual union supercharges your sense of a *We*.

That intimate place is the heart and soul of any great *We*. As you can see, intimacy is different than having a mere bond. Eventually, as a relationship grows, the *We* becomes a place of deep familiarity where both partners can talk about what is truly between them, as well as what is inside each one. Intimacy is not just about sharing your inner states. It's about sharing the wonders of the *We* too.

Intimacy is more than having a mere bond.

The experience that secure love creates is the inestimable joy and value two partners experience by simply being with each other. Both feel important, cherished, and infinitely lovable. With a full *Right to Love and Be Loved*, each partner extends their own deep sense of being wonderfully lovable to the other. This is why having a reference feeling of *Lovable* is so important. Once you feel lovable, you have the ability to make somebody else feel lovable. You feel in your core being what a *treasure* you are. Moreover, you look for that same treasure or lovability in your significant others. Is this not what feeling loved is all about?

Again, not everybody is given a right to experience *fully embodied lovability*. When this right is not validated it gets *split*, much like the *Right to Separate and Belong*. The split may happen at two levels. First is the emotional level. You may have a right to love fully, but not to be properly loved in return. Alternatively it gets split in the opposite manner, so you get permission to be loved, but not to love others. This is the other missing right for many narcissists.

Second, the right may also be split sexually. Here, one gets little or no right to be sexual within an emotionally close relationship. Hot, steamy sex is reserved for extramarital affairs. Passionate sex is quickly lost in any relationship, because you don't have a right for both. When the right is split in this way, you may hear a person say, "Why can't the hot ones and the good ones be in the same package?" or, "Why can't I have love and great sex in the same deal?" That's usually a split *Right to Love and Be Loved* sexually talking.

Heavy porn users often have a problem with this right. Not only do they not have a right to have emotional and sexual connection in the same loving package, but they don't have much of a right for full body contact and sensuality either. When this right gets split, intimacy at every level is at risk. Let's explore how a split *Right to Love and Be Loved* shows up in adult relationships.

How Passion and Partnership Gets Split

Over the course of our first few sessions, we explored the roots of Sabrina's split right. The words *extreme*, *shame*, and *not enjoying* rang like a refrain throughout her early stories. "My mother was jealous—*extremely* so. No matter what I did," Sabrina said, "my mother made me feel *ashamed* about everything, especially my looks and my relationship with dad. My mother was jealous of me. I didn't realize it, but dad was seeking the love he missed from his wife in me. Nothing I could do would ever win her love back once she realized that my father loved me more than he loved her. Eventually, my mother *and* sisters noticed Dad loved me more than he did any of them. Then things got really *extreme . . .*"

I probed more about her relationship with daddy. "They were jealous of my looks, to be honest," she blurted out with not a small amount of dismay. "When I was very young, I was put in a little girl's beauty pageant. My father bought a pretty red dress and enrolled me in it. Mom was *extremely* jealous of me after that. Nothing I did was without some *shaming* comment. Whenever I had fun with dad, she would say in an *extremely* sarcastic voice, "Did you *enjoy* playing with daddy today?" Every time I had fun with my dad, I paid dearly for it. Eventually, *I couldn't accept any attention from my father.* So I pushed him away. I could *never enjoy* his attention." So, what happens when a little girl is caught in this kind of a trap? Something has to give, and that's the *Right to Love and Be Loved.*

Sabrina learned early on from her mother and sisters that she could not fully *enjoy* the attention of a man she loved. *Enjoying* her father was off the menu. In her family of jealous women, little Sabrina was caught in a terrible Catch-22. If she were loved by daddy, she lost being loved by mommy. Moreover, she dare not *enjoy* a man's attention if they loved her. She had to shut it down. Her brain took the best deal possible. Sabrina's system toned down being loved by a man to keep her mother's love. More specifically, the message was, "You cannot *enjoy* the love of a man."

In Sabrina's early world, her brain learned to associate love and survival with extreme states like jealousy, drama, and shame—*the very same states* created by constant infidelity. By having affairs, which included feeling lots of drama, jealousy, and shame, her brain was returning to its original template learned early in childhood. Sabrina's affairs were predictable and understandable if you understood the templates for love that her brain received.

Moreover, enjoying a father's love was strictly taboo for Sabrina. Later, that template would preclude her from sexually enjoying any man who loved her. Conversely, *if there was going to be any enjoyment, it would have to come from a man who did not love her.* Thus, the right to enjoy a man sexually *and* be loved by him got split in Sabrina's early template for love.

In this we can perceive what can split a *Right to Love and Be Loved*. Sabrina was caught up in the *third wheel syndrome*. Her mother and father never had a great relationship. In this situation, it's not uncommon for a father to unconsciously seek the attention from a daughter he doesn't receive from his wife. When a wife notices her daughter has the love she can't get from her husband, frequently the mother feels jealousy toward the child. At this point, the child can't win for losing. If she is loved by daddy, she loses mommy's love. When the roles are reversed, the same thing can happen to boys as well. If they're loved by mom, but dad feels he's in a loveless relationship, the father may relentlessly belittle the son; especially their sense of masculinity. This will split the right for them as adults.

When a child is a third wheel in their parents' marriage,
it creates a win-lose situation with love for the child.

Using a tool called *re-imprinting* we worked on reconnecting the missing dots between love and enjoyment for Sabrina. We restored Sabrina's right to *enjoy* the love of a man who fully loves her. Later, we also cleared up that third wheel thing going on for her inner little one.

Eventually, the gates of pleasure were opened up between Sabrina and John. The affairs naturally stopped when the passion began. One day John asked why there was such a difference in their sex life. That was the day we brought John in for an update. At first he was shocked and hurt. However, once he understood how all of this got wired into Sabrina's brain from childhood, compassion replaced the judgment he held about his wife. John was every bit the loving husband Sabrina described. In our last session, he told me, "I have a better wife now. Lately, our sex life has been amazing. Sabrina is a wonderful wife and mother. It's great to finally have the passion *we* always dreamed about."

Our work together raised their level of intimacy, too. In working through this, Sabrina and John learned to share their hearts in ways they never imagined. Sabrina's decision to work on her split right before she got *caught* saved her marriage. If you're ensnared in such a loop, please muster up the courage to reclaim your full right. You and your partner deserve the kind of love that Sabrina and John reclaimed after doing deep work, and of course, a lot of forgiveness.

Affairs can be a great catalyst for increasing intimacy in a couple. For many couples, there's a silver lining of great closeness and truly knowing each other, perhaps for the first time, on the other side of all the sharing it takes to heal an affair. Both partners will need to look at what truly led to the affair from their side of the street. When there's a crisis like there was for Sabrina and John, it can break down the walls that once stood between two partners. The sharing it takes to heal and restore trust opens up new depths of intimacy. If you approach affairs this way, a split *Right to Love and Be Loved* can be an avenue of great closeness if you do the work together.

Not everyone with a split *Right to Love and Be Loved*, even those with *third wheel syndrome*, will be prone to having an affair. In fact, it can go the opposite way. One woman with a very similar background as Sabrina's complained that during any sex act she felt numb *down there*, as she put it. She too had a lot of sexual shaming from her parents. The euphemism *down there* was very telling of how her split *Right to Love and Be Loved* literally cut her off from feeling any vaginal sensations during love making.

For men, it shows up in the sexless marriage where they're used as, "a paycheck with a pat on the back," as one male client described it. At other times, a split right has no sexual component at all. Rather, one just feels deeply unworthy to be loved fully. You see it in couples who have experienced long-term conflict and heartache. After years of relationship pain, distance, or *locking horns*, neither partner feels worthy of love. This split right has a wide range of manifestations. To understand that, you need to know how this right gets wired in the first place.

Lovable Wires Our Brain

The *Right to Love and Be Loved* is the crown jewel of your attachment system. All of the previous rights build up and point to this beautiful, summarizing right. It's no accident that the last right to come online is not some right to be fully *self*-actualized. Rather, your attachment system ends in a crescendo of *love*'s possibilities for your life. What caps off all this brain development is the right that gives you full permission to be *loved*. It's the final statement by your attachment system as to whether you're empowered to create secure relationships or not. The ultimate destination for those earlier rights is to create a home in your heart for love.

The Right to Love and Be Loved is the crown jewel of your attachment system. All of the previous rights build up and point to this beautiful, summarizing right.

Each of the five previous rights exists to support the *Right to Love and Be Loved*. If you understand that creating love is the ultimate intention for every proceeding right, you'll grasp how closely aligned each right is with the goal of supporting love. Like the needle on a compass, this right directs you to create intimacy and a deep bond with those you love.

The brain's cortex and limbic regions continue to develop in terms of sophistication and connectedness at this time. During the third year of a child's life, the number of synapses continues to grow. By the end of the year, a child's brain will have approximately double the number of synapses as an adult brain. Of course, these will be pruned by further relational experience as time goes by.

Complex thinking further evolves. A child at this age has much improved recall memory. They're better able to interpret past and present events. With more complex thinking, children begin to grasp the nature of cause and effect in terms of their actions or the actions of others. This results in a greater range of thinking and cognitive flexibility. Like the last two rights, the *Right to Love and Be Loved* has a more upper brain, cortical edge to it.

However, while they grasp the rudiments of cause and effect, children are not quite doing *logic* yet. Around the end of the third year, the prefrontal cortex comes online. This ushers in the era of *magical thinking*. Think the boogieman, Easter Bunny, Santa Claus, and a whole bunch of non-rational explanations for why things happen. Within this *magical-*

logical context, a child's brain comes up with its first explanations for all that preceding experience.

We call these explanations for one's missing rights, *limiting beliefs*. If you factor in the influence of magical thinking, you may begin to realize just how *off*, and perhaps even quixotic, most of these original explanations are. Many of your limiting beliefs are remnants of this first level of magical, causal thinking. So, how accurate could they truly be? Personally, I'd rather trust the tooth fairy.

Sometimes this right is split due to a brother or sister being born at around age two or three. This is especially the case if they're the first born. It's a variation of the *Paradise Lost* pattern. The child's brain makes a fatal leap of logic that says they aren't worthy of love, simply due to a sibling needing the spotlight of care. That's not logical yet the birth of a brother or sister can deeply impact a child's right to feel lovable. This is so prevalent that if you see a split *Right to Love and Be Loved*, you might want to look here first. Here's the good news; if you understand the rights below the beliefs, you can work *directly* with what's shaping your experience with love.

With these ever increasing mental capacities coming online, a child begins to notice the subtleties of family life. They observe and respond to things like parental rivalry, the sexuality that's present in many aspects of daily life, that there are rules for belonging, whether or not the parents are distant or close, and so much more. The amount of attuned, emotionally warm and responsive points of contact with the little one plays a big role in how this right forms.

Many of the more subtle nuances of this right are due to the concerns that arise when parents are socializing their child sexually, socially, and otherwise. How a child's budding sexuality is mirrored and accepted is the key to understanding much that lies behind this right. Any negative parental attitudes toward human genitalia, a child's natural curiosity about sex, fondling of their private parts, or interest in pleasuring themselves will damage this right.

Children need their naturally loving, sexual energy to be supported and approved. Whenever a parent rejects the natural sexuality of a child, it deeply impacts their later right to be fully sexual within a loving relationship. They will negate or cut off their sexuality in hopes of gaining parental acceptance and love. In other words, love's template becomes, "I must not have my sexuality to be loved." This will utterly disable their future romantic relationships.

More abusive are the instances where a parent is overtly seductive with a child or uses them for romantic purposes that fall just short of overt sexual advances. Sometimes, this right gets injured when a parent inappropriately leaks sexual energy with a child. Any instances of incest or molestation will disastrously split this right.

Sometimes, as with Sabrina, a child will be caught up in the bidding war that parents have for each other's attention. The Neo-Reichians refer to these children as *the exploited child*. Here, parents use the child to express their displeasure to the other spouse. A jealous mother who withdraws her love from *Daddy's Little Princess* or an envious father who rejects a son for being *Mommy's Little Man* will be devastating to a little one. A child learns that in order to gain one parent's love they must lose the other. The template for love becomes a zero sum game where loving equals loss.

Thus a child may learn they cannot have altruistic, caring love *and* sexual, romantic love in the same package. It's as if the *heart* and the *genitals* cannot be present together. Just so, they learn to be deeply loving but not loved by their partner. Or, they may learn to play it safe with love by not reciprocating. Here, they hedge their bets against losing love by never investing in the first place. That's the other way to deal with relationships when the brain learns that love is a rigged zero sum game.

If there was a sexual wound, some learn that deeply erotic sex and more compassionate *love-making* cannot cohabit together. They learn to be asexual, or alternatively, hypersexual outside a strong bond. Some sexual addictions come from this split deep within someone's sexual psyche. Whenever a child does not receive parental responses that are attuned both relationally and sexually at this age, the full *Right to Love and Be Loved* will be placed in jeopardy.

Relationship Patterns

The common denominator behind these patterns is holding oneself back in some energetic way from a full connection with loved ones. The Neo-Reichians therefore call this the *rigid* or *up tight* pattern. This can be done in either an avoidant or an anxious way. For those with an avoidant love style, they tend to be close, and then disappear or choose to tone down the level of emotional access, sharing, and intimacy. For the anxious, they'll pick partners who can't sustain closeness. In response, they may opt to be *situationally avoidant* by withdrawing from their partner with angry or depressed protest. When the *Right to Love and Be Loved* gets split, a cat and mouse game with closeness develops.

When the Right to Love and Be Loved gets split,
a cat and mouse game with closeness develops.

Those without a *Right to Be Loved* may *compensate* for its loss by seeking to be very attractive, extremely accomplished, or both. They seek love by putting their looks, sex appeal, money, status, or career to the forefront, hoping these will *buy* them love. Their common delusion is that attractiveness or accomplishments will make them worthy of love. This of course, is the *false self* for a split *Right to Love and Be Loved*. Not feeling a true right to be loved, *they will settle for attention rather than an attuned, secure relationship.* Long ago they learned that being loved was above their pay grade.

There are five major ways that compensation shows up. First, if somebody is the recipient of genuine love, they'll find ways to ward it off or not let it in. Being loved by a partner will set off all the alarm bells in their brain. Here you often find the avoidant *Barbie* or *Ken* who think all they have to offer is their looks. When fitness or beauty is done in the service of *compensation for one's lack of lovability*, it crosses the line into non-secure love.

Second, some opt for economic prowess or status to compensate. Physically *looking good* isn't the only avenue of compensation. Men especially compensate for their *lack* of *lovability* by offering economic status as a way to *look good*. Some studies have suggested if a man is below average in looks, height, and build that he can still date a woman considered to be a *9* or *10*. However, it will take an extra $250,000 of income above *normal* to do so. So, the strategy does indeed *work*. But does anybody ever see real love in these types of arrangements?

Third, if the *attractive* partner ever loses their beauty or other compensating quality, a crisis descends on the relationship. Underneath is a template that seems to say, "I won't be loved if I ever lose my attractiveness." A variant is "I must be sexually or financially exploitable to be loved." With those sorts of templates and beliefs, it's no wonder so many with this split right are prone to depression. For many, love is a series of infatuated highs followed by desperate lows when love turns disappointing. Those with an anxious love style may be attracted to difficult, unavailable partners and then try desperately to keep them.

In all of this, what one does not see is a full right to receive only true love and to give only true love. When someone with a secure love style is physically or economically blessed in life, rarely do we witness them choosing a partner based solely on looks or status. Nor do they choose to *barter* themselves like this. When you feel *Lovable* to your core, there's no sense of *compensating* in order to be loved. The full *Right to Love and Be Loved* is about finding someone who truly is your best friend and passionate lover all rolled up into one soulmate. Those with a secure love style will skip the spinning wheels of extreme attraction or economic status in lieu of someone who truly loves them for who they are—flaws and all.

Fourth, those with this wound often have a void in the middle of their relationships. While they may look extremely good or successful on the outside, underneath there's a *profound feeling of sadness and loneliness*. That's the baseline state for everyone with this split right. As a result, they'll become the masters of the *hollow relationship* simply because they don't have the rights for anything more intimate or profound. Their greatest fear is that if they were ever in an intimate relationship, their un-lovability would be exposed. Thus it's preferable to stay *shallow and safe*.

The baseline state for every split Right to Love and
Be Loved is a profound feeling of sadness and loneliness.

A fifth pattern can be seen when somebody is very seductive, erotic, and skilled in the early sexual phases of a relationship. Then they mysteriously lose their sexual interest and arousal. One client observed they had "Olympic sex" all the time—at first. Yet, when the relationship called for a deeper emotional connection and commitment, *Olympic sex* turned into a strange form of sexual and relational *dodgeball*. Olympic sex was merely a substitute for real intimacy. However, in all secure relationships intimacy is the cake while sex is the icing. Of course, every great cake has both.

This pattern may occur because there's been some form of early sexual molestation, but certainly not always. Because of this early experience with a parent or family member (usually), their brains learned to split those who truly love them from those who are sexual with them. Thus they learn to either shut it down completely or else flip to the other extreme, becoming salacious flirts who lose their sexual boundaries. All of this is done in an effort to heal the original wound. These two adaptations are often love's fate for the *exploited child*. Their brain splits people into two different camps; those who may love them, and those who may be sexual with them.

As in the previous two rights, the young brain will split the unloving parent into two mental *objects*. However, the split for this right isn't between the bad parent and the good parent, as we see in the *Right to Assert*. Here, the brain splits the parent into the sincere, loving parent and the sexually exploitive parent. This split between love and sex then becomes the dominant template for all of their intimate relationships going forward. Research has shown that one in four women and one in five men have been molested by the time they're 18 years old. However, since this is self-reported research, you can probably estimate that somewhere between 40 to 50 percent of women have actually been sexually abused. Once again, splitting allows the child's brain to take the best deal available. However, you can train your brain to create a better deal where sex and love can belong with the same person.

One tragic trend for those with this split right is to wait until the marriage is nearly over to reach for professional help. The right is so compromised they can't reach for proper support until there's a real crisis. Often, the partner must threaten them with leaving before they get the message that the drain of their constant problems has completely worn down the spirits of their spouse. Beneath their pattern of accepting bitter disappointments as a normal way of relating, you'll often find a person who's afraid of intimacy. Some are scared that if anyone finds out who they truly are, they'll be quickly rejected. So they preemptively reject any attempts at getting professional help.

Often a person is afraid of intimacy because they fear if anyone finds out who they are, they'll quickly be rejected.

They fear that somebody may discover how flawed or unlovable they truly are. Ultimately, they aren't avoiding therapy to be dismissive of their partner. Rather, they're trying desperately to keep the relationship alive by hiding their faults. When people feel this unlovable, it's a terrible self-fulfilling pattern. By accepting disappointment as the norm for love, they set the stage for even more disenchantment and disillusionment.

There are three big soul lessons for those with this wounded right. One is to learn the difference between attention and love. A second lesson is to grasp how lovable they are simply because that's our birthright as human beings. A third lesson is that feeling lovable is not based on being flawless. Rather, flaws allow us to invite someone into that tender, intimate place within us.

John Gottman's research points out that every couple must learn to navigate each other's *enduring vulnerabilities*. Everyone comes to the game of love with *baggage*. The trick is to find someone who will help you unpack that baggage with grace, understanding, and kindness. When true love looks at our *enduring* vulnerabilities, it sees nothing but *endearing* vulnerabilities. Intimacy with a secure partner gives you the inner freedom to be your fullest self. When those with this split right reclaim their full humanity as a lovable person, miracles happen in their relationship. The depression and sadness lift. Depth becomes the norm. Intimacy becomes a safe, rich, and wonderful thing. The relationship grows the deep roots that make love grounded, resourceful, and lasting.

One big soul lesson for those with this wounded right
is to learn the difference between attention and love.

The litmus test for knowing this right has been restored is when a person allows the full range of intimacy into their relationships. Base chakra meets crown chakra in a fully erotic, completely soulful rendezvous of sensual delights. Both sincere and sexual love happens naturally. They stop using manipulative strategies based on attractiveness, flirtatiousness, or any other thing that compensates for an unlovable self. Women stop gravitating toward sugar daddies or avoidant, distancing partners. Men stop salivating when the classic femme fatale walks by. When we have a full *Right to Love and Be Loved*, the games stop and distancing techniques cease, while full emotional and sexual intimacy begins. Then a truly miraculous thing happens. You get a *bonus* right from your attachment system—the right to have your soulmate.

"I Care About You" Love

If you want to see how the typical split *Right to Love and Be Loved* shows up, watch season nine of *The Bachelorette*. Toward the end, Desiree had narrowed the field of twenty five original suitors down to three potential mates. At first, she chose the dashing Brooks, even though he clearly didn't love her. Out of all the bachelors, it was noticeable that he was the only man who couldn't drum up the courage to say the words, "I love you." All he could muster were lame confessions like, "I *care* for you." Inexplicably, Desiree chose Brooks, who would promptly reject her. Eventually, Desiree went on to choose Chris, who married her just over a year later. So, what do you think was behind that original, surprising, and seemingly *inexplicable* choice?

My insight is that Desiree probably had a split *Right to Love and Be Loved*, and Brooks probably did too. Earlier in the season, Desiree told the story of how she had left her family early because there was "no love" there. During their breakup, Desiree tells Brooks, "*I don't know what it's like to be reciprocated with love. I never have.*" Desiree chose Brooks because his, "I *care* about you," line perfectly matched her missing right for love to be reciprocated.

At one point Desiree said to Brooks, "I love you regardless. I do." That was her split right talking, which didn't allow her to be loved back. Later Brooks said, "Do you know I *care* for you? I *do*." However, that wasn't the, "I do," she was hoping to hear. Desiree finally got it, "Yes, because you don't *love* me."

In an exit interview, we also saw Brooks' possible split *Right to Love and Be Loved*. "I'm so surprised," he reflected. "The love she has for me!" Why was he so *surprised*? Brooks' brain seems to have deleted the obvious. Not much was given about his childhood. If I were to take a guess, Brooks may have been running a *Paradise Lost* pattern. Or he might have deleted all the signs that Desiree loved him because he had a split *Right to Love and Be Loved*.

A brain that has a damaged right to be loved typically deletes a lot of signals. Desiree deleted the obvious signs that Brooks was Mr. Wrong for her. Her brain just as clearly deleted the signs that Chris was Mr. Right. Meanwhile, Brooks deleted the clues that Ms. Right was standing right in front of him with her heart on a silver platter. This wasn't an accident. Your brain deletes anything it doesn't have the rights to experience. Our perceptual filters always match our rights.

A brain that has no Right to Love and
Be Loved typically deletes a lot of signals.

In the finale, Chris stands before Desiree while she explains the last few weeks after her breakup with Brooks. Looking into his eyes,

Desiree shared, "I feel like . . . I hate it, but I feel like I was *blindsided* by my feelings for Brooks." Then, still gazing into Chris' eyes she said, "*I couldn't see* that the one thing I always needed was standing right in front of me. You have been by my side from the very beginning. You never lost sight of what could be. And for that I'm so grateful. Thank you for never giving up. You mean the absolute world to me. I love you so much." They kissed and sealed their love. Somewhere in the aftermath of the entire Brooks ordeal, Desiree reclaimed her right to be fully loved. We also notice that was the moment she reclaimed her right to have a soulmate. While I don't usually see such rapid recoveries outside of reality TV, we simply notice the good things that recovering this right can do.

The Tofu Right

Over the years, I have informally noticed that what *first* presents itself for many clients is a missing or split *Right to Love and Be Loved* by almost a factor of two over any other missing rights. A naive practitioner could easily assume someone simply had a split *Right to Love and Be Loved*. Since this is a *summarizing right*, it's wiser to look for the exact flavor of missing rights below it. In some respects this right is like Tofu—it picks up its flavor from what it's cooked with.

For instance, do you remember that Gwen also had a split *Right to Love and Be Loved*? She also had a whopper of a missing *Right to Have Her Needs* running underneath. Gwen's exact flavor of a split *Right to Love and Be Loved* was peppered with the feeling of *unworthy*. One could never reset her split right unless they first restored her *Right to Have Your Needs Met*.

Personally, I had a missing *Right to Exist*, split *Right to Separate and Belong*, and a missing *Right to Assert* below my *split Right to Love and Be Loved*. Therefore, my split right had a different flavor than Gwen's did. It's this way for every split *Right to Love and Be Loved*. There's a *domino effect* of earlier rights upon later ones. The *Tofu* tastes different for every split *Right to Love and Be Loved*. Every split *Right to Love and Be Loved* will have its own signature feel and taste based on the exact pattern of missing rights below it. After all, it's a *summarizing right* that's unique to you. To reset this last right, you must work with all the rights below.

Rights of the *We*

The *We* also has a *Right to Love and Be Loved*. As your energetic third partner, the *We* must be loved. In turn, it will amplify the love that's between you. The *We* reciprocates the energetic love given to it. So what does it mean for a couple to love the *We*?

As your energetic third partner, the *We* must be loved.

First, loving the *We* means both partners need to check to see if they've fed it the *Four Feelings of Secure Love*. Then it remains a loving conduit of secure energy. I remember as a child staying for weeks at a time on my uncle's farm. At first, very little was asked of me. Days were spent riding the ponies, feeding carrots to the horses, eating corn on the cob, running through the forest, and playing in the big barn where my cousins had built elaborate tunnels in the hay loft. I loved driving the tractor while sitting on my uncle's lap.

When I was nine my uncle changed the game on me. "Wake up, city boy," my uncle said to me one morning at four a.m. "It's time you learned how to be a farmer. Farmers feed the animals and milk the cows. Those animals you love so much need your care too." I learned each animal had its own specific diet. Horses needed hay and a malted corn meal that smelled like pancake syrup. The rabbits liked a food that looked like green pellets. Pigs loved table scraps.

Just like the animals, the *We* must be cared for, fed, and loved on a daily basis. Moreover, just as each animal has its own specific diet, the *We* has its preferred diet—the *Four Secure Feelings*. Your job is to make sure that your brain dines only on the six rights of secure love. If you want to feed your *We*, make sure both of you have all of your secure rights so that the feeding of the *We* goes well. Make sure you feed the *We* all of its rights, too.

Second, the *We* needs you to step into its *mind* the same way you would with your partner, child, or friend. Get to know the state of your *We* intimately. That means knowing its needs and dreams, its dark side and light side, its limitations and potentials, as well as its enduring and endearing vulnerabilities. Did you check in with the *We* this morning and ask how it's going between you? In the evening, do you ever wonder what sort of day your *We* had?

Treat your *We* in a secure fashion. Be attuned with it. Watch over it like a shepherd. Get to know it intimately. Respond by turning toward it rather than turning away or turning against it when it has a need. Develop empathy for how it's doing in your common life.

The *We* needs you to step into its *mind* the same
way you would with your partner, child, or friend.
Get to know the state of your *We* intimately.

Third, the *We* wants both partners to love each other in reciprocal ways. That's the dream of every great *We*. Its greatest vision is to have both partners feel loved and loving in equal measure. Its big dream is to make sure that everyone feels lovable and loved. The more you support and enable its dream to ensure that secure love abounds for everyone, the more you love your *We*.

Fourth, make sure you create strong, *daily rituals of connection* that mix together your highest values and dreams as a couple. Design them together as a team. The masters always create daily rituals of connection like kisses at the start and end of the day, the *check-in*, and so much more! Sometime each week, a couple needs to sit down and check-in with the *We*; together, and compare notes and observations. Then, lovingly pair up to do something empowering for the *We*. Dare to let go of any old visions that don't serve the *We* and your union. Are there are any better versions of your selves it wants to support? In other words, get attuned with the *We* in a connected, empowering way.

Fifth, the *We* deserves to be sensual and sexual. Everyone on the planet needs *contact comfort*. Our attachment systems are wired to expect physical contact and closeness. Otherwise, the bonding goes awry. Our attachment systems need close, warm, bodily contact to remain *attached*. Never forget that truth.

Some men make the mistake of assuming that if they bring home the bacon it should be enough. However, if men don't offer their wives both the *non-erotic cuddling* and sexual intimacy that all women need, they run the danger of becoming an uncomforting mate in the eyes of their woman's attachment system. Conversely, many women don't realize that men seek sex because it's one of the few ways we're allowed to have feelings of closeness. Sex is the primary way men are allowed to *attach* given the strictures of the male sex role. Both women and men have needs for emotional closeness and physical touch, though they're calibrated differently for the sexes.

Men, if you want a better sex life, start kissing your woman in more romantic ways when the outcome *won't* be sexual intercourse. Research shows that when we hold a kiss for six seconds, both partners get a hit of oxytocin. Also, make sure you cuddle with your beloved in non-sexual ways often. When men are non-cuddlers, only 6 percent of the time will their sexual advances be met with a *Yes*.

In addition, a woman will have an orgasm through intercourse alone only 30 percent of the time. You'll need to learn a few things about her anatomy to keep a woman interested. It's important to know all about her clitoris, cervix, and how to stimulate them. There's also a G-spot, an A-spot, and a U-spot to catch up on if you want to be a happy man with a sexually satisfied woman. Above all, *stay north* for a while, guys! If you treat a woman like this, research shows that 75 percent of the time you make a sexual advance you'll be a happy man.

Loving and Intimate Skill Set

Depth is the blood that runs in the veins of every great *We*. Soulmates need a profound grounding to sustain lasting love. For a couple to remain soulmates, they must cultivate a deep, grounding container for their love. Love needs deep sharing and intimacy.

Looking at intimacy, my mind returns to the research of Dr. John Gottman. Every couple has *enduring vulnerabilities*. In fact, 69 percent of the problems a couple has are *perennials*, i.e., flowers that come back year after year. Most of a couple's problems will track for the duration of the relationship. Since most problems are *perennials* rather than *annuals*, i.e., flowers that bloom and then go away in the fall, it requires sincere and sustained depth to deal with them effectively.

The masters of relationships are good at dealing with the enduring wounds and foibles of their partner in a way that invites dialogue and understanding rather than crippling judgment. This is never easy for any couple. Learning how to be intimate with your partner is about discovering ever more gracious ways we can deal with their early wounds. In every troubled couple I have ever dealt with, their core wounds are almost always ground zero for their recurring struggles. The deeper problem is that their judgment overshadows their graciousness, kindness, and understanding for each other.

The *Right to Love and Be Loved* depends upon empathy and kindness to be fully present in a couple's inner life. Sometimes, I will simply tell a couple to just be kind with each other. The wisdom of St. Paul still applies; *Love is patient, love is kind*. Couples need to keep their attention on the fact that their partner is not the *enemy*. Rather, the *problem* or the *pattern* is the enemy. I then invite them to be kind to the enduring vulnerabilities they see in each other beneath the conflict.

How do we grow depth of intimacy in a relationship and graciously deal with each other's enduring vulnerabilities? First, couples need to realize that love is not a defensible position. If you're living behind a wall, it will be difficult to cultivate an intimate relationship. On the other hand, couples need proper boundaries so they can share their true selves. There's a *Goldilocks Zone* here as well.

Second, realize when you're utilizing an *Identity Castle* to protect yourself. Intimacy depends upon vulnerability. That can't happen when you build a wall around yourself. Couples must deal with their armoring to create intimacy. Everybody has some castle walls around them. It's perfectly normal to say, "Yes, I can live behind a castle sometimes." Such castles defend us against hurt and painful feelings. If you want to build up intimacy within your relationship, you'll need to open the gate to your identity castle.

If you want to build up intimacy within your relationship, you'll need to open the gate to your identity castle.

Here's the exercise I do with couples to help them open up with each other, and identify their identity castles. Identity is something we declare ourselves to be; "I'm a farmer," "I'm a perfectionist," "I'm the jealous sort." So, *what is the identity that protects you from past relationship pain?* Let's go through this exercise together.

First, identify your typical *Identity Castle*. Here are a few popular ones that are trending in many couples today.

The Angry One	Controller
Troublemaker	Drama Queen/King
Peacemaker	Seductress/Player
Entertainer	Righteous One
Warrior	Overachiever
Rational/Analyst	Interrogator
Rescuer	Good Girl/Boy
Victim	Strong, Silent Type
Diplomat	Perpetrator
Fixer	Rebel
Other _____	

Second, be honest with yourselves. Who are you when you *really* get hurt (pissed, sad, upset, etc.)? What's your *go to* identity when you want to defend yourself against any pain? Or when you sense an approaching attack? Personally, I'm prone to duck behind the protective walls of *The Righteous One*. The other identity castle I prefer is the *Rational One*. What about you? Take a minute to look at this list. Get honest about *who you are* when you're under pressure, attacked, stressed, hurt, disappointed, etc.

Third, *reflect on what good thing comes to you when you live in your identity castles.* Take a few moments and get into rapport with this part of you. If you're a couple, share the results. It's useful for couples to know how each partner deals with hurt, and why that painful identity is so precious to their brain. When you share, it's important for the listener to just listen and not to judge. Notice how this builds up intimacy and vulnerability naturally.

Bear in mind that every identity castle serves a very good purpose. No part of your brain ever constructed an identity castle for the sole purpose of being evil or troublesome. Making sure I was found *right* was my utter salvation as a child. If accused of something, one had to prove they weren't wrong, or else you could be severely beaten. Later on, I learned that sometimes being rational would do the trick too. Strangely, being rational in high school could confuse my mother. When I discovered that my mother could get confused and therefore I could avoid a beating, being rational looked very appealing.

The good thing my brain gets from these two identity castles is I can avoid a beating. Except the beating was forty plus years ago! Now, flash forward. These two identities feel condescending or dismissive to a loved one. None of these identities feel attuned to anyone. I'm much better at noticing my two favorite identity castles these days. Yet sometimes, I still have to watch myself from going there.

Please notice how many of our *Identity Castles* are actually very young versions of ourselves trying desperately to protect our earlier hurts and missing rights. Underneath many identity castles is an adaptive five year old child trying to avoid childhood pain. Except, those adaptive childhood strategies rarely work in adult relationships. Here's a big truth; most couple fights are actually two adaptive children running their favorite identity castle at each other. Loving couples must protect each other from their adaptive child, who if left unchecked can do real harm to the relationship.

Fourth, *come up with a better identity castle for each painful one.* Remember it's *not* your responsibility to come up with an identity for your partner! One of my favorite new identities is *The Attuned One.* For some, it may be *The Trusting One, The Open One,* or *The Secure One.* Others could be *The Welcoming One, The Worthy-ing One, The Cherishing One,* or even *The Empowering One.* Find a new identity that's designed for a more loving you.

Fifth, *share that new identity with your partner.* Give yourself time to build a new identity castle in your mind. Remember, no castle was ever built in a day. When you both have more loving, secure identity castles, your relationship will be embedded in a protective cocoon of *We-ness.* When intimacy gives you a cocoon rather than a castle, that's when you feel securely loved.

When intimacy gives you a cocoon rather than
a castle, that's when you feel securely loved.

Love Equals

One final consideration about the meaning of *love* needs to be mentioned. Everyone has very specific ideas of what it means to *be loved.* In NLP circles, these are called *complex equivalences.* We usually get these equivalences from childhood. Have you ever heard someone say, "If you loved me, you would never be late?" Buried beneath that sentence is a complex equivalence for love, where love equals *being* on time, not *wasting* my time.

Gary Chapman talks about the *five love languages.* These may be considered complex equivalences for love too. Here, things like words of affirmation, quality time, physical touch, acts of service, or gifts may be key indicators for when someone feels loved. In my own work, I tend to accent core emotional needs such as certainty, significance, fun and diversity of experience, or physical connection as key signals for when someone feels loved.

Everyone has a very unique configuration of equivalences that tell them when they're loved. That means for every person, the *Right to Love and Be Loved* has been encoded with a very specific set of signs and indicators. It's important to figure these out for yourself and discuss them with your partner. Couples must learn to negotiate these differences. If you can each understand how your brain configures love and then *communicate* those signals to each other, the sky's the limit for how loving you can feel with each other!

Everyone has a very unique configuration of signs that tells them they're loved. These complex equivalences must be successfully navigated by any couple.

It's just as important, however, to make sure your relationship is not held captive to your complex equivalences for love. Just because you have a sign for love, doesn't mean it's the absolute truth about love, or that it should ever be the *law* in your relationship. Part of being a secure partner means you can gracefully respect each other's different equivalences. Don't judge your partner because they have a different set of signs for love. Giving the *We* some good old fashioned behavioral and mental flexibility can do wonders for your relationship. Graciousness is more loving than being demanding or judgmental. If your partner misses some of your complex equivalences from time to time, learn to be gracious.

My Right to Feel Lovable and Loved

Here's the drill one final time. Find someone who knows you well. Say, "*I have a full Right to Love and Be Loved*." Continue as before.

If you don't have a full *Right to Love and Be Loved*, you'll want to find somebody who can help you reset those missing rights. In the meantime, you may want to create a new perceptual filter for yourself. On a 4 by 6 index card write:

Ways I Can Feel OK to Be Completely Lovable and Loving

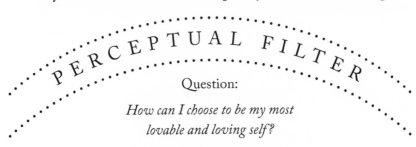

PERCEPTUAL FILTER

Question:

*How can I choose to be my most
lovable and loving self?*

So that:
- *I can create a powerful "We" (if you are a couple)*
- *I can find my soulmate (if you are single)*

For the next few weeks, read this card two to four times a day. Read it in the morning and just before you lay your head on the pillow at night. Notice any ways that you're already being loved in life. You might notice that you have more lovable and loving moments than you normally remember. Look into the mirror and say, "I am a lovable and loving self." Remember, love *is* your birthright.

If you would like to feel more *Lovable* and start reclaiming your *Right to Love* and *Be Loved*, go to *www.garysalyer.com/lovemanual*. Once more, you'll find additional, customized filters designed to help you create a cozy and warm experience with your natural right to feel securely loved.

Nine

The Soundtrack and the Soul Lesson

I vividly remember opening boxes of Cracker Jacks as a child, joyously looking for the *mystery prize* inside each box. I'd eat through the whole box looking for that toy. If I were very impatient that day, I'd push my young fingers all the way through to the bottom searching for it. Then one day I realized something very important. The prize was never at the top of the box. After years of eagerly looking for the prize, I began to notice a pattern for every single box. The prize was always found at the *bottom* of the box.

Every experience with love or deep attachment creates an *emotional soundtrack* for your life. That's what *The Four Feelings* do; they create the music of love for your life. What if buried deep within the emotional soundtrack of your life is a very important treasure? In dealings with clients, I have discovered that their emotional soundtrack always carries the life-long *love lesson* they must learn to create the love they deserve. Learning that lesson is often the last big thing they need to do in order to reclaim a secure love style.

Like the prize at the bottom of the Cracker Jack box, this lesson is buried deep down in your attachment system. Each person signs up for their own tailor made lessons about life and love. Here's the really good news about that prized lesson. Once you learn your soul's lessons, it frees you to find your soulmate. If you're a couple, it equips you to create a satisfying, deep, and lasting relationship.

A Bonfire of Hope

Evelyn felt totally hopeless about finding love. So much so, that her brain wouldn't allow her to make any pictures about a potential soulmate. To protect her from rejection and abandonment, Evelyn's brain couldn't even imagine what she wanted from love in our first session. When I asked Evelyn what she wanted, all Evelyn could say was, "I'm sorry. I just feel so *hopeless*. I actually don't know what I want. I would like to find love, but I'm afraid to ask for it."

A bit later, Evelyn talked about the moment she lost all ability to hope, "I was placed in my first foster home when I was five where I had a pet rabbit, Angel. One day while playing outside she started to hop away. Angel was my only symbol of what it felt like to have a home. As she started hopping across the yard, I called and called but Angel just kept hopping away. I screamed for help but nobody came. After that, I knew that help was never coming. I never wanted to *hope* for help or love again." That was the pain Evelyn's brain was blocking by not making any pictures of the future. It all made perfect sense. When her brain thought of the *future*, it was actually remembering her foster care *past*. So why go there?

Evelyn and I worked several sessions on her sense of hopelessness. We would restore hope but it would fade before our next session. When there is such deep abandonment, there are often several *imprints* to clear up before a brain will feel completely safe. One day, I realized it was time to add some resources from higher self to the mix. Hope needed a stronger resource to make it all stick.

Evelyn's concept of a higher self had not one iota of a metaphysical quality about it. It was more along the lines of one's best self on a good day. That understanding was sufficient to open the portal of resourcefulness she needed to recover a healthy right to hope. Evelyn learned, "I can overcome anything," including an avoidant love style. Once we did higher self work, a bonfire of hopeful resourcefulness took up residence in her life. Before then, finding a resource that would allow hope to stay put in

Evelyn's brain was difficult. By accessing higher self with my guidance, she was able to side step that vexing problem. Here's the bigger story; the right resource is always available when my clients access their higher self.

A bonfire of resourcefulness can take up residence
in your life when you access your magical higher self.

In this chapter, you'll learn how accessing higher self opens the portal to all the resources you need to find and create the love you deserve. There's never a reason to not be hopeful about love. Everyone will learn how painful experiences provide the necessary contrast you need to discover a prized lesson about love. You'll also learn why couples need alignment with each other's higher values, and sometimes, bigger purpose to create lasting love.

Help for Creating Secure Love

There's a wide range of ways people experience or conceptualize their higher self. I've never met a single person who can't resonate with some definition of it. *However you understand the idea of a higher self is perfectly fine for our purposes.* Susan Ariel Rainbow Kennedy utilizes the concept of an *inner wise self.* I use the generic term *higher self.* If you have another term, that's fine too.

For some, *higher self* refers to any version of them which is more ethical, balanced, rational, caring, loving, or in some way represents their *best* way of being in the world. For others, higher self has more metaphysical roots. For them, this higher self is both pre-existing and post-existing. If they're more religious, they may refer to it as their *soul.* Still others bring a re-incarnational worldview to our work together. They choose to see their higher self as a pre-existent identity that has been through *many lives with many masters* as Dr. Brian Weiss might put it.

This work is not religious unless you choose to see it that way. Higher self work is simply utilizing the resources of our best, higher identity (however you see that identity) to align our brains with love. *HELP* in the form of *Higher Energetic Loving Presence* is available to us all. There's absolutely no right or wrong definition of a *higher self*. You already have what you need for taking full advantage of this chapter.

While I cannot say that I've done higher self work with every client or couple, I can say that it's often a powerful means of putting *closure* on the painful episodes in our life. Once my work with clients is well under way, and a secure love style starts to show up, higher self work acts like the third stage booster rocket. It's the work that puts them into *orbit* so they don't return to their old, painful patterns around love. Higher self work has kept many of my clients from crash landing again on the launch pad of love.

When a client can isolate the four or five most common, repeating feelings or states over the course of their lifetime, they usually see a dominant pattern. From that painful pattern, there's a higher self lesson that unlocks the doors for your future with love. I refer to such repetitive emotional feelings and states as your *emotional soundtrack*. Thus buried deep within your soundtrack is a prized lesson, just like there's a prized toy in every Cracker Jack box!

If you do the deep work and take a bird's eye view of your life, you can isolate the big lesson you need to learn about love. Your soundtrack carries a wonderful soul lesson for you to master. Here's the really great news! The *answer* you seek about love can actually be found in the *problem*.

To be honest, I have a more metaphysical understanding of my higher self. However, if you have a more naturalistic notion, please be patient for a little bit. For me, my higher self incarnated to learn specific lessons about love. I hold an incarnational view about my higher self. Although I have never definitively figured out if there are any past reincarnations for me, I have found that holding a more purposeful view of my life has greatly empowered me to write a more secure story. I believe that my higher self/best identity chose the path I have trod to learn exactly the lessons in this book.

When I learned that lesson, it knocked the crippling *victim* stance right out of my official story. A good part of those lessons also came from doing scholarly research and listening carefully to the experiences of my clients. I also had some beautiful *lesson partners* whose experiences have taught me many things about love. Then of course, there was my borderline mother who provided me with so many early experiences that would inform the questions which lie behind parts of this book. Eventually, I learned to appreciate my childhood and all of its pain for the great lessons it taught me. Yes, I learned to appreciate even my mother. This in turn allows me to hold the stance I need with my clients.

There is yet another gift in this realization about your soundtrack. If your soul lesson is carried in your soundtrack, that means no part of you is hopelessly confused. Your higher self made sure to give you the solution to whatever you have experienced about love. That's very good news, isn't it? *The new experience with love you desire is already available in your soundtrack and higher self.*

That secure love style you want to create, along with the soulmate relationship that comes from it, is obtainable *now*. It's just a matter of doing the deep work and learning your big soul lesson about love. This means in the long run, that your soundtrack and higher self may be aligned in a way that frees you to create all the love you have ever desired. In turn, this makes everything you have ever wanted from love available and already inside of you *now*.

It's not just that your experience is adjustable.
The new experience with love you desire is
already available in your soundtrack and higher self.

Balancing Resources

Connecting to your higher self has four main benefits. Summarily, it balances any painful equations in your brain, provides the positive resources of wisdom and love, allows you to integrate your brain, and gives you the resources you need to recover a secure love style.

First, connecting to higher self balances the equation in your brain. What equation is that? It's the equation between your unconscious mind and your conscious mind. The unconscious mind processes much more information every second of your life than your conscious mind does. That leaves a huge imbalance. Your unconscious mind gets about two million bytes of information per second. Your conscious mind—that part that says it's *you*—gets only 138 bytes per second. However, when you connect to your higher self, *you* can access more information and resourceful states to balance that unfair equation. Luckily, you can open a portal to your higher self. In that place are all of the resources *you* need to create a calm, loving, integrated, and attuned emotional soundtrack.

Second, higher self provides the positive counterbalance of wisdom and love which act as corrective, restorative states for all that stuck programming running in your brain. Your brain matures from the bottom first, and then upwards and forwards. The arc of a young brain's development starts in the reptilian brain, with just a skeleton crew in the mammal brain. Later, the higher levels of the limbic system come online. Eventually, more and more of the cortical brain, i.e. the primate brain begins to come online. Finally, the pre-frontal cortex activates last, a.k.a. your human brain. The downside is a lot of negative programming gets *grandfathered* into the system. This means that the earlier, more primitive parts of your brain carry a lot more energetic weight for creating love.

However, what if you could balance that negative, energetic flow coming from deeply buried implicit memories with something more positive? That way you could restore all those missing rights with loving energy, right? Well, that's exactly what higher self energy does. It provides the positive resources of wisdom and love, which act as balancing, restorative states for all those missing rights running at the base of your brain. The process looks like this:

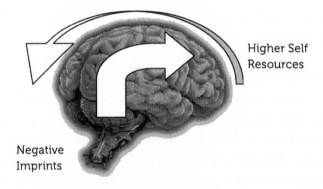

Higher Self
Resources

Negative
Imprints

Love is the goal for every human brain on the planet. Everything about our evolution as a species and our individual development has an arc of expansion. That arc of brain evolution and development acts like an arrow pointed toward love. Early rights were but a stepping stone to your *Right to Love and Be Loved.* As many cosmologists have observed, all of the magical abilities of your pre-frontal cortex point beyond themselves. Each successive part of your brain developed to produce better bonding states that were more conducive to supporting love. Lastly, your human brain with its pre-frontal cortex evolved to open an access portal to something more loving beyond itself. That access portal we call *higher self.* What's more, as so many masters, prophets, priests, priestesses, poets, and sages have told us, that portal is always about love.

Third, higher self access allows us to integrate our brains and love styles in more loving, authentic, and attuned ways. As Dr. Daniel Siegel points out, a healthy and securely attached brain is a well-integrated brain. Integration is the true mark of a secure love style.

Now, if you think about it, one brain did not create the six rights you experience on a daily basis. If you grasp the brain development underneath each right, a sobering truth comes to light. In actuality, *five different brains created six rights* from the ages 0 to 3. Each of those brains had very different emotional and cognitive capabilities. The brain that learned it had a *Right to Exist* could not have learned it had a *Right to Love and Be Loved.* Neither could it have understood the *Right to Separate and Belong.* That early brain was neither cognitively nor emotionally developed enough to grasp these later rights. Thus it is for all the rights as they develop.

Later, your brain was tasked to integrate the experiences of those early five brains. That's like an IT professional being asked to integrate the early computers from the 1940s with the super sophisticated computers of today. Seen this way, secure integration is a rather large task for the later adult brain to do with wisdom and grace. Your brain is one big neural network tasked with integrating the experiences of some very early *emotional programs* from your past. To do that well, you'll not only need a great professional guide, but the guiding wisdom of higher self as well.

Fourth, higher self gives access to the hitherto unavailable resources we need to recover a secure love style. Some years ago, after doing the deep work, I was fairly at peace with my mother. No longer was I carrying a life debilitating grievance. While journaling, I wrote that I may never truly know what it feels like to be loved by a mother, yet I was okay with that. Somehow, I was at peace with it all.

However, for my higher self, or perhaps even Source, being *at peace* was not enough. About a week later, a client came in for a session. We were doing a very intuitive piece of work called *Family Constellations* work. To do this work, I'm required to step intuitively into the experience of family members in order to restore the proper *orders of love* in the family. Toward the end, I had Karen imagine a long line of her maternal ancestors—her mother, grandmother, and great grandmother—standing in a line behind her, beaming all of their great love back into her attachment style.

When I stepped into the energy of her maternal ancestors, a feeling of such caring love swept over me. I was blown away by the purity of the love from such a great lineup of mothers that I was intuitively feeling on her behalf. That moment felt like *Mother's Day* on cosmic steroids. It was an awesome moment for both of us.

A few hours later, while journaling about that feeling I heard the voice of higher self saying, "This is what it feels like to be loved by a mother." In a single moment, the great mystery of my life was gone. I now knew what feeling loved by a mother felt like. There was no longer a void to be compensated for by other loving experiences where *mother* once stood. I now had a new, secure resource brought to me courtesy of the providential wisdom of higher self.

This is what I mean by higher self bringing resources that will balance the equation, lead you to the next, higher level of your personal evolution, and integrate your brain in a secure way that's more than you can imagine.

The resources you need to restore a secure love
style are always available from higher self, even
if those resources are not currently on your map.

Contrast Creates the Soul Lesson

What sets up a soul lesson in the first place? In a word, *contrast*. Contrasting states are the heart and soul of every higher self lesson, all puns intended. All learning needs contrast so we can distinguish one thing from another. Similarity is a part of learning, yet for the purpose of understanding our big life lesson about love, nothing is as strategic as seeing our emotional soundtrack as contrastive fodder for learning. We need *black* to grasp the significance of *white*. We understand *young* only in terms of *old*. Did you ever notice in the dictionary that it first gives the definition and then the *antonyms*? That's because we can't fully understand any word if we don't also have a firm grip on what its opposite is.

When I do this work, I tell my clients, *The Parable of the Angel Who Wanted to Understand the Light*. A long time ago, there was a young angel in heaven who was very curious about the light. Every time the little angel saw a bright light such as a star or a moon, she marveled at what it all meant. One day, the little angel came before the chief of angels, asking if she could incarnate into a human life to learn all she could about the light. The chief angel smiled at her and said, "Of course. I'll arrange for it right away."

Her incarnation, however, featured nothing but darkness for the entirety of the little angel's life. After her life, the little angel was no longer curious. She was furious about the trick that had been played on her. Immediately upon reentering heaven, she stormed the chief angel's throne. In utter exasperation, she exclaimed, "I asked to understand the light, not the darkness! All I got were shadows and dark places in that life! How was I supposed to learn about the light from all that gloom?"

The chief angel lovingly looked at her and said, "Little one! You asked if you could learn about the light. I gave you that opportunity. How can you understand the light unless you know what darkness is? Do you remember that time while you were in college when you got lost in a blizzard? All you could see was the light. As a result, you suffered from snow blindness because there was only light with nothing to contrast against it. I gave you that experience so you would learn that you can't see a thing if all you have is light. Without darkness no one truly understands or appreciates the light. So what did you learn from the darkness about the light?"

We need contrast to understand anything. Even in the dictionary, we need the antonym to understand a word.

I then tell my clients that the negative, *repeating* emotions on their emotional soundtrack are the contrasting states needed to understand their higher lesson about love. (Yours can be found in the exercise at the end of Chapter One.) Only if a client has done a substantial amount of work on their emotional soundtrack, are they ready for this kind of transformational work. It's amazing how people stop fighting their life experiences and get into deep rapport with their life when they do higher self work. Our remaining sessions go much faster after that. If there was any victim or grievance stuff going on before, it usually goes away soon thereafter.

Resources to Love and Be Loved

As it so happens, higher self access can do wonders for couples. Do you remember Jennifer and Todd from Chapter Six? Well, it turns out they had perfectly symmetrical and complementary soul lessons to learn from each other. As a couple they had *dueling rights*. That meant they also had *complementary soul lessons* buried deep in their emotional soundtracks. Their soul lessons fit each other like a glove. Seen from a higher perspective, there was a reason they contracted to love each other.

Jennifer and Todd both had a split *Right to Separate and Belong*, except they were split in the opposite way. Jennifer had no right to belong while Todd had no right to separate. As part of their couple work, I eventually did higher self work with both of them. Jennifer was always invisible to her parents. No one ever noticed her much or truly included her. She was always on the lookout for when she would be on her own. As a result, she was dying to be included in a strong, protective *We* with Todd. However, due to his split right, all he wanted was to keep some distance. This drove Jennifer crazy. Having very little right to separate, real intimacy was almost a toxic state for Todd. This led to much marital frustration between them.

With my guidance, Jennifer reflected from that place of accessing higher self. When she learned her lesson, she shared, "So that's the big picture. I've never felt *all in*, and so I've never been *all in* either. Just as importantly, I need to experience someone being just as committed to me. That's the big lesson for my life; *I came to learn about being fully loved and loving.* My life makes more sense now. This will change a lot of things between Todd and me." When you look at your relationships with this level of clarity and honesty, things change. Later, Jennifer confided she felt more belonging than she had ever felt in her life. She also felt incredibly more loving.

Todd then needed to embark upon his own journey to higher self in order to keep up with his partner. In all healthy relationships, both partners are actively growing with each other. Todd's soul lesson was to learn there is *power and freedom in belonging.* Each in their own way was never quite *all in.* Both felt the same intense lack of belonging underneath it all. When Todd learned to create a *We* in the key of power and freedom, Jennifer experienced being fully loved. In turn, when she felt fully loved, Jennifer could love Todd in a way that empowered Todd with freedom. In their own ways, Jennifer and Todd were learning about being *all in.* Once they learned their dovetail soul lessons their *We* got a long overdue upgrade. The soul lesson each learned gave the other the exact prize at the bottom of the Cracker Jack box for which they were looking.

When couples learn their soul lessons, they can
give each other the prize of secure love.

Evelyn, Jennifer, and Todd all had different takes on higher self. Unlike Evelyn, Jennifer had a more metaphysical concept of higher self. She would sometimes refer to *Source energy* during our sessions together. Todd had still another concept of higher self. Personal beliefs play very little into the effectiveness of my higher self work with clients. What matters almost exclusively is the ability to create more resourceful states in your life.

Resources to Feel Worthy

Carla was a woman who had a pattern of going back to a painful partner once too many times. She would go back and back and back until one day, she collapsed in utter exhaustion from the relationship. Her relationships often ended in an ugly point of no return. It's been my observation that when people keep returning to a painful relationship, it's often a sign that buried deep within the relationship is a lesson both have refused to learn. However, there's a way to move beyond such *lesson partners* to find your soulmate.

A mid-forties hair dresser, Carla owned a very upscale and posh shop. When Carla was introduced to Terry at a party, he seemed to have it all—the looks, the job, and the charm. Five years later they had been through six breakups all due to the same reason—cheating on his part. Each time, she would break up with him in a tearful fury. A few weeks later, Terry would say the magic words, "I was a jerk. Please forgive me. I'm sorry." Carla would then take him back and the cycle would repeat itself.

One thing Carla noticed in our higher self work was that in many of her relationships, she was only worthy of *crumbs*. As she began to see the bigger picture of her life, Carla exclaimed, "Wow! My relationship with Terry is just a bunch of crumbs, just like it was way back then for my ten year old, my high school kid, and even in my first marriage. That's the pattern! I settle for crumbs and then the connection goes away. That sucks."

When we did the higher self work Carla ruminated, "I now see that I have the power to create a worthy connection. Moreover, these connections are unlimited." Then she added, "My soul lesson is kind of simple now that I see it more clearly. I have the power and *I have the right to create only worthy relationships*." With her lesson learned so beautifully, she did not take Terry back. Carla's soul lesson was about worth and power, two contrasting states one would expect to learn from a missing *Right to Your Needs* and a missing *Right to Assert* one's truth.

As you learn your soul lesson, you will
naturally stop going back to painful relationships.

The Neurological Journey of the Soul

You may be asking—how does this work, neurologically? In light of all the science and attachment theory invoked up to this point, you may be wondering how all of this ties together with neuroscience. While I don't have all the answers, one can invoke some preliminary conclusions.

First, we observe that higher self work is not much different than re-imprinting. It adds emotional resources to stuck states by imagining and feeling more resourceful states, while the client is simultaneously feeling a stuck state. When learning these lessons, the experience is not just an intellectual exercise. One of the keys for the effective practitioner is to make sure that the stuck state is in the room *and* that the client is *feeling* the higher self resource. In terms of the neuroscience, your unconscious mind, i.e. your reptile and mammal brains, doesn't know the difference between reality and imagination. That's why you can go to a theater and feel your heart start pounding during a scary movie. You know perfectly well the T-Rex isn't actually there. That's a bug in your brain, but it can be taken advantage of in order to create new states.

The same thing applies when you imagine positive emotional states during re-imprinting. If a state can be imagined, it can be added to a stuck state. This effectively teaches your brain to chain states by firing off a stuck state, and then, immediately firing off a better, more resourceful state. Eventually, the brain learns to fire off just the better states automatically. That's how NLP does its magic—it utilizes this neurological bug to rewire your brain. Something similar is happening during higher self work. Once the future resource from higher self is in the room, we then take it back to the stuck states on the timeline. Higher self work is a neurological way we download imagined future resources into our past and present.

Higher self work is the neurological way we download imagined future resources into our past and present.

Second, do I think that imagination is all there is to this work? No, not really. I do believe that there's something more going on here. I've seen too many uncanny things happen during this work that were truly outside the existing maps of my clients when they began our session.

Admittedly, this is where neuroscience crosses paths with spirituality. I personally believe there is a *field of consciousness* that permeates reality with a wise, loving presence. Somehow, I think your higher self is a part of this reality. This is one place we can observe with the great linguist, Ludwig Wittgenstein that, "Sometimes language goes on vacation." Even the field of quantum mechanics has begun to posit a consciousness running underneath reality. So, I'm not the only one who perceives a place where science, spirituality, and personal reality intersect.

However, if you don't agree you can simply accept that there's a sound neurological reason it works and leave it at that. In either case, you get to drive the bus for love rather than your early programming, i.e. any missing rights. Or, you can believe as I do that when you access your higher self, you empower yourself to complete the neurological journey of your soul. Either way, you can learn to love and be loved in a better way. It's a win-win situation no matter how you view things. All that truly matters is that you find your resources to love in more secure ways.

Dreams Guide Us Too

Yet another time honored way that higher self may speak to us is through our dreams. Sometimes we receive dreams that are meant to give us a resource or to teach us a soul lesson. I've had a lot of these dreams. Every time I began to do serious work on myself, dreams would come at important junctures. You may want to pay more attention to your dreams. With one client, the moment we began our work together she started bringing dreams to me nearly every session. It actually helped speed up the work we were doing.

Sometimes, dreams from higher self are meant to give us a much needed *resource* state. About twenty five years ago, I had a dream that I can still see in my mind's eye. I was walking a stone path during what seemed like the Roman period. Beside me was this beautiful figure of a woman named Celeste. She wore a long, purple gown like you see on Greek goddesses. I could sense she was my mother and I was her son. We were looking at flowers on a sun lighted path. Without a word, Celeste was teaching me what those flowers meant. The feeling of the dream was a warm feeling of being loved by a mother. In the figure of

Celeste, I was actually dreaming of what a secure relationship would feel like with a mother. When I woke up, I had a sense of being loved by a mother where before, there was absolutely none.

Other types of dreams are meant to *reframe* our reality. About a decade ago, a spectacular dream came to me that completely changed the way I looked at my life. In that dream, I was watching a play. Standing just off stage, I was viewing the play from beside the curtains. Eventually, it became apparent that the actors on stage were my family! All of my uncles and aunts were playing various parts. In the middle was my mother. She was taller and darker than anyone else in the play. The feeling was of foreboding and darkness. My mother also carried a psychological weight that was unmistakably larger, more aggressive, and more somber than the others.

At one point, I was totally confused by the play. There didn't seem to be any point to it. My uncles and aunts were walking about in a circle but the script seemed to have no plot. I said to myself, "They must be doing this just for me." Everyone on stage stopped dead in their tracks, and looked at me. One of my uncles stared me straight in the eyes and said aloud, "He's finally got the point of it all." My family was playing different roles to teach me something.

As they were all exiting off the stage, my mother was walking with them. When she got to the middle of the stage, she stopped and gazed directly at me. Then my mother said the most stunning thing. "I played the part you asked me to, Gary. It was a hard part, but I played it for you." The feeling I felt from my mother was that this role was a huge sacrifice for her. The part she played was just as painful for her to perform as it was for me to watch.

The dream taught me that somehow my mother had been of service to me. This was about the time I was looking at my entire life, seeking to find a way to tell a more secure story. While I can't explain it logically, some part of me calmed down after the dream. I realized that my painful family had served a bigger purpose from a soul level viewpoint. From that higher self perspective, my family gave me what I needed. Afterward, I was at peace with my life. Most of all, my official story changed dramatically.

Had I not done all the attachment rewiring of my brain, this dream would have had no effect. But in its perfectly proper timing, higher self offered it with providential precision. These sorts of dreams are no accident. Read the works of Carl G. Jung and you'll see how others have perceived this same truth. The point is to notice your dreams as a resource or reframe for painful experiences. The resources are always available in ways that you can't control, yet are always in your favor. In the end, it helps to have a bond with your higher self if you want to reclaim a secure love style.

Aligned Values

In every great relationship, there's a deep alignment between both partners. They match each other's values in substantial ways. Extraordinary couples also naturally complement and support each other's higher purpose, however that may be construed. Such alignment is implied in the *Rights of the We*. Without alignment, relationships are doomed to conflict and dysfunction. Even if two people have a secure attachment, *The Four Feelings of Secure Love* need alignment to make it last.

It's therefore important to know and share your core values and your big life purpose with your partner. If you're single, this is so absolutely essential to explore on dates. Strong couples need similar values concerning things like spending, finances, sex, child rearing, and so much more. Other important values include how they schedule time, the importance of work versus play, prioritizing each other versus your family, and so forth. All the secure feelings in the world will not compensate for the frustration if one partner wants to live in a tent in the woods while the other wants a posh mansion.

As Dr. Tad James teaches, a key element in creating your future is to completely understand your values. To create a lasting relationship, it will be very important to get crystal clear on your values, highly valued criteria, the core beliefs supporting your values, as well as the source of those values and beliefs. It's essential to know where your values come from. Do they come from family, friends, your religion, broader culture, social class, or your educational training?

In addition, some people have values that are laid down like the law. For others, values are treated as principles of life organization. Moreover, how your partner reasons about their values is just as important as what they value. Are they willing to have values for you and values for them, or do they mean to enforce their values on you? All of these things must be considered well before you enter into the practicalities of actually living together.

In Dr. Gottman's sound relationship house theory, *shared values* are the highest level. All great couples dialogue about core values, and then co-create their own unique rituals of connection, the meaning of holidays, anniversaries, etc. If you want an extraordinary love, start by creating more of those rituals of connection. Above all, make sure those daily rituals are designed and birthed by the values that stir each of your souls. Put the *Right to Create Your Own Experience* to work. Design a relationship that's bound together by *small meanings* often. All secure couples do this.

Aligned Purposes

The other thing that matters is whether or not you have a larger purpose, and does it match the higher calling of your partner if they have one. Both established couples and potential partners need to do significant amounts of higher self clarification with each other. One thing that creates real tragedy in love is when one person's purpose calls them in a different direction than their partner. It's important to figure out if you have a sense of a larger calling, if your partner does too, and to get perfectly clear on how you may securely support each other's higher self purpose. Sometimes, couples fall in love even when their higher life path will not support a life together.

A secure relationship must be able to empower, with perhaps some work and negotiation, both people's dreams and calling. Supporting each other's dreams is one of the higher levels of Dr. Gottman's *sound relationship house.* Unfortunately, society has gone too far in the direction of empowering individuals to pursue their dreams at the expense of prioritizing a securely loving relationship. However, a secure experience with higher self will at least give the *We* a chance if there are differences between you and your beloved.

To sum up, love has some deep challenges in a human brain. It can be difficult to fix those problems at the same level of the problem. Albert Einstein advises us, "No problem can be solved from the same level of consciousness that created it." Higher self is the higher level of consciousness needed to solve the problems we find in our brains. People ask why I can be so confident that we can be *Safe to Love Again*. It's because I know reality has a level where there's no problem for love. In fact, that level is pure love. From that place, you can access resources to resolve any issue around love. When you train your brain to access this higher level of identity, you can be *Safe to Love Again*. Always!

> Reality has a level where there's no problem for love.
> You can access resources to resolve any issue.

Accessing Higher Self

As Deepak Chopra makes a point in his *Super Soul Sunday* interview on the Oprah Winfrey Network, your higher self is the observer who's above your inner observer. There, you'll find a place where the pain doesn't exist. Moreover, you'll discover a place of infinite resources. So, take a few minutes when you're alone and read these next few paragraphs. Acquaint yourself with that wonderful place of refuge and resources called your higher self. This too is your natural birthright as a human.

Sit down with your feet on the floor. Take a few breaths. Breathe in and out slowly for about five breaths. Ground yourself. Turn your attention inward. Next, notice the part of you that's noticing your experience. Step into the place that's noticing the noticing of your experience. That's what it's like to access your higher self.

Step fully into the part of you that notices the one who's noticing that experience. Ask, "Is there any pain in that place? Is there any pain in that version of me?" (If you're fully in that observer zone, or accessing the higher self version of you, the answer should be *No*.) Sit in that place for a while. Notice its calming power.

Now notice that your higher self not only offers you a place of refuge, but also resources. Notice how there's always a place where you can not only escape the pain, but indeed access the resources and bigger outlook to experience your most secure self. Finally, notice what resources are available here. Notice how you might love better if you allowed these resources into your consciousness. Just sit with the resources. When you're ready, come back to now.

Relax into this experience of your higher self for a while. Perhaps repeat it a few times. Come back and journal for ten minutes on this portal of resources. Answer these few simple questions:

1. What is a higher version of me that I can experience right now? (Even just a bit is good!)
2. What is the better experience of love I can offer to my loved ones if I were to access this place within me more often?
3. What specific resources can I tap into from this place?
4. Are there any higher self lessons available for me to learn?

Just know you can always access that place where love has no pain, but only the resources and lessons to love and be loved fully. Good job! It's almost time to wrap up this journey with a nice, tidy bow. Just one chapter to go!

Ten

Let's Change
Your Generation's Fate with Love

Love needs a little help these days. So I'm going to ask you to become part of a movement for secure love. If you have read this book, I know you're invested in love for yourself and others. We all need support to love in more secure ways. Everyone needs inspiration and a compassionate, helpful hand to deal with the ups and downs that come with every relationship. We are, after all, just human. That means we were born with the need for an encouraging community. It takes a village to change a love style. I'm calling this movement, *The Extraordinary Love Invitation*.

Are you ready to change your generation's fate with love?

Secure love is at risk of becoming an endangered species if we aren't careful. There's just way too much heartache out there. Many people are shabbily treated in their relationships. It's not just married couples and their 50 percent divorce rate. Singles are constantly getting dumped for someone *better* by the most insensitive of means. *Fear of Missing Out* (FOMO) is far and wide. Ghosting is rampant and painful. These breakups are wreaking havoc on our brains. Neurologically, when we experience a breakup, our brain registers the relationship pain in the same area as physical pain. This is the case whether it's a legal divorce or a rude breakup as a single.

⌐ue to our attachment systems, your brain registers the pain from a breakup on the same level as *breaking a leg*. Some studies have suggested that each time we breakup with someone, our brain has the same pain as if we were in a *severe car accident*. Now factor in that some singles are experiencing these sorts of breakups up to 3 to 4 times a year. How many of you would willingly submit your brain to the pain of 3 to 4 car accidents a year? How many times would you allow your legs to be broken in a year?

Yet that's what we're doing to ourselves when we go online, meet someone, date for a few months, fall in love, and breakup. This kind of society wide, cavalier attitude towards the human heart is just not survivable for our brains. We deserve to treat each other much better. It's going to take a movement to change these patterns.

> We deserve to treat each other much better. It's going to take a movement to change our dating patterns.

Fear of Missing Out is causing singles to miss out on so much. This is more than ironic. It's downright catastrophic. The most common complaint I've heard from women ages 28 to 35 is that they can't find a man who will commit to building a family. For a woman of child bearing age, this trend is more than heartbreaking; it's downright soul crushing. My heart was moved by two women in Phoenix and Newport Beach who were in tears sharing the excruciating pain of wanting to find that one man who would create a family with them. These young women were painfully aware that their biological clock was ticking and they were ready for real love.

To explain this trend, many have pointed a finger at the reticence of younger men to become husbands and fathers. Some claim this is due to *perpetual male adolescence*. That may well be in play for some guys. However, I've heard another story from men who are trying to find a secure mate, just like their women peers. While speaking in Sacramento, a professional singer opened up the event. James was a man about 35, extremely tall and handsome, with a definitely secure love style. After I shared on the topic of *Safe to Love Again*, James wanted to talk backstage. In the half hour we spent together, I learned that he had a happy childhood with wholesome parents who stayed married and a great career. He was a real gem of a man.

It was telling what James shared with me, "Gary, I like what you had to say. Yet to be honest, dating is tougher out there for guys like me than you know. I heard what the women tonight were saying, but they don't understand what it's like on our side. Many of them have had four or five breakups in the past few years from some jerks out there. Many were lied to, cheated on, and otherwise treated badly. My father raised horses and we took in some abused ponies from time to time. Some of these women are like those ponies. They're high strung and want to buck you all the time because of what the last guy did. I want to find a woman to marry, settle down with, and start a family. Yet what I'm seeing out there are a lot of scared ponies in the women I've dated the past few years. So, where can I find these secure women you speak about?" What I'm hearing is a huge *attachment* problem that's now a multi-generational phenomenon.

> Our generation has a huge attachment problem
> that's now a multi-generational phenomenon.

We now have several generations that are not *Safe to Love Again*. Moreover, all of these attachment antics by the 50 percent of the population who have avoidant or anxious love styles are affecting everyone. We're laying waste to each other's love styles when we *give BS* and *take BS* with each other. It's time to stop the BS that's been socially sanctioned in the dating trenches.

Moreover, it's time to start being attuned, compassionate, and kind with each other, even when the relationship isn't meant to continue. It's okay to offer some appreciation for each other, even when you know a second or third date isn't on the table for you. However, big changes must first happen on a societal level. If we're ever going to help each other find that secure place in ourselves, it's going to take a movement where things begin to change on a very big scale.

First, let's take a big breath and stop making each other wrong.

Nothing good comes from harsh or even subtle, politically correct judgment between the sexes. Everyone in this predicament has a brain that's taking the best deal available. So let's not get into the whole *men are wrong, women are wrong* trap. That being said, as seen from the perspective of your attachment system, what's currently going on is patently absurd. There isn't a conspiracy out there, but there sure is one very big attachment dilemma. Simply put, every single deserves a break from these dating shenanigans.

You deserve to have your heart treated with care, reverence, and attunement. If we're going to create a society wide respect for each other's hearts, we'll need a bigger solution than *dating sites* and *apps* can offer. We need a *movement* to support people who can date, relate, and marry in more attuned, thoughtful, and loving ways from first date to the diamond anniversary and beyond.

> We need a movement to support people who can
> date, relate, and marry in more attuned, thoughtful, and
> loving ways from first date to the diamond anniversary.

Join the Party for Secure Love

Modern Society has a huge missing *Right to Have Our Heart Needs Met* and one very big split *Right to Love and Be Loved.* These missing rights play themselves out every Friday and Saturday evenings. I know because I've listened to the hurt from my single clients during the mid-week. Because it's a societal and generational thing, we need a movement to get beyond this needless pain and frustration. So, consider yourself invited to the party for love.

Are you willing to show up for love, join the movement, and change the way your generation dates?

The first way you can join the party if you're single is to consider being kinder and more open on dates, especially the first and second dates. Furthermore, the ghosting must stop. Did you know that the single most destructive and abusive thing anyone can do to another person's attachment system is to cut off a relationship without any contact or warning? The amount of stress and damage that ghosting does to our love styles is off the charts from the clinical research. When I say we should be kinder to each other, I'm thinking of those sorts of things. *Safe to Love Again* needs these common graces. We need to become a more attuned dating society.

Try to practice *The Four Feelings* with each other in at least some small ways. When someone breaks up or decides not to date further, *we owe it to the next person who dates them to protect their heart for somebody else.* We don't want them turned into an *abused pony* in their next relationship. When singles treat other singles, first dates, and potential spouses with kinder and more attuned responses, that's what I call an *extraordinary single.*

Extraordinary singles treat other singles with kinder and more attuned responses on dates.

Second, I want to invite couples to the party for love as well. We all need support from *crib to coupledom* when it comes to love. When singles become a couple, they often soon discover that they've signed up to learn a few more lessons. I've had the privilege of helping many singles find their soulmate. Nevertheless, sometimes after they get into a relationship, they realize they have more skills to learn. Sometimes they discover other hurts they never even knew existed that need healed. That's when they come back to finish their journey to secure love.

Established couples also need the support of a loving community that's committed to helping couples make love last. I've had the privilege of helping many couples overcome their issues to create a wonderful lasting love. Some come in very distressed. Others only know that the passion and romance has been dulled in their relationship. Before they lose their romance, these couples just want to get back to being the passionate couple they remember.

Those daring, brave souls are *extraordinary couples.* These precious souls work hard at staving off the dreaded 50 percent divorce statistic. All of them worked on becoming more secure. When you show up for secure love in your marriage, you're virtually reversing the dreaded divorce rate. Instead of having a mere 50 percent chance of keeping your love alive, when you show up for secure love you gain a 75 percent chance of keeping your relationship loving, passionate, and strong. We don't have to accept divorce as simply *what happens to most couples after a while.* When couples show up for love, everyone wins—especially the children. If you practice *The Four Feelings* along with more attention on aligned values and purposes, I think we can raise that to a 90 percent chance of making your marriage last.

If you're a couple, are you ready to join the movement and find the support that you and your beloved deserve?

Extraordinary couples with a secure love style divorce only about 25 percent of the time. With The Four Feelings, we can reduce that to about 10 percent.

Will You Show Up for Love?

When we show up for love, we never know how it will affect others. After my son was born, it petrified me that I might not be a good father. There was no father in my past to copy. Adults rarely played with me while I was growing up, except for my grandmother. As a result, I felt awkward around children. When my wife announced she was pregnant, it concerned me that I wouldn't be a good dad. I wanted very much to give my child a loving, wonderful childhood. Yet I also knew I didn't have a clue how to play with a child.

After Kenny was born, my worst fears were confirmed. I knew I needed outside help when my wife looked at me playing with our son and said, "Are you playing with Kenny the same way you play with the dog?" I tried to get out of that one but it didn't work. At the time, I was about to embark on my first year of being a college professor. Soon thereafter, I discovered a class on *How to Be a Parent* in a converted house next to the Hall where I was teaching. Moreover, the class was right after my 7:30 class, beginning at 9:00! What a stroke of luck. Or higher self! So, I signed up.

I'll never forget that first day of class. I came *prepared* in my gray pinstripe suit with all manner of paper and pen supplies to take copious notes. Looking around, something seemed *off* though. I noticed that all of the students seemed a bit *young* for college students. Moreover, all of them were women with children. They turned out to be unwed teenage mothers. Of course, all of them were playing just fine with their sons and daughters. When the teacher came over, she saw me in my suit, ready to take notes. Looking amused, she said to me, "Gary, where's your son?" I looked up and said, "My son? Why would I bring my son? How would I take notes with my son here?" She laughed and said to me, "Gary, you can't learn to play with Kenny unless he's here. This is a *hands-on* class. Please bring him next time."

Here's where the story gets interesting for love. After about six weeks, I had figured it out. Playing with a child was so simple! It didn't take rocket science or extensive notes. All you had to do was follow their lead, play in the sandbox, enjoy the textures of everything, smile a lot, and just have fun on their level. When I found out how simple being a good father was, I figured staying any longer in the class was a waste of my time.

When I told one of the teachers that Kenny and I wouldn't be there next week, a concerned look came over her face. She looked me straight in the eye, saying, "Right now, all of these young girls have a very jaded view of the men who got them pregnant and deserted them. Gary, you have no idea what you mean to these young girls. We need you to stay so we can convince them that someday, it might be worthwhile to trust a man again and perhaps to even fall in love. It's not easy being a teenage mother. Part of preparing them for the real world is helping them to get over these wounds. So, please stay. It will mean the world to us and the girls." So Kenny and I stayed.

At the end of the last class, a young woman approached me. Gloria was the one who from the beginning didn't seem to like me much. I'll never forget what she said, "Gary, thank you for showing up for your son. I'll have to say, I hated men when I came to this class. I figured they all wanted just one thing before they would cut and run. You, however, have taught me that there are good men out there. Thank you, Gary. You don't know what this means to me. We all feel this way about you. *Now that I know what a good man looks like, I won't miss my mark the next time."* What an honor!

I was floored. From the look in her eye, there was no doubt that would be true. My showing up for Kenny affected her, the man she would one day marry, their children, her children's children, and onward. A big lesson about love was revealed to me so many years ago. *When you show up for love in any way, you never know who it will affect, and how it will change their life.*

When you show up for love, you never know
who it will affect, and how it will change their life.

Whenever we show up for love, it affects people all around us. One act of love can have a reach that goes on for generations. Every act of love can have a *butterfly effect* where the good it does affects ever more people in a never ending domino effect of positive energy. You never know how far the ripples will go. This is why I want to start a movement for secure love. Each act of love can have an enormous effect on your world and the world of others. Politics, economies, and even the environment can be positively changed by empowering secure love styles in each other.

So, will you join me? Will you help me forge a movement that will change the way love shows up for generations?

Discovering Fire for the Second Time

Love is the key for our common futures. As Pierre Teilhard de Chardin once boldly proclaimed, *"Someday we shall harness the energy of love and for the second time in history, humanity will have discovered fire."* It's time for humanity to discover the fire of secure love. It's time, time indeed, for love's seekers to be able to bask safely in the warmth of its tender flames. The time is long overdue for our generation to experience the fires of love's passion without the fear of painful, recurring heartache. *Safe to Love Again* is all about discovering the secret code that will allow everyone to reclaim their rightful birthright to love in ways that are unchained of fear's debilitating effects. We can learn to love again without all the trappings of the past. For many of my readers, your hearts know it's time to harness the energy of *secure* love and discover, for perhaps the first time, the fiery wonders of what love can be.

Real love is a daily, earthy, grounded, simple as dirt yet profound as poetry experience. What tells us we're loved is uncomplicated—like the sound in someone's voice, a kind deed or gesture, or just plain hanging out and having fun together. And yet, it's the most profound of all human experiences. If my book has any lasting message it's this; love doesn't have to be as difficult as we make it. It's all adjustable. *Together*, we can make love happen for all of us.

What I'm proposing is to join the movement for love. Consider this an invitation to make love your personal mission in life. If you want to make a difference, *here's the link to join the movement:*

www.garysalyer.com/lovemovement

It's time to make a bond with each other to help love out. When you sign up for Love's Movement, you'll be connected to other love seekers just like you. Nobody was meant to change their love style in isolation or by themselves. It takes a community of support and encouragement to create the love you deserve. Why not join with other love seekers like yourself and receive the support you are so worthy of?

Sign up for Love's Movement at
www.Garysalyer.Com/lovemovement.

All my best, highest intentions and love go with you. Just know, that I wrote this book holding the purpose that you would find what you need to create the magnificent, safe, and loving relationship you deserve. May you find love's richest blessings and love well.

Many blessings and much love,

Gary

Acknowledgements

It takes a village to write a book. To be honest, I never knew I was so loved until countless people showed up to support me. First, I'd like to thank SARK and Dr. Scott Mills for their incredibly skillful, soulful, and dare I say it, *succulent wild coaching* for the writing of this book. Susan, you mentored me as a writer, daring me to be more vulnerable and open. Scott, you asked me to show up in life with more *yin* energy, which allowed me to write in a softer, more inviting way. Without your friendship, coaching, and skillful chiding, this book would never have come to press.

Thank you so much, Dr. John Gray, for mentoring me on how you wrote *Men Are From Mars, Women Are From Venus*. The principles you shared about how to write a compelling book on love stayed with me. A big call out also goes to Marci Shimoff for suggesting the title of this book!

Big kudos go to Paul Carrick Brunson for writing the Foreword. From our first conversations in a Berkeley pub after being on stage together, you believed in my message. Thank you for inspiring me to be a thought leader, my friend. You and Jill are true *love heroes*, the epitome of everything I write about.

To my *editing angel* and good friend, Andy Spyros, I owe you a mountain of appreciation. It was your careful eye and dutiful spirit that cut the original 622 page draft down to something manageable for my final edits. I truly can't thank you enough for co-editing this book to make it more powerful, deep, concise, and clear.

Thank you Star Ladin for imploring me to make the book useful for both singles and couples, especially couples with great marriages. Much gratitude goes to Kristen Moeller whose author mastermind got me started on this path so many years ago.

Then there's my final editor, Jo Spring, who turned my words from *wine into smooth brandy*. Of all the editors I interviewed, you were the one who felt *called to birth* my book. Your soul and heart brought the true intentions of my words into soulful clarity. A big round of applause goes to Michelle Radomski who designed the book cover, James Hummel for designing my new website and Steve Cozart for the new professional pictures. Appreciation also goes to Francine Brevetti for her skillful proofing eye.

I wish to thank Dr. Dianne Frost for your continuing inspiration while I wrote this book. Our deep connection, conversations and your expert input as a Depth Psychologist helped me to stay focused. Thanks also go to Rebecca Hall Gruyter, Jesse Koren and Sharla Jacobs for their support over the years. Bill Baren and Patrick Dominguez also merit a big call out. The incredible Lisa Garr is owed a big round of applause for inviting me to play a higher game as an "aware" thought leader. Then there are my lifelong friends whose love guided and supported me during the *searching* years; Dr. Lysha Albright, Steve Chiles and Ken Fairbanks. I'd also like to mention my son Kenny and my daughter-in-law, Jayne. Seeing your love blossom and grow into a wonderful, committed marriage has warmed my heart. I'm so proud of you!

Knowledge is always a collaborative effort. A good many mentors stand behind this project. First, I want to thank Dr. Carl Buchheit for the best NLP training I could ever imagine. You showed me that it's all adjustable. Most of all, you changed my incarnation. I'd also like to thank Dr. John Gottman and Dr. Julie Gottman for their lifelong research on couples and the wonderful clinical trainings they afforded me. Gratitude also goes to Dr. Daniel Siegel and Terry Real for their trainings and work on attachment theory and couples respectively.

Finally, I'd like to thank Source and all those *guides* who intuitively showed up to inspire so many ideas that came to me at 4:00 a.m. This book sprang into my mind as *downloads* in the middle of the night. *Safe to Love Again* was entirely guided by a collaborative effort with an utterly conscious, gracious, and loving Universe. We truly live in a loving, cosmic *We*. Lastly, thank you Andrea Bocelli, whose love songs got me in the mood for every chapter I wrote!

About the Author

Steve Cozart

Dr. Gary Salyer has spent a lifetime learning how to step into a secure love style. All of his relationships have taught him things about what makes love work well. Dr. Gary's path to creating a secure love style has opened his heart in a thousand different ways, and now his passion is to share those lessons with everyone. He has been dedicated to "changing a generation's fate with love" since he was seven and first noticed that not everybody feels happy and loved.

As a father, his goal was always to pass along a secure love style to his children. Watching his son Kenny create a fabulous relationship with his wife Jayne is, without a doubt, his life's greatest accomplishment. Hearing them promise each other at their wedding, "to nurture your dreams, because through them your soul shines," was his lifelong dream come true.

For the last decade, Dr. Salyer has been in private practice offering heart-centered transformation to clients across the country so they can re-write the rules for love in their brains, and step into the most loving version of themselves. Dr. Gary also speaks to a national audience as a featured expert on a variety of stages across the country as well as various TV and radio shows. He is the creator of the Safe to Love Again Workshop, the Extraordinary Singles Retreat, and the Extraordinary Couples Retreat. For more information or to contact Dr. Gary, go to his website at www.garysalyer.com.

Love Takes a Commitment

What are your commitments from each chapter?

Chapter 1 – The big question I'll answer about love is...

Chapter 2 – The missing feelings for love I'll restore are...

Chapter 3 – The false self I've created around love is...

Chapter 4 – I will train my brain to feel more welcomed by...

Chapter 5 – I will train my brain to feel more worthy by...

Chapter 6 – I will train my brain to feel more cherished by...

Chapter 7 – I will train my brain to feel more empowered by...

Chapter 8 – I will train my brain to feel more loved and loving by...

Chapter 9 – I will learn my soul lessons for love by...

Chapter 10 – I will join the movement and support love by...